A
BOOKSHELF OF
OUR OWN

A Century of Women

*The 100 Most Influential Women
of All Time*

*Fifty Jewish Women Who Changed
the World* (with Diana Rosen)

A
BOOKSHELF OF
OUR OWN

Works That Changed
Women's Lives

DEBORAH G. FELDER

CITADEL PRESS
Kensington Publishing Corp.
www.kensingtonbooks.com

CITADEL PRESS BOOKS are published by

Kensington Publishing Corp.
850 Third Avenue
New York, NY 10022

All Kensington titles, imprints, and distributed lines are available at special quantity discounts for bulk purchases for sales promotions, premiums, fundraising, educational, or institutional use. Special book excerpts or customized printings can also be created to fit specific needs. For details, write or phone the office of the Kensington special sales manager: Kensington Publishing Corp., 850 Third Avenue, New York, NY 10022, attn: Special Sales Department, phone 1-800-221-2647.

First printing: January 2005

10 9 8 7 6 5 4 3 2 1

Printed in the United States of America

Library of Congres Control Number: TK

ISBN: 0-8065-2614-9

For Nina Louise

Nothing, I am sure, calls forth the faculties so much as the being obliged to struggle with the world.

—Mary Wollstonecraft, *Thoughts on The Education of Daughters*, 1797

CONTENTS

Foreword to come (2 pages)

PREFACE

Women's history is more than simply a catalog of the social and political events that have shaped women's lives over the centuries. There is a unique quality to every age in the history of women that can be understood and appreciated in the context of the fiction and nonfiction works of each era. *A Bookshelf of Our Own* attempts to present an overview of women's history from the perspective of literature written by and about women. I have chosen the authors and works featured in this volume because I think they offer valuable insights into the cultural and historical experience of women as they have been, as the epigraph to this book suggests, "obliged to struggle with the world."

The struggle of women to forge individual, social, and political identities, to gain equality, to demand and obtain respect, to love and be loved, to confront and challenge the circumstances that have constrained them, and to question, and sometimes reject, the lives they have chosen is evident in the works chronicled here; each character, subject, and author's perceptions and voice tells us something distinctive about women past and present. The authors' voices are not exclusively female: some of fiction's most extraordinary and memorable women protagonists were created by male writers and are discussed here in essays on four of the greatest nineteenth-century novels in world literature and one revolutionary play from the same century (Henrik Ibsen's *A Doll's House*). I have also included an Honorable Mentions list of fifty additional works for readers to consider. This list broadens the base of women's experience and includes more plays, as well as more fiction from the past twenty-five years. Poetry, that most singular of literary genres and the one that, as Russian poet

Yevgeny Yevtushenko put it, "ignores all frontiers," deserves a book of its own and thus has not been included, although a poem by Emily Dickinson appears to punctuate the essay on Charlotte Perkins Gilman's 1892 story of madness and enlightenment, "The Yellow Wallpaper." Due to obvious limitations of length, I have focused primarily on Western literature as it relates to women's history, but I nevertheless urge readers to seek out significant works by women authors from other cultures.

Although there are several remarkable women characters in classical literature, such as Medea, Antigone, and Hecuba, I have chosen to begin *A Bookshelf of Our Own* in the medieval period, with Murasaki Shikibu's *The Tale of Genji* and Christine de Pisan's *The Book of the City of Ladies*, the first major literary creations of women writers. Separated by culture and category, each work has its own special place in the history of women's writing. The *Genji* has the honor of being regarded as the first great novel in world literature; the fact that it was written by a lady of the Japanese court adds to its distinctiveness. Pisan's work, considered by some scholars to be the first true feminist treatise, is both a defense of women against the misogyny that was a feature of European life in the middle ages and a catalog of famous women whose attributes and contributions belie the then widely held notion of female inferiority.

Major novels by and about women would begin to appear in the eighteenth and nineteenth centuries. Prior to then, we have one groundbreaking novel, *The Princess of Cleves*, by Madame de La Fayette, which, although written in seventeenth-century France during the reign of Louis XIV and reflective of the Sun King's court, is set in the Renaissance at the similarly glittering court of Henri II, where "love was always allied to politics and politics to love." Madame de la Fayette offers readers an illuminating look at the concept of courtly love, as well as the morals and political maneuverings of the nobility. For a work of the eighteenth century, a time of political turmoil, revolutionary fervor, and the idea of inalienable rights in France, England, and the United States, I have chosen Mary Wollstonecraft's *A Vindication of the Rights of Woman*, which includes a call for the education of women that will produce individuals with reason, knowledge, and virtue. An insightful and important pronouncement of woman's rights, *Vindication* would become a foundation text in the struggle for women's liberation and gender equality.

By the nineteenth century, the novel had become the dominant form of Western literature. The century marked the emergence of women as strong, central protagonists in the novel, and for the first time in literary history, male novelists explored female consciousness in the context of a patriarchal society. Hawthorne's Hester Prynne, Flaubert's Emma Bovary, Tolstoy's Anna Karenina, and Hardy's Tess Durbeyfield challenged the expectations of the ways in which women were expected to conduct their lives, with ostracism and death as the inevitable punishments for such violations of convention. Unlike the characters mentioned above, Ibsen's Nora Helmer, in what is as much a polemic as it is a drama, decides her own fate when she ultimately rejects the role as a wife and mother that has kept her submissive, childlike, and irresponsible in favor of an uncertain new life of freedom.

During the nineteenth century, the voices of women writers were being heard as well, beginning with Jane Austen, whose social satires provide contemporary readers with a glimpse of the courtship manners and mores of her time, exemplified in this volume by Austen's 1813 novel *Emma*. With *Jane Eyre*, Charlotte Brontë would take the novel into the realm of interior consciousness, and by the 1860s and 1870s, George Eliot, then the dominant intellectual novelist in England, would add social awareness to psychological exploration, most notably in her masterwork *Middlemarch*. As the nineteenth century gave way to the twentieth, women writers offered provocative challenges to the male-dominated world view in works by Charlotte Perkins Gilman, Kate Chopin, Colette, Edith Wharton, and Willa Cather.

At the same time, women were working for equality and empowerment in the move toward suffrage. The history of the first wave of the women's movement is featured here in a profile of Eleanor Flexner's masterful *Century of Struggle: The Women's Rights Movement in the United States*. With the vote won for women in the United States and in England after World War I, an important political goal in the quest for equality had been realized. However, there was more work to be done if women were to achieve full creative and autonomous parity, as novelist and essayist Virginia Woolf made clear in 1929's *A Room of One's Own*. In Dorothy Sayers's 1936 novel, *Gaudy Night*, the central female character, Harriet Vane, is a best-selling detective novelist who questions whether it is possible for her to successfully combine creative autonomy with the commitment required for a successful marriage.

Virginia Woolf's call to women to achieve their full potential would be answered in the influential critical work *The Second Sex*, by Simone de Beauvoir, the novel *The Golden Notebook*, by Doris Lessing, and in Betty Friedan's *The Feminine Mystique*. Friedan's 1963 treatise on the discontent experienced by women because of their treatment as second-class citizens in post-World War II America served to launch the second wave of the women's movement. The women's liberation movement of the 1960s and 1970s resulted in a burgeoning of women's fiction and nonfiction by such writers as Sylvia Plath, Kate Millett, Germaine Greer, Molly Haskell, Erica Jong, Susan Brownmiller, Adrienne Rich, Tillie Olsen, Judith Rossner, and Cynthia Ozick, all of whom offer important perspectives on the social, political, psychological, and sexual status of women in the last decades of the twentieth century. The same decade also brought forth a multicultural perspective which added to the rich canon of women's writing and is represented here in works by Maxine Hong Kingston, Angela Davis, Isabel Allende, Toni Morrison, and Zora Neale Hurston, a once largely forgotten novelist of the 1930s and 1940s who received deserved recognition during the 1970s and whose novels continue to be taught in college courses on African-American literature, women's literature, and twentieth-century American literature.

The 1980s and 1990s saw the stirrings of a post-feminist consciousness in a reevaluation of the gains in equality made by women in the wake of the women's liberation movement. By the 1980s, women were earning graduate degrees and entering the work force as never before, while at the same time they were having children and endeavoring to balance the demands of the workplace with those of family life. The 1980s myth of the "super-woman" who could "have it all" was seized upon by the media, which, according to journalist Susan Faludi, mounted a "counterassault on women's rights, a backlash, an attempt to retract the handful of small and hard-won victories that the feminist movement did manage to win for women." Faludi explores this phenomenon in *Backlash: The Undeclared War Against American Women,* published in 1991. As examples of post-feminist literature, I have selected Cathi Hanauer's anthology of essays by women, *The Bitch in the House,* and the very entertaining *Bridget Jones's Diary,* by Helen Fielding. The experiences of new generations of women will determine how women's literature will evolve in the twenty-first century.

Readers will undoubtedly have their own choices for the works they feel best illustrate the history of women through the centuries. I have offered my choices for consideration in what is also a book about literature and the extraordinary pleasure, as well as the illumination, which can be derived from experiencing it. *A Bookshelf of Our Own* can serve as an introductory volume in the compilation of a library of writings on women that will hopefully grow and continue to instruct and entertain readers through the years with what Virginia Woolf called, "that complete statement which is literature."

Finally, I want to thank my editor, Margaret Wolf, for her support and her patience during the preparation of this book, and my husband, Daniel Burt, whose scholarly perspective was an invaluable resource in my own reconsideration of the works profiled here.

A
BOOKSHELF OF
OUR OWN

THE TALE OF GENJI

by Murasaki Shikibu

The first great novel in the history of world literature, *The Tale of Genji* is celebrated as one of the supreme masterworks of Japanese prose fiction and one of the most accomplished works of the imagination ever written. Adding to the novel's originality, as well as its significance in the history of women's literature, is the fact that it was written by a lady of the eleventh-century Japanese court.

Little is known about Murasaki Shikibu (c. 978–1031), the author of *The Tale of Genji*. Her father was a provincial governor and a member of the middle rank of the Japanese aristocracy. The name "Shikibu" ("Bureau of Ceremonial") designates a position once held by her father, and "Murasaki" ("purple") may have stemmed from the nickname of a female character in the *Genji*. Although her family was not prominent or powerful, it was distinguished by literary achievement. Murasaki Shikibu's great-grandfather helped compile the first imperial anthology of Japanese verse, and her father was a poet and scholar of Chinese classics, an essential qualification for a successful bureaucrat in the male-dominated public life of the time. As a child, Lady Murasaki's literary skills were evident but unappreciated. Her diary, in which she describes her experiences at court from late 1008 to early 1010, also records one method of childhood study, as well as the fact that her father, who noticed her capacity for learning, lamented that she had not been born a boy: "When my brother . . . was a young boy learning the Chinese classics, I was in the habit of listening to him and I became unusually proficient at understanding those passages which he found too difficult to grasp. Father, a most learned man, was always regretting the fact: 'Just my luck!' he would say. 'What a pity she was not born a man!' "

Around 998, Lady Murasaki was married to her cousin, a member of the imperial guard. Her only child, a daughter, was born in 999, and she was widowed in 1001 (some sources say 1011). In 1002 or 1003, she began the fictional narrative that would bring her notoriety and, it is thought, helped secure for her a position at court as lady-in-waiting to the Empress Shōshi. Despite the circumscribed and cloistered life of noblewomen during the period—they lived a sedentary life behind walls and screens, most had no public function, and their names were rarely recorded—it is not surprising that a woman did produce such a brilliant literary work as the *Genji*. Following Chinese tradition, only poetry, history, and philosophy were regarded as distinguished literary genres. Chinese art and culture was the exclusive province of men, who devoted themselves primarily to writing in Chinese, the official language of religion and government. The Japanese vernacular was left largely to women, with the result that women writers dominate the literature of the period and are credited with developing an indigenous literary style. There were two vernacular prose genres for women to choose from. One was the literary diary, a record of activities, observations, and feelings, of which Murasaki Shikibu's own diary is a leading example. The other available prose form was the *monogatari*, fanciful, often supernatural, storytelling derived from the folk tradition. Murasaki's great innovation was to combine both genres, creating a prose narrative infused with real situations and psychological insights. Murasaki Shikibu's literary talent was no doubt a major asset in her court service—she had the time and leisure to create her tale, together with access to the court world, both of which she used to full advantage in producing her epic. *The Tale of Genji* gradually evolved from chapter installments enjoyed by a small aristocratic audience into a narrative twice the length of Tolstoy's *War and Peace*, another novel renowned for its size as well as its brilliance.

Completed around 1013, *The Tale of Genji* is a massive fifty-four-chapter work that ranges over a period of seventy-five years and three generations, includes nearly five hundred characters, and chronicles the lives and careers of the nobleman Genji and his offspring. Genji is the son of the emperor and a "lady not of the first rank," who, as a consequence of her lover's indiscretion, is hounded to an early death by one of his senior wives. Beloved by his father and known as "The Shining Prince," Genji is in many ways a paragon of manly virtues, possessing wit, sophistication, and great physical attractiveness. At the beginning of the novel, the emperor wants to designate his son crown prince, but he lacks the political support to achieve this. In addition, a Korean soothsayer has warned that disaster will befall the country if Genji becomes emperor. Reluctantly, the emperor decides to reduce Genji to the status of mere subject, although he retains for him the rank of nobleman to ensure that he will have an official career. Thus dispossessed, Genji begins a lifelong quest to obtain compensation for his loss of royal rank. This takes the form of a search to find the perfect woman and to achieve redemption through love, even as he pursues affairs that challenge social mores and complicate his search for self-fulfillment. His early idealism is tested in his disastrous extramarital affair with his father's consort, which causes his exile, and in his relationship with the character Murasaki, who, like his mother, is a woman of unsuitable rank. Unlike a conventional romantic hero, Genji is humanized by his shortcomings and redeemed by his vulnerability and emotional needs.

In *The Tale of Genji* Murasaki provides intense and nuanced character portraits in which political pressure, custom, and individual identity join together to generate the novel's drama. An equally interesting facet of the novel is the author's penetration into the psyches of the various women whom Genji encounters. Rather than representing the expected fulfillment of love and redemption through their relationships with the highborn, captivating hero, Murasaki's women, bound by the customs and values of the author's time, suffer from their dependence on a man's unsteady devotion and are fearful of betrayal and abandonment. In the world of the *Genji* (which was the world of Murasaki Shikibu), women are expected to be submissive and to sexually acquiesce to the demands of men. But the author explores a psychological insight lurking behind the submissiveness: for example, the young

Murasaki finds Genji's sudden advances toward her "gross and unscrupulous" because she is disconcerted by the awakening of her sexuality in a situation that shows a man at his most selfish. Ultimately, Genji is the mirror through which Murasaki Shikibu's women see themselves; that the image is not necessarily the reality adds depth to the characters and situations.

After chronicling Genji's adventures up to his return to the city, restoration of his rank (his son becomes emperor, and Genji is promoted to government minister), Murasaki's death, and his death at the age of fifty-two, Murasaki Shikibu devotes the final thirteen chapters to the succeeding generation. The remainder of the novel focuses on the relationship between Kaoru, Genji's putative son, and Genji's grandson, Niou, as they compete for the affections of three sisters. The two young men "were thought by the world to be uncommonly handsome, but somehow they did not shine with the same radiance [as Genji]." The patterns of passion and betrayal established in previous generations by the emperor and Genji are repeated in the third generation but remain unresolved in the end, as the disaffected Niou and Kaoru fail to find the self-fulfillment that Genji has obtained.

Murasaki Shikibu's saga of Genji and his children offers the reader a true, deep understanding of human nature and experience in an open-ended, indeterminate manner that reflects human weakness as well as existential uncertainty and anxiety. It would take many more centuries for western writers to attempt what Murasaki accomplished in *The Tale of Genji* and to discover what she articulated in her epic: that the art of the novel "happens because the storyteller's own experiences of men and things, whether for good or ill—not only what he has passed through himself, but even events which he has only witnessed or been told of—has moved him to an emotion so passionate that he can no longer keep it shut up in his heart."

THE BOOK OF THE CITY OF LADIES

by Christine de Pisan

The Middle Ages in Europe, a period stretching roughly from 400–500 A.D. into the fifteenth century, was an era notable for a fear and mistrust of women inherent in Judeo-Christian tradition, which subscribed to the biblical assertion in Genesis that Eve was the perpetrator of Original Sin, and from medical science dating from the Greeks, which viewed females as anatomically defective males. These views were reflected in the literature of the age: medieval treatises, religious texts, romances, and *fabliaux* (a genre of short comic tales) portrayed women as lustful, treacherous, disobedient, garrulous, and inferior to men in every way. One woman who dared to directly confront the literary misogyny of the age was Christine de Pisan, whose discourse in defense of women, *The Book of the City of Ladies* (1405), is a masterpiece that some scholars have called the first true feminist treatise.

In an age when a woman's influence, limited at best, was generally characterized by her royal status (Eleanor of Aquitaine) or religious inclination (Joan of Arc, Hildegard of Bingen), Christine de Pisan stands out as a literary figure of remarkable depth. France's first woman of letters, Christine wrote poetry, biography, a book on etiquette for women, treatises on pacifism, the arts, government,

5

and war, and biblical commentary. She achieved renown for her writing during her lifetime and was the first medieval female author to earn a living exclusively from her work.

Born in Venice, Christine de Pisan (c.1364–c.1430) was the daughter of Tommaso di Benvenuto da Pizzano, a noted physician, astronomer, mathematician, and astrologer. Both of her parents were from prominent Italian families. When Christine was four years old, the family moved to Paris, where her father served as court astrologer to Charles V (1338–1380), although in her biography of Charles, she described Tommaso as "philosopher, servant, and counselor" to the king. Against the wishes of her mother, Christine was schooled by her father in Latin, philosophy, and various branches of science not usual in a medieval girl's education. At fifteen, according to the custom of the time, she was married to a man chosen by her father. Her twenty-five-year-old husband was Etienne de Castel, a courtier who became secretary and notary to the king. In 1390, after ten happy years together, de Castal suddenly died while on a trip to Beauvais in what may have been an epidemic of the Black Death. Left the sole support of three children, her mother, and a niece, Christine turned to writing to gain the patronage necessary for financial security.

To prepare for the task of earning a living by her pen, Christine embarked upon an extensive course of self-education. She studied history, science, and the art of poetry, and during this period she may also have worked as a manuscript copier. She began her career writing lyric poetry, composing *ballades* and *rondeaux* in the conventional forms popular at the time. The tone of her work was personal, with a poignant, emotive quality particularly evident in the poems about her widowhood. Christine's poetry gained favor with princes and nobles, and by the end of the decade she was earning a steady income. She began composing longer narrative poems, including fashionable "love debates" presented to a "court of love" for resolution, and the more serious *Long Road of Learning* (1403), a utopian dream-vision in which Christine visits the Court of Reason to discover who should rule a better world. Around 1400, she began writing long prose works, such as the biography of Charles V (1404), *The Book of Three Virtues* (1405), and *Christine's Vision* (1405), a cryptic semiautobiographical dream-vision that analyzes the ills of French society, not the least of which was its concept of womanhood.

Christine had previously criticized men's behavior toward women in *The Letter of the God of Love* (1399) and in attacks on Ovid and Jean de Meun, one of the authors of the hugely popular medieval romance, *The Romance of the Rose*. *The Book of the City of Ladies* may have had its origins in a series of letters Christine exchanged, between 1400 and 1402, with other leading intellectuals of the day debating the merits of *The Romance of the Rose*. This long poem expresses the concept of courtly love (a medieval philosophy of love and a code of rules for lovemaking) through the story of Amant ("Lover"), who attempts to pick a beautiful Rose guarded by such allegorical figures as Danger and Jealousy. Begun by Guillaume de Lorris around 1230, the poem was completed by Jean de Meung from 1275–80. Jean de Meun, sometimes referred to as the Voltaire of the Middle Ages, satirizes courtly love by making women personify its hypocrisy and falsity. His section is filled with attacks on women, whom he blames for humanity's departure from the ideal. Unlike her opponents, who considered Jean de Muen's *Rose* a work of the highest literary and moral merit, Christine criticized it as extremely vicious and vitriolic in its characterization of women and unChristian in its view of the relations between the sexes. Critic Rosalind Brown Grant has observed, "Christine sought to prove misogynists such as Jean de Meun wrong by arguing that what unites men and women as human beings—their rationality and possession of a soul—is more important than what divides them as sexes. . . . At the heart of Christine's defense of women, both in her letters on the *Rose* and in the *City of Ladies*, was her profound conviction that it is a *human*—and not a specifically *female*—trait to be prone to sin."

The Book of the City of Ladies is a biographical catalog, a genre from classical antiquity that celebrates the lives of famous men and women. In the allegorical framework of the dream-vision, in which Christine is the protagonist, she presents a catalog of renowned heroines from the past and present, including pagan, Greek, Roman, and biblical figures, as well as saints. Christine's vision comes to her as she is sitting in her study reading *Lamentations*, a thirteenth-century diatribe against marriage, which characterizes women as depraved and malicious, and vilifies them for making men so miserable. A depressed and weeping Christine wonders why men "are so unanimous in attributing wickedness to women" and why "we should be worse than men since we were also created by God." Three ladies personifying the virtues of

Reason, Rectitude, and Justice come to comfort her, and they suggest that she write a book refuting, point by point, misogynist accusations that women are evil. Reason tells Christine, "The female sex has been left defenseless for a long time now, like an orchard without a wall, and bereft of a champion to take up arms against in order to protect it." With the help of Reason, Rectitude, and Justice, the foundation, walls, towers, and streets of an allegorical "city of ladies" will be built to house illustrious women and defend them against the misogynists.

The City of Women is divided into three parts in which the Three Virtues give examples of renowned women in response to Christine's questions concerning the inferior political, social, and intellectual status of her sex. In Part I, Reason presents pagan women noted for their soldierly courage, artistry, or inventiveness; in Part II, Rectitude cites ancient Hebrew and Christian women celebrated for their gifts of prophecy, chastity, or devotion to family and country; in Part III, Justice recounts the steadfastness and religious devotion of the female saints. In the last chapter, Christine, seeking to dignify her female readers and to raise their self-esteem, addresses all women and informs them that the city is complete:

> All of you who love virtue, glory, and a good reputation can now be housed in great splendor inside its walls, not just women of the past but also those of the present and the future, for this city has been founded and built to accommodate all deserving women. Dear ladies, the human heart is naturally filled with joy when it sees that it has triumphed in a specific endeavor and has defeated its enemies. From now on, my ladies, you have every reason to rejoice—in a suitably devout and respectful manner—at seeing the completion of this new city. It will not only shelter you, or those of you who have proved your worth, but it will also defend you and protect you against your attackers and assailants, provided you look after it well.

The Book of the City of Ladies might have languished in obscurity were it not for the efforts of feminist scholars during the last decades of the twentieth century to recover previously unknown and unheralded literary works by women. Because of Christine's emphasis on the traditionally passive female traits of respectfulness, virtue, and devotion, there has been some controversy among scholars over whether *The Book of the City of Ladies* can be considered a true feminist text. Christine de Pisan was certainly not a feminist in the modern sense. She did not question the medieval hierarchical social order but sought to prove that women deserved to hold an honored place within it and that virtue and morality were not exclusively male preserves. *The Book of the City of Ladies* is a foundation text that marks the beginning of a canon of women's literature dedicated to elevating the status of women that would continue nearly four hundred years later with Mary Wollstonecraft's *Vindication of the Rights of Woman* and come to fruition in the equality-driven political and social women's movements of the nineteenth and twentieth centuries.

THE PRINCESS OF CLÈVES

by Madame de La Fayette

In 1678, during the reign of Louis XIV, a short historical novel titled *La Princesse de Clèves* appeared in Paris bookshops. Its author
was anonymous, which was probably just as well, given that the
novel, although set in the late sixteenth-century French court of
Henri II, mirrored in many ways the court of the Sun King. *The
Princess of Clèves* caused a sensation for its brevity, which was revolutionary in an era when historical romances (*romans*) were
loosely constructed, episodic, and might run to seven thousand
pages in length, as well as for the author's anonymity. A treatment
of courtly love and the conflict between love and duty—a favorite
seventeenth-century theme—*The Princess of Clèves* would go on to
be considered the first classic French novel.

Madame de La Fayette (1634–1693) was born Marie-Madeleine
Pioche de La Vergne. Her father, a military engineer, was a member of the minor French nobility. He died in 1649. Shortly afterwards, Marie-Madeleine's two younger sisters, left without dowries,
entered a convent, as was a custom of the time. A year later, her
mother married a more prominent nobleman, the Chevalier
Renaud-René de Sévigné. The match allowed Marie-Madeleine's
mother to secure for her daughter a place at court, as a lady-in-

waiting to Anne of Austria, the widowed queen of Louis XIII and the regent for her son, Louis XIV, who had ascended the throne in 1643, at the age of five. Marie-Madeleine would also develop a lifelong friendship with her stepfather's niece-in-law, the Marquise de Sévigné, whose massive correspondence with friends and family would become renowned as a monument of French literature. Another friend was the young Henrietta of England, sister of the exiled Charles II, who would marry Louis' eccentric brother, Philippe, the Duc d'Orléans. Madame de La Fayette later wrote a biography of Henrietta, which was published after her death.

In 1655, Marie-Madeleine was married to Jean-François Motier, comte de La Fayette, a provincial nobleman with estates in the remote, mountainous region of the Auvergne in central France. Madame de La Fayette lived with her husband in the Auvergne until 1659, when, after producing the second of the couple's two sons, she returned to Paris. She would remain in the capital for the rest of her life, occasionally visited by her husband. She raised her children in Paris, became the hostess of a fashionable salon that attracted many of the leading intellectuals and writers of the day, and began her writing career. Her first publication, the only one to appear under her name during her lifetime, was a portrait of her friend, Madame de Sévigné, published in a collection titled *Divers Portraits*, in 1659. Her first fictional work, *La Princesse de Montpensier*, a depiction of court life during the reign of Charles IX, appeared anonymously in 1662, and she collaborated with her close friend La Rochefoucauld on the romance, *Zaïde*, set in ninth-century Spain, which appeared in 1670. In 1672, Madame de La Fayette began to research the historical background of *The Princess of Clèves*; she completed the novel six years later. It would be the last of her works published in her lifetime.

The Princess of Clèves begins: "The last years of Henri II's reign saw a display of opulence and gallantry such as has never been equaled in France. The King himself, charming to look at, the very flower of his race, was a great lover of women. His passion for Diane de Poitiers, Duchesse de Valentinois, had begun over twenty years before, but it was nonetheless dazzling. He excelled at all forms of sport; much of his time was given up to it; every day there was tilting at the ring, hunting, tennis, ballets, and the like." The physically well-favored, amorously inclined Louis XIV was soon to discard his second mistress for another "favorite," but the courtiers who frequented Versailles would have recognized their king, their sport, and their lavish milieu right away in these opening sentences. By chronicling the recent past rather than the present, Madame de La Fayette achieved a tactful, objective distance from which she could safely reflect the court world of Louis XIV in the reign of Henri II. To underscore *The Princess of Clèves*'s blend of fact and fiction, she called the novel a *histoire*, an ambiguous term which means both "history" and "story."

At the beginning of *The Princess of Clèves*, the author details the political and romantic rivalries at court, leading the reader to expect either the extravagances of the *roman* or the private scandals of the powerful. Instead, into this web of court intrigue comes Madame de Chartres, hoping to marry her beautiful young daughter to a high-ranking nobleman, preferably a prince of royal blood. The preliminary description of the intrigues at Henri's court provides the backdrop to the process of wooing that commences. Mademoiselle de Chartres, "one of the most eligible heiresses in France," has all the qualities of the romantic heroine: "She was absolutely dazzling. Indeed there was nobody to touch her, with her white skin, golden hair, classical features, and general aspect of sweetness and charm." In order to achieve an advantageous marriage in the complicated court network of political and romantic alliances, Madame de Chartres must guide her innocent sixteen-year-old daughter through a world in which glamour conceals motive and appearance disguises reality. She cautions her daughter not to be deceived by appearances, since what she will see is almost never real or true. The conflict between appearance and reality, the difference between the way people act and what they truly feel, generates the novel's drama. On the subject of love, Madame de Chartres is blunt: "She told [her daughter] that men were not very sincere, not very faithful, and not above deceit; she spoke of the unhappiness that love affairs can bring to a family, and then, on the other hand, she showed her the life of a good woman, happy, serene, and enjoying the particular glamour that attaches to noble birth when there is also virtue."

Mademoiselle de Chartres's character will be tested after marriage, as she accedes to her mother's wishes and agrees to wed the much-older prince of Clèves, whom she does not love. She tells the prince that she will try to love him, but that she feels no real passion for him or for any man. The new princess is dutiful toward her husband and maintains a spotless reputation in a court where, in the tradition of courtly love, extramarital attachments are the norm. The princess's behavior not only traduces this tradition, it cheats the courtiers out of the possibility of a new scandal to enjoy. One evening, at a court ball, the princess is ordered by the king to dance with a late arrival, the duc de Nemours. Described in the novel as "nature's masterpiece," the duke is the most handsome, gallant, and accomplished nobleman at court. He falls in love with the princess, and she, for the first time, feels passion for a man. The princess of Clèves is conflicted as she attempts to cope with her feelings for Nemours while recognizing her responsibilities to her husband. Her conscience will not allow infidelity, and, although she tries to hide her true feelings behind a decorous public mask, she experiences a split between her outward behavior and her inner desires. Driven to resolve this conflict, she confesses her feelings to her dying mother, who acknowledges that her daughter is "on the edge of a precipice." After her mother dies, the princess turns to her husband—the only authority figure available to her—and in the novel's most controversial scene, she courageously but naively confesses her attraction to the unnamed Nemours. Instead of receiving the emotional and moral support she so desperately needs, she is confronted with the prince's distrust and anxiety. Disappointed by his inability to provoke a passionate response from his wife, the prince is increasingly consumed by jealousy, insists upon knowing the name of his rival, and becomes obsessed with uncovering evidence of the princess' betrayal. Incapable of believing his wife's protestations of innocence, beyond what she feels for her would-be paramour, and convinced of her infidelity, the elderly prince languishes and dies.

The way is cleared for a happy romantic ending to the novel, since the princess of Clèves is now free to give in to her passion for Nemours. But this is no ordinary romance, and appearances, as Madame de La Fayette has cautioned the reader, are deceiving. The author has endowed her title character with qualities beyond that of any romantic heroine of the era, and she has presented moral dilemmas that make up the challenging, ambiguous world of the novel. The duc de Nemours prevails upon the princess's uncle to intercede on his behalf, and the uncle arranges a meeting between the two lovers. When Nemours de-

clares that his love for the princess is "true and strong" and proposes an attachment, she is adamant in her refusal, stating:

> I confess . . . that my passions may govern me, but they cannot
> blind me. Nothing can prevent me from recognizing that you were
> born with a great susceptibility to love and all the qualities re-
> quired for success in love. You have already had a number of pas-
> sionate attachments; you would have others. I should no longer be
> able to make you happy; I should see you behaving towards an-
> other woman as you had behaved towards me. I should be mor-
> tally wounded at the sight and I cannot even be sure I should not
> suffer the miseries of jealousy. . . . I must remain in my present
> state and stand by the resolution I have taken never to abandon it.

The princess submits passion to the cold logic of reality.
Nemours has deceived before; like all men, he will do so again.
The princess of Clèves recognizes that she has a central duty to
herself, not to her lover. She rejects marriage and gratified passion, and instead retires from the court and the world to her estate in the Pyrenees. The novel closes with a brief memorial to her
life there: "She spent a part of each year in the convent and the
rest of it at home but living in even greater austerity, with even
more saintly occupations than in the strictest of orders. Indeed,
her life, which was not a long one, provided an example of inim-
itable goodness." As for the duc de Nemours, he "did everything
imaginable to make her change her mind. At last, after the passage of whole years, time and absence healed his grief and his
passion died away."

The Princess of Clèves was an immediate success. Paris book-
sellers were unable to meet the demand, and provincial readers
were forced to wait months for a copy. The novel sparked a search
for the identity of its author, as well as a lively debate over its merits as a work of art and its truthfulness. Madame de La Fayette,
after denying that she was the author, offered her own review of
the novel, declaring it to be "most agreeable, well written without
being extremely polished, full of wonderfully fine things that even
merit a second reading." She praised the novel for its "perfect imitation of the world of the court and the way one lives there," but
she was careful to add that it "should properly be regarded as a
memoir." One of the great ethical debates of the era followed the
novel's publication and concerned the scene in which the princess

of Clèves tells the prince that she loves the duc de Nemours. The Paris journal *Mercure Galant* invited its readers to vote on whether the princess was right or wrong to confide in her husband. Opinion was overwhelmingly against her, thus blurring the distinction between art and life—as in so much popular fiction, past and present.

Considered the first psychological novel, *The Princess of Clèves* influenced later generations of French novelists, from Rousseau to Camus. Because it is a novel by a woman about a woman, it can also be regarded as a study in women's issues. *The Princess of Clèves*, with its focus on inner conflict, moral complexity, and human truth, has earned an honored place alongside the works of the great women novelists of the nineteenth century and beyond.

A VINDICATION OF THE RIGHTS OF WOMAN

by Mary Wollstonecraft

Mary Wollstonecraft's feminist manifesto, *A Vindication of the Rights of Woman* (1792), is the first major pronouncement of women's rights, a foundation text in the struggle for women's liberation and gender equality, combining the force of the Declaration of Independence with that of the Emancipation Proclamation. In an era in which women had virtually no legal standing, in which their intellectual abilities were denied, and their roles and identities defined by the requirements of obeying and pleasing men, Mary Wollstonecraft argued that a woman was not a kind of superior domesticated animal but a rational human being. She insisted that women's mental and moral capabilities must be recognized and encouraged, and their independence and autonomy nurtured. In a revolutionary era in which despotism was challenged and the rights of man asserted, Wollstonecraft radically called for the extension of rights and liberties to women as well. Although others had written on behalf of women's rights before Wollstonecraft, her book is the first comprehensive argument affirming the necessity for women's education and diagnosing the social and moral implications of gender inequality.

Mary Wollstonecraft (1759–1797) was, in the words of her

friend and admirer the poet William Blake, "born with a different Face." During her brief, tempestuous life, she rebelliously refused to adapt herself to the conventional standards applied to women, contending with every limitation imposed on them. As Virginia Woolf observed in her memorial to the impact of Wollstonecraft's life and work, "Many millions have died and been forgotten in the hundred and thirty years that have passed since she was buried; and yet as we read her letters and listen to her arguments and consider her experiments . . . and realize the high-handed and hot-blooded manner in which she cut her way to the quick of life, one form of immortality is hers undoubtedly: she is alive and active, she argues and experiments, we hear her voice and trace her influence even now among the living." Mary Wollstonecraft first identified the challenges women faced and still face in reaching their full potential, and *A Vindication of the Rights of Woman* is an essential work that remains one of the most influential texts ever written in the history of women's liberation.

Wollstonecraft's theories on women's education and status were based significantly on her own experiences as a daughter, single woman, mistress, mother, and wife. In each role she defied conventions and challenged traditional assumptions. Her father, Edward, gave up his trade as a silk weaver and moved his wife and six children from London to Yorkshire, where he tried his hand at farming. From an early age, Mary cultivated her intellectual development although intellectual attainments were generally thought beyond women's capabilities. Edward Wollstonecraft's failure as a farmer caused him to become increasingly bitter and violent, and he began to drink and to abuse his family. As Wollstonecraft's husband and first biographer, William Godwin, writes, Mary "would often throw herself between the despot and his victim, with the purpose to receive upon her own person the blows that might be directed against her mother." Mary observed and experienced firsthand the unequal power dynamic between husband and wife, father and daughter, and it became clear to her that she would have to earn a living to support herself and her family. Characteristically, she chose self-reliance and independence over the security afforded by marriage. "I will not marry," Wollstonecraft declared, "for I do not want to be tied to this nasty world, and old maids are of so little consequence that, let them live or die, nobody will laugh or cry. It is a happy thing to be a mere blank and to be able to pursue one's own whims where they lead without having a husband and half a hundred children at hand to tease and control a poor woman who wishes to be free."

At the time, professional options for respectable women were few: a woman could work as a companion, a teacher, or a governess. Wollstonecraft tried all three. At nineteen, she left home to become the live-in companion of a Mrs. Dawson and accompanied her to the resort town of Bath, where Wollstonecraft was exposed to the superficial high life of the fashionable at leisure; she was both bored and appalled at the superficial and frivolous behavior of the fashionable ladies of the day. In 1783, Wollstonecraft interceded on behalf of her younger sister, Eliza, whose marriage was duplicating the pattern of domestic violence of their own family. With the aid of her close friend, Fanny Blood, Wollstonecraft took Eliza away from her husband, and the three opened a school in Newington Green. There she wrote *Thoughts on the Education of Daughters* (1787), in which she argued that a girl's intellect should be developed. This radical notion, which forms the core of the leading pedagogical ideas of *A Vindication of the Rights of Woman*, challenged the popular contention of French philosopher Jean Jacques Rousseau in his novel *Emile and Sophie: Or, a New System of Education* (1762) that rational pursuits belong to men alone and that women should be educated only in the ways and means of pleasing their husbands. The school eventually foundered, and Wollstonecraft next accepted a position in Ireland as a governess to the children of Lord and Lady Kingsborough. She entered service at the great Kingsborough mansion (as she later recalled from the perspective of a supporter of the French Revolution), "with the same kind of feeling as I should have if I was going to the Bastille." Her independence, rebelliousness, and her sensitivity to the inequities of wealth made her service as a governess intolerable, and she eventually left for London, where the publisher Joseph Johnson gave her lodging and sufficient editorial work reviewing and translating to support herself. Johnson encouraged Wollstonecraft to try to become a professional writer—a radical option for an eighteenth-century woman. In her own words, she aspired to become "the first of new genus," a woman writer who dared to grapple with the major issues of the day and refused to be relegated to the sphere of irrelevant frivolity and superficiality that was the common lot of other female writers then. While Wollstonecraft's contemporaries such as Fanny Burney and Jane Austen wrote anonymously, and subsequent writers such as

Anne, Charlotte, and Emily Brontë, as well as George Eliot, chose male pseudonyms to help assure that their work would be taken seriously, Wollstonecraft openly proclaimed her identity as an author and entered fully into the intellectual debates of the time, subjects no previous English woman had attempted in print before.

Wollstonecraft's mentor, James Johnson, was at the center of intellectual London, and his circle included the political theorist Thomas Paine, scientist Joseph Priestly, philosopher William Godwin, painter Henry Fuseli, and poet William Blake. Most were freethinking radicals, and Mary, who shared their interests in challenging orthodoxy, began expressing her views in Johnson's *Analytical Review.* The central event that absorbed Wollstonecraft and her circle was the French Revolution. At first, the English greeted the overthrow of an outdated despotic regime with enthu-siasm. However, Edmund Burke's conservative treatise, *Reflections on the Revolution in France* (1790), which argued in favor of the English monarchical status quo over the upheavals in France, helped turn English opinion against the Revolution. Wollstonecraft's *A Vindication of the Rights of Men* (1790) was among the first rebut-tals of Burke's position. In it, she challenged Burke's denial of the natural rights of man in favor of law, custom, and tradition. For Wollstonecraft, liberty and self-determination are basic attributes of human nature, and mankind's drive to resist subjugation and oppression is morally and religiously sanctioned. Wollstonecraft's treatise was her first popular success and one of the earliest polit-ical essays by a woman.

If the implications of the French Revolution provided the stim-ulus for *A Vindication of the Rights of Men,* they also formed the ini-tial motivation for the similarly titled *A Vindication of the Rights of Woman.* Her essay is dedicated to the French diplomat and states-man Talleyrand, whose report, in 1791 on public education, given to the Constituent Assembly that was drafting the new French constitution, had restricted a proposed system of free education to men only. *A Vindication of the Rights of Woman* attempted to make a case why women must be included in a reformed educational sys-tem of an enlightened republic. As Wollstonecraft makes clear in her dedication: "Contending for the rights of woman, my main ar-gument is built on this simple principle, that if she be not prepared by education to become the companion of man, she will stop the progress of knowledge and virtue; for truth must be common to all, or it will be inefficacious with respect to its influence on general practice." To make her case for the necessity of women being properly educated, Wollstonecraft begins by attempting to establish the key commonality between men and women that will drive the logic of her argument:

> In what does man's pre-eminence over the brute creation consist? The answer is as clear as that a half is less than the whole; in Reason.
>
> What acquirement exalts one being above another? Virtue; we spontaneously reply.
>
> For what purpose were the passions implanted? That man by struggling with them might attain a degree of knowledge denied to the brutes; whispers Experience.
>
> Consequently the perfection of our nature and capability of happiness, must be estimated by the degree of reason, virtue, and knowledge, that distinguish the individual, and direct the laws which bind society: and that from the exercise of reason, knowledge and virtue naturally flow, is equally undeniable, if mankind be viewed collectively.

If the essential attribute of human nature is reason, which is perfected by knowledge, then education is central to forming a virtuous individual and society. And if this is true for men, Wollstonecraft points out, it must also be true for woman. "For man and woman," she argues, "truth . . . must be the same. . . . Women, I allow, may have different duties to fulfil, but they are *human* duties, and the principles that should regulate the discharge of them, I sturdily maintain, must be the same." If the purpose of life for all mankind is the perfection of one's nature through the exercise of reason, then, according to Wollstonecraft, it is immoral to deny women the opportunity to gain both knowledge and virtue.

A Vindication of the Rights of Woman goes on to analyze the positives that flow from the education of women and the negatives that exist through women's exclusion from education's benefits. In their present state, women are "barren blooming" flowers due to a "false system of education, gathered from the books written on this subject by men who, considering females rather as women than human creatures, have been more anxious to make them alluring mistresses than affectionate wives and rational mothers; and the understanding of the sex has been so bubbled by this specious homage, that the civilized women of the present century, with a few exceptions, are only anxious to inspire love, when they ought to cherish a nobler ambition, and by their abilities and virtues exact respect." Women's typical education produces a "puerile propriety," an immature individual incapable of orderly thought and, therefore, easily influenced. Such training ill-equips women from being good wives or mothers. Marriage, Wollstonecraft argues, must be grounded on mutual respect, which can only be achieved when women are encouraged to develop their intellectual abilities; otherwise subordination, inferiority, and inequality are inevitable and ruinous in forming virtuous wives and mothers:

> Taught from their infancy that beauty is woman's sceptre, the mind shapes itself to the body, and, roaming round its gilt cage, only seeks to adorn its prison. Men have various employments and pursuits which engage their attention, and give a character to the opening mind; but women, confined to one, and having their thoughts constantly directed to the most insignificant part of themselves, seldom extend their views beyond the triumph of the hour. But were their understanding once emancipated from the slavery to which the pride and sensuality of man and their short-sighted desire, like that of dominion in tyrants, of present sway, has subjected them, we should probably read of their weaknesses with surprise. . . . It is time to effect a revolution in female manners— time to restore to them their lost dignity—and make them, as a part of the human species, labour by reforming themselves to reform the world.

To bring about this revolution Wollstonecraft proposes establishing government schools "in which boys and girls might be educated together" up to the age of nine. After that, "girls and boys, intended for domestic employments, or mechanical trades, ought to be removed to other schools, and receive instruction, in some measure appropriate to the destination of each individual, the two sexes being still together in the morning; but in the afternoon, the girls should attend a school, where plain-work, mantua-making, millinery, &c. would be their employment." Young people of superior abilities, male and female, would pursue their academic training together. "In this plan of education," Wollstonecraft asserts, "the constitution of boys would not be ruined by the early debaucheries, which make men so selfish, or girls rendered weak and vain, by indolence, and frivolous pursuits."

Wollstonecraft concludes her argument with an enumeration of the various follies and weaknesses that proceed when women are allowed to remain ignorant, and recommends corrections that extend beyond proper education. Women, Wollstonecraft argues, must be able to support themselves if a husband or family member cannot. Women also should have the full legal rights of citizens, including the right to own property, have custody of their children, and participate in governmental affairs. She ends with a plea and a warning:

> Let women share the rights and she will emulate the virtues of man; for she must grow more perfect when emancipated, or justify the authority that chains such a weak being to her duty. . . . Be just then! O ye men of understanding! and mark not more severely what women do amiss, than the vicious tricks of the horse or the ass for whom ye provide provender—and allow her the privileges of ignorance, to whom ye deny the rights of reason, or ye will be worse than Egyptian task-masters, expecting virtue where nature has not given understanding!

Initial reaction to Wollstonecraft's essay was generally temperate and favorable. Opinion, however, shifted markedly when the details of Wollstonecraft's subsequent life were made known following her death, in 1797. In 1793, Wollstonecraft visited Paris to observe firsthand the progress of the Revolution and its increasing violence during the Reign of Terror. There, she met a number of the Revolution's leading political figures. She also began an affair with American adventurer Gilbert Imlay, who deserted her after she gave birth to a daughter, Fanny. Despondent, Wollstonecraft returned to England and attempted suicide by jumping off London's Putney Bridge into the Thames. She was rescued by passersby. In 1796, she married philosopher William Godwin. One year later, Mary Wollstonecraft Godwin died within days of giving birth to a second daughter, Mary, who would later marry the poet Percy Bysshe Shelley and create a literary classic of her own, *Frankenstein*. To memorialize his wife, Godwin published *Memoirs of the Author of a Vindication of the Rights of Woman*, which revealed to the public that Wollstonecraft had borne a child out of wedlock, was deserted by her lover, attempted suicide, and engaged in sexual relations with Godwin before marriage. Many, scandalized by these revelations, found confirmation of the immorality and dangerousness of her ideas in her unconventional lifestyle. One writer declared, "Her works will be read with disgust by every female who has any pretensions to delicacy; with detestation by everyone attached to the interests of religion and morality, and with indignation by anyone who might feel any regard for the unhappy woman, whose frailties should have been buried in oblivion." Another would resort to verse:

> Whilom this dame the Rights of Women writ,
> That is the title to the book she places,
> Exhorting bashful womankind to quit
> All foolish modesty and coy grimaces,
> And name their backsides as it were their faces;
> Such license loose-tongued liberty adores,
> Which adds to female speech exceeding graces;
> Lucky the maid that on her volume pores,
> A scripture archly fram'd for propagating whores.

And he summed up his views in the following couplet:

> For Mary verily would wear the breeches
> God help poor silly men from such usurping b– – – – –s.

Wollstonecraft's impassioned argument on behalf of women's rights and aspirations, and her often rebellious attempt to live out the full implications of her ideas, would prove to be too far ahead of their time, too radical an assault on the accepted certainties of gender assumptions. It would take almost a century for Wollstonecraft's life and work to be rediscovered and appreciated during the pursuit of the women's rights goals she first articulated. As critic R. M. Janes has argued, "Wollstonecraft's particular contribution was to state and enact the major topics of feminist discourse. In the positions she articulated and the life she led, she touched upon almost every topic that has since been raised. Everything is there."

EMMA

by Jane Austen

Emma is not Jane Austen's most popular and endearing novel—that distinction belongs to her 1813 work, *Pride and Prejudice*, with its winning heroine and noble hero, and the satisfying resolution of their romantic dilemma. *Emma* features a noble hero (with a name to match his character—Mr. Knightley) and a gratifying romantic resolution, but it also possesses a more complex—and flawed—heroine in the title character, as well as more intricate situations that showcase the fullness of Austen's maturity as a novelist. Published in 1816, *Emma* is the fourth of Austen's six novels and the one that most demonstrates her exceptional skill as a social satirist, psychologist, and dramatist. It has also been chosen for this volume because it is considered to be the finest novel by one of the greatest novelists of all time.

Jane Austen (1775–1817) is the ideal example of the maxim that an author should write about what he or she knows best, and that everyday experience can be the source of great and enduring art. Austen was born into the English gentry class, whose customs she exclusively detailed in her novels. She was the youngest daughter of seven children of Reverend George Austen, the rector of Steventon in Hampshire, and Cassandra Leigh Austen. Jane

Austen and her older sister, Cassandra, were educated privately and at schools in Oxford, Southampton, and Reading. Austen grew up well read in English classics, prose, and poetry, was reasonable well versed in languages, and was also skilled in such traditionally feminine pursuits as music and needlepoint.

In 1801, George Austen, accompanied by his family, retired to Bath. After his death, in 1805, the family moved to Southampton to be closer to the two youngest Austen sons, who were in the navy. The Austens returned to Hampshire, in 1809, settling in the village of Chawton, where Jane remained until her death from Addison's disease at the age of forty-two. She shared a room with her sister all her life and had no personal acquaintance with any other important writers of the day. All her novels concern the central domestic drama of matrimony, but Austen never married, although her biographers have speculated that there were several romantic attachments and know of at least one marriage proposal. Rather than imitating her heroines and securing a husband and the property that went with him, Austen involved herself with her wide circle of friends and relatives, helped to run the family household (one of her duties was to oversee the sugar stores), and concentrated on her writing.

Jane Austen's writing career is divided into two distinct periods. Her earliest work, written in Steventon during the 1790s, includes fragments, satires, literary burlesques, and the first drafts of what would become her early novels: *Pride and Prejudice*, *Sense and Sensibility*, and *Northanger Abbey* (published posthumously). Then came a twelve-year lull, during which Austen wrote little. After the family's relocation to Chawton, Austen reworked her first three novels and composed her last three: *Mansfield Park*, *Emma*, and *Persuasion* (also published after her death). She wrote between domestic chores and social events at a tiny table in her drawing room. Austen chose for her subject the world she knew best and once told a niece who was thinking of writing novels, "Three or four families in a country village is the very thing to work on." Her novels—socially sophisticated, sharply rendered comedies of manners—were described by her as "the little bit (two inches wide) of Ivory on which I work with so fine a Brush, as produces little effect after much labour."

Emma, the longest of Austen's novels and the only one named for the central protagonist, is the most psychologically rich, with its closest focus on the inner development of its heroine. The novel depicts a year in the life of Highbury, a Surrey village in which nothing unusual generally happens beyond the natural cycle of births, deaths, engagements, and marriages, and the various unexceptional day-to-day occurrences of a self-contained, provincial community. Like all of Jane Austen's novels, *Emma* charts the progress of its protagonist to the altar, but unlike Austen's other novels, *Emma*'s heroine is unhampered by the lack of fortune and status, with only the disadvantage of her own immaturity to complicate her destiny: "Emma Woodhouse, handsome, clever, and rich, with a comfortable home and happy disposition, seemed to unite some of the blessings of existence; and had lived nearly twenty-one years in the world with very little to distress or vex her." Emma's mother is dead, her older sister is married and living in London, and her father is a hypochondriac and self-proclaimed invalid. Emma is the uncontested mistress of Hatfield, the most prominent household in Highbury, which she dominates. Only her sister's brother-in-law, Mr. Knightley, is willing to criticize her, and so Emma is afflicted with the "power of having rather too much her own way, and a disposition to think a little too well of herself."

The novel opens with Emma left on her own for the first time after her companion and former governess, Miss Taylor, marries the Woodhouses' neighbor, Mr. Weston, and leaves Hatfield. Emma flatters herself that she has successfully arranged the match, and she looks for another opportunity to try her hand at matchmaking. She befriends the impressionable Harriet Smith, "the natural daughter of somebody," and recklessly decides that she is the perfect mate for the local vicar, Mr. Elton. But to make the match happen, Emma must convince Harriet that her attachment to a local farmer, Robert Martin, is beneath her, and she intimidates Harriet into rejecting his proposal. Indulging in a romantic fantasy, Emma commits a series of social blunders that underscore her thoughtlessness, vanity, and snobbery. Her encouragement of Mr. Elton on behalf of Harriet is misconstrued by the clergyman as Emma's own interest in him, and she is comically blindsided by Mr. Elton's marriage proposal following a Christmas party that concludes the novel's first volume. Mr. Elton's drunken impertinence exposes Emma's errors of judgment in which the exaggerated sense of her own importance, together with her sense of infallibility and her snobbish prejudices, prevents her from correctly seeing the reality of social situations or the true nature of those around her. She ends this first stage of her development vowing never again to engage in matchmaking. Emma has played with love and romance by proxy through Harriet; however, the stakes will increase as she allows her own affections to be engaged and when she finds herself the victim of another character's scheming and manipulation.

Emma's superiority, assumed rather than earned, will also be challenged, as three newcomers arrive to help Highbury awake from its moribund routine, as well as to help Austen's heroine shed her complacency and complete her education. One is the estimable Jane Fairfax, the talented young niece of Miss Bates, a garrulous, slightly foolish Highbury spinster. Brought up and educated by Colonel and Mrs. Campbell as a companion to their daughter, Jane has returned to Highbury to visit her aunt and grandmother after Miss Campbell's marriage to Mr. Dixon. The modest Jane is Emma's equal (or superior) in everything but fortune; consequently she is not one of Emma's favorites. The second newcomer is Frank Churchill, Mr. Weston's son, who has arrived in Highbury to pay his respects to his father's new bride. The attractive and agreeably sociable Frank flirts with Emma, and the pair enjoys a secret joke at Jane's expense, alleging that she has had an unhappy love affair with Mr. Dixon, who seems to be the only possible source for the gift of a piano that Jane has received. The third character to arrive at Highbury is the former Augusta Hawkins, now married to Mr. Elton. An ill-bred parvenu, Augusta Elton challenges Emma for social dominance in Highbury and provides a mirror that reflects her own tendency toward vanity and snobbery: "Mrs. Elton was a vain woman, extremely well satisfied with herself, and thinking much of her own importance. . . . She meant to shine and be very superior, but with manners which had been formed in a bad school, pert and familiar." The bad breeding and behavior of both husband and wife is evident at the long-awaited ball at the Crown Inn, where they snub Harriet. Mr. Knightley forgoes his previous reluctance to dance and saves the embarrassed Harriet by becoming her partner (thus chivalrously living up to his name). It is a fateful moment for Emma, who acknowledges Mr. Knightley's superior nature and begins to see him as a potential romantic partner as well. The following day, Harriet is bothered by a band of gypsies (the novel's only melodramatic event) and is rescued by Frank Churchill. Harriet later confesses to Emma that she is now over

Mr. Elton and prefers someone more superior, leading Emma to think that she must mean Frank. Matchmaking yet again, Emma willingly accedes to her friend's preference.

As summer arrives, the complicated tangle of relationships reaches a critical point. Jane prepares to accept a governess position arranged by Mrs. Elton; Frank is inexplicably out of humor at the news; and Mr. Knightley decides to revive the social life of his estate, Donwell Abbey. A visit to Mr. Knightley's home stimulates a more ambitious picnic to Box Hill, where Frank caters to the worst of Emma's imperious tendencies by proposing a game in which each of the party is commanded to entertain her by saying one clever thing, "or two things moderately clever—or three things very dull indeed." The garrulous Miss Bates chooses the last, prompting Emma's unpardonably rude remark, "Ah! ma'am, but there may be a difficulty. Pardon me—but you will be limited as to number—only three at once." This witty remark at Miss Bates's expense crystallizes all of Emma's shortcomings and is the climax of the novel. Emma's deficiencies of character are made painfully clear to her in Mr. Knightley's later rebuke. Mortified by the hurt she has caused an old family friend who deserves her respect and compassion, and distressed at eliciting Mr. Knightley's poor opinion of her behavior, a repentant Emma visits Miss Bates the next day to apologize. This act of reformation, together with the acknowledgment of her error, paves the way for the comic conclusion of the novel, which depends on Emma's maturation.

In rapid succession, complication gives way to clarity, romance, and marriage. It is revealed that Frank has been secretly engaged to Jane all along, and his duplicity and manipulation are the final telling comparison with Emma's own behavior, which at times has also been far from open and honest. Emma's first thought, however, is for "poor Harriet," who is assumed to be in despair over the news. Instead, in the novel's great comic revelation, Harriet admits that, encouraged by Emma to aim for a husband of a higher station, she has set her sights on Mr. Knightley and not on Frank—it was Mr. Knightley's chivalrous behavior at the ball, not Frank's rescue of Harriet from the gypsies, that has engaged her affections. Emma is shocked into the recognition of her own blindness and folly: "With insufferable vanity had she believed herself in the secret of everybody's feelings; with unpardonable arrogance proposed everybody's destiny. She was proved to be universally mistaken. She had brought evil on Harriet, on herself, and she too much feared, on Mr. Knightley." Equally powerful is her realization "that darted through her with the speed of an arrow that Mr. Knightley must not marry anyone but herself." Initially misperceiving the other's feelings—Knightley, that Emma is in despair over Frank's engagement, and Emma over the presumed affection between Knightley and Harriet—the couple comes to a satisfactory understanding in the end, as Knightley proposes and Emma accepts. To add to the happy conclusion of reconciliation and unity, Harriet receives and accepts a second proposal from the hapless farmer, Robert Martin.

At his request, Jane Austen dedicated *Emma* to the Prince Regent (later George IV), who was a fan of the novelist. It sold quickly in its first edition of 1,500 copies, but a second edition was not published until 1833. Jane Austen herself had misgivings about her novel, fearing that "to those readers who have preferred 'Pride and Prejudice' it will appear inferior in wit, and to those who have preferred 'Mansfield Park' very inferior in good sense." Even more troublesome was her concern that she had created a heroine "whom no one but myself will much like." It is true that the most liked of Austen's heroines is undoubtedly Elizabeth Bennett, and *Pride and Prejudice* is the Austen novel most often read, as well as filmed—from the 1940 Hollywood version starring Greer Garson and Laurence Olivier to two miniseries as well as the 2001 comedy takeoff of the novel, *Bridget Jones's Diary*. But *Emma* has had its modern-day aficionados as well. During the 1990s, there were two well-executed versions of the novel: one a film starring Gwyneth Paltrow and the other a British miniseries. Perhaps the most artfully rendered and appealing film adaptation of *Emma* was Amy Heckerling's 1995 satire, *Clueless*, which updated Austen's novel to present-day Beverly Hills and changed Emma's name to Cher. This version speaks to the timelessness of the novel, which is, after all, essentially a story about a young woman who must learn painful lessons about human nature and bring her ego in line with reality in order to mature. Emma, like the reader, is schooled in the complicated matters of life and love, in which wisdom and clarity replace self-deception and confusion.

JANE EYRE

by Charlotte Brontë

Charlotte Brontë's novel of an independent-minded, principled young governess who comes to love her morally ambiguous, emotionally tortured employer, *Jane Eyre* (1847) is a romantic, psychological, and feminist classic that in fundamental ways revolutionized the art of fiction, with its assault on conventional nineteenth-century morality and its challenge to the novel's accepted methods of storytelling. The literary precursor of the modern gothic suspense novel, *Jane Eyre* also inspired such authors as Daphne du Maurier, whose best-selling *Rebecca* (*see* Honorable Mentions) began the twentieth-century genre of romance novels featuring an unassuming though plucky heroine and a dark Byronic bad boy ultimately redeemed by love.

Charlotte Brontë's life had a gothic quality that informed her work. Born in 1816, she was the third daughter of Patrick Brontë, the vicar of Haworth in the West Riding of Yorkshire, a picturesque but isolated region of impassable roads and desolate, windswept moors. After their mother's death, in 1821, the six Brontë children were cared for by an aunt and their puritanical, tyrannical father. Charlotte's biographer, English novelist Elizabeth Gaskell, wrote of Patrick Brontë, "He did not speak when he was annoyed or displeased, but worked off his volcanic wrath by firing pistols out the back door in rapid succession." After the two eldest Brontë daughters died of tuberculosis contracted at school, Charlotte and her sister Emily, also at school, were brought home. There, together with their younger sister Anne and brother Branwell, they were largely left to themselves. The major imaginative moment of their young lives occurred when their father brought home a set of wooden soldiers for his son. The toy soldiers became the *dramatis personae* in an ever-lengthening series of fantasy stories in which the children created the imaginary kingdoms of Gondal and Angria, and populated them with invented and historical figures. Charlotte's first stories, written in minuscule script in tiny homemade books, recorded the various lives and adventures of the characters in these fantasy kingdoms and provide an essential key to her artistic vision as a novelist.

The siblings' imaginative play continued well beyond childhood, but economic circumstances forced the Brontë children to abandon their fantasy empire of wish fulfillment to make their way in the world. Both Charlotte and Emily worked as teachers, and Anne became a governess. Branwell, whom it was hoped would succeed as a portrait painter, became instead the family disgrace, succumbing to drink and opium. To keep the family together, the sisters hatched a plan to open their own boarding school, and to perfect their French, Charlotte and Emily left Yorkshire to attend a school in Brussels. Left on her own when Emily's homesickness drove her back to Haworth, Charlotte developed an emotional attachment to the school's owner, whose wife quickly stepped in and stopped the infatuation. Charlotte returned to Yorkshire, where she and her sisters collaborated on a volume of poetry, published at their own expense under the names Currer, Ellis and Acton Bell. Only two copies were sold, and the sisters next turned to the commercial possibilities of the novel.

Charlotte Brontë's first attempt, *The Professor*, a one-volume realistic story based on her time spent in Brussels, was rejected by at least seven publishers. However, one sympathetic publisher suggested that "a work in three volumes would meet with careful attention," and she recast some of the elements of her childhood fantasy stories into a new novel in which she "endeavored to import a more vivid interest." In August 1847, a year after it was begun, *Jane Eyre* was published. The London season's literary sensation, a second edition of the novel was published three months after the first, and a third two months after that, an extraordinary success for the first book of an unknown author. *Jane Eyre* was published with the pseudonym Currer Bell to match Anne and Emily's Acton and Ellis Bell because, as Charlotte explained, "We had a vague impression that authoresses are liable to be looked on with prejudice." Anne's *Agnes Grey* and Emily's *Wuthering Heights* had been accepted for publication before *Jane Eyre*, but both novels did not appear until December 1847, when their publisher, hoping to profit from Charlotte's success, suggested in advertisements that their works were by one Mr. Bell, "the successful New Novelist." Anne's and Emily's novels, mistakenly believed to be the cruder, apprentice efforts of Currer Bell, were ignored. By 1848, *Jane Eyre* was a popular success. That same year, Branwell died, and at his funeral, Emily caught a cold that developed into tuberculosis. She died at the end of the year. Anne Brontë also died of tuberculosis, in the spring of 1849, leaving Charlotte alone. Charlotte wrote two other novels, *Shirley* and *Villette*, and in 1855, she married her father's curate. She died of tuberculosis while pregnant. Patrick Brontë survived all of his children, living to the age of eighty-four.

Jane Eyre, the story of a heroine, in Charlotte Brontë's words, "as plain and small" as herself, traces the title character's development from her troubled childhood to independence as a governess. In the care of her widowed aunt, Mrs. Reed, Jane is mistreated and neglected in favor of the three spoiled Reed children until her anger at her situation prompts a violent outburst that causes her to be delivered to the equally oppressive charity institution, Lowood Asylum. There, amidst the poor living conditions and repressive atmosphere, her rebellion recurs. Eventually she learns to harness her egoism and passion, which establishes the novel's dominant conflict between assertion and restraint, as well as love and duty. Jane makes friends at the school and eventually becomes a teacher there before accepting a position as a governess at Thornfield Hall, the country estate of Edward Rochester. Her task is to care for Rochester's illegitimate daughter, Adele Varens, a sweet, timid child. Despite Jane's homeliness and lack of status and sophistication, Rochester's brusque, cynical, world-weary manner, and a series of strange and alarming occurrences, including the sounds of maniacal female laughter, the burning of Rochester's bed, and the wounding of a mysterious visitor, Jane and Rochester develop a mutual regard for each other and eventually fall in love. Jane discovers that a disturbed woman lives on the locked third floor of the mansion; the night before her wedding to Rochester, the woman appears in her room. Rochester tells Jane that the woman is the household's unsavory seamstress, Grace Poole, but he has not told his bride-to-be the truth, and at the altar his sensational secret is revealed: concealed in Thornfield's attic is a madwoman named Bertha Mason, whom Rochester had married in the West Indies fifteen years earlier. Crushed by Rochester's deception, Jane departs Thornfield, and after nearly perishing on the moors is taken in by the Reverend St. John Rivers and his sisters. Jane calls herself Jane Elliott and returns to teaching. She rejects Rivers's proposal of a loveless marriage and a life as a missionary's wife. The claims of her former love prove stronger than her sense of duty to the honorable but emotionally shallow Rivers. After a telepathic vision in which she hears Rochester call her name, Jane returns to Thornfield to find the mansion burned, Bertha Mason dead, and Rochester blinded and maimed. With the moral and legal obstructions conveniently eliminated and Rochester sufficiently punished and penitent, the pair is reunited, and in one of most famous lines in fiction that begins the novel's final chapter, Jane records, "Reader, I married him." Rochester's sight returns and he is able to see the son born to him and Jane several years later.

In *Jane Eyre*, Charlotte Brontë recast the elements of the nineteenth-century gothic romance—its dark secrets, presentiments, coincidences, and eerie atmospherics—into a moral and psychological journey of a soul to fulfillment. At the center of the novel's drama is an unconventional heroine, never seen in fiction before. Jane is lowly and plain; she is forced to earn her living in a society of limited possibilities. Her hard-earned reward of the heart is played out against her struggle toward independence and emotional equilibrium. It is not surprising that Jane and her creator have been cited as early feminist models. Readers of today's romance novels would recognize a standard theme in Brontë's story of a lowly governess who falls in love with her wealthy employer, accepting him despite his rake's history and sensational secret. For the many nineteenth-century readers captivated by the novel, *Jane Eyre* was unique and daring, both for its story and its style, as well as for its intense exploration of the narrator's private thoughts and feelings (previously the province of poetry, not the novel). The popularity of Charlotte Brontë's first-person narrative of development was no doubt a factor in Charles Dickens's decision to launch his own first-person bildungsroman, *David Copperfield,* and influenced William Thackeray's similar attempt in *Pendennis.* For Thackerary, *Jane Eyre* hit even closer to home, when Charlotte Brontë, who greatly admired the novelist, dedicated the second edition to him. Thackeray was rumored to be Brontë's model for the character of Edward Rochester; it was also alleged that she was Thackeray's mistress.

Not all of the novel's first readers were delighted with the book, however. Jane's frank avowal of love for the morally suspect Rochester, as well as her rejection of the conventional role of the passive, relenting female in favor of independence and a self-determined morality, presented a challenge to Victorian orthodoxy and authority. Some found the book's sentiments, in the words of a contemporary reader, "un-Christian or worse." One appalled reviewer delivered the ultimate Victorian coup de grâce, charging that the book "might be written by a woman but not by a lady."

It is tempting for modern readers of *Jane Eyre* to filter their view of Charlotte Brontë's great work through celluloid and video images. The subject of at least thirteen film and television adaptations (one in every decade of the twentieth century since 1914), *Jane Eyre* shares—with Dickens's *David Copperfield* and *Great Expectations,* Flaubert's *Madame Bovary,* Hugo's *Les Misérables,* and Twain's *The Adventures of Huckleberry Finn*—the distinction of being one of the most often filmed novels. However, such adaptations should not replace or obscure the achievement of the original. The remarkable power of *Jane Eyre* derives as much from its intimate exposure of the narrator as from its melodramatic plot, with its sensational central secret and its deviations from reality through the heightened aura of the uncanny, which lends the novel a poetic, symbolic expressiveness. Rejecting the restriction of the novel to a surface imitation of life, Charlotte Brontë grafts onto her story a poetic method and intensity to achieve a depth of feeling and interior awareness in the stages of her heroine's moral and psychological development, linking each stage, as in a poem, through association, imagery, and symbolism. *Jane Eyre* brings to the reader the inner world of the psyche and the heart's private longing.

THE SCARLET LETTER

by *Nathaniel Hawthorne*

The great Victorian novelist Anthony Trollope once described the experience of reading Nathaniel Hawthorne: "He will have plunged you into melancholy, he will have overshadowed you with black forebodings, he will have almost crushed you with imaginary sorrows; but he will have enabled you to feel yourself an inch taller during the process." Hawthorne's genius, unique in American letters, is unfaltering in its moral seriousness; both bleakness and ecstasy can be experienced in his fiction. He addressed the Puritan obsession with the wages of sin, using it to focus it upon the hidden recesses of human nature, the consequences of moral transgressions, and the conflicts between authority, personal freedom, and responsibility. In *The Scarlet Letter* (1850), pride, guilt, retribution, and the alienation of the individual from society are explored in the story of Hester Prynne, who, despite the novel's setting in mid-seventeenth-century Puritan Boston, can be considered the first feminist central character in what is America's first great novel.

Nathaniel Hawthorne (1804–1864) was well versed in the culture of Puritan society. The Hathorne family (Hawthorne added the *w* after leaving college) could trace its ancestry to a member of John Winthrop's Massachusetts Bay Colony who moved to Salem, in 1636. One ancestor was a judge in the Salem witchcraft trials, and, according to family legend, one of the victims placed a curse on Judge Hathorne and all his descendants before her execution. Hawthorne's father was a ship's captain, and his mother was the daughter of Richard Manning, a blacksmith who became the proprietor and manager of the Boston and Salem Stage Company. When Nathaniel was only four, his father died in Surinam of yellow fever, and the family was absorbed into the large Manning clan. Nathaniel's childhood was spent between Salem and Maine, where the Mannings owned property, and he felt somewhat lost in the practical bustle of the large family. A sensitive child, Hawthorne decided by the age of seventeen that he would become a writer: "I do not want to be a doctor and live by men's diseases, nor a minister to live by their sins, nor a lawyer and live by their quarrels. So, I don't see that there is anything left for me but to be an author."

After graduating from Bowdoin College, Hawthorne returned to Salem, where, from 1825 to 1837, he lived a reclusive life, reading voraciously, particularly in the history of colonial New England, and emerging from his room only for evening strolls and occasional walking trips around Massachusetts. His first published work was the novel, *Fanshawe,* based on his experiences at Bowdoin, which appeared anonymously, in 1828. The novel was ignored and so dissatisfied its author that he would later seek out available copies to destroy. Hawthorne devoted the next twenty years to the shorter form of the prose tale and sketch. In the absence of an international copyright agreement, native novelists struggled in the marketplace because American publishers were able to pirate the best English writers, like Scott and Dickens, for free with impunity and therefore had no financial incentive to cultivate homegrown talent. But Hawthorne did find a market for his short fiction in New England magazines and newspapers, as well as in *The Token,* a Boston gift book annual, where most of the works collected in *Twice-Told Tales* (1837) first appeared. He worked hard at perfecting his craft, learning to project onto fictional characters and situations the moral and existential themes that fascinated him. Hawthorne's early tales, such as "The Gentle Boy," "Young Goodman Brown," "The Minister's Black Veil," "The Birthmark," "Ethan Brand," and "Endicott and the Red Cross," all illustrate a preoccupation with the psychological canons of the Puritan past—the ambiguity of sin, the conflict between heart and head, and the corrosive power of guilt—as well as the character types and settings that he would return to in *The Scarlet Letter.*

In 1842, Hawthorne married Sophia Peabody, and, unable to earn a sufficient income from his writing to support his growing family, he secured a position as an official at the Salem Customhouse from 1845 to 1849. Hawthorne's was a Democratic political appointment that he lost with the Whig election victory of Zachary Taylor. His dismissal, prompted by false allegations by Salem Whigs of "corruption, iniquity, and fraud," received national attention and contributed to the success he would later achieve with *The Scarlet Letter.* After losing his position, he returned to writing in earnest to make up for his lost income. In September 1849, he began *The Scarlet Letter* as a tale for a projected new volume to be titled *Old-Time Legends: Together with Sketches, Experimental and Ideal.* The novel's themes and situations reflect ideas recorded earlier in his notebook. Hester Prynne, his heroine, is anticipated in the entry: "The life of a woman, who, by the old colony law, was condemned always to wear the letter A, sewed on her garment, in token of her having committed adultery."

James T. Fields of Ticknor and Fields, the book's publisher, read the uncompleted manuscript and encouraged Hawthorne to expand the story and publish it as a separate work. It was finished in February 1850, and it became an immediate popular success, with the first edition of 2,500 copies selling out in three days. Two more editions appeared before the end of the year, and—although only 7,500 copies would be sold in Hawthorne's lifetime, earning him a grand total of $1,500—*The Scarlet Letter* has never gone out of print since it first appeared, becoming, along with *Moby-Dick* and *The Adventures of Huckleberry Finn*, an enduring classic and a continuing subject of serious critical literary scrutiny.

The Scarlet Letter centers on Hester Prynne, an attractive, apparently widowed young woman who has shocked and angered her rigidly Puritan community by taking a lover and bearing a daughter by him. Hester has been convicted of adultery—a crime against society that is punishable by death—but the Boston magistrates have decided to be merciful to her and have decreed that she stand before the townsfolk on the scaffold near the marketplace for three hours with her infant in her arms. To mark her as a sinner, she is also to wear on the bosom of her dress, embroidered in red cloth, the letter *A*—for "adulteress"—for the rest of her life. Governor Bellingham, Reverend John Wilson, and Reverend Arthur Dimmesdale, a young and eloquent minister, plead with Hester in vain to reveal the guilty man's identity. She refuses, much to the relief of Dimmesdale, since it is he who is Hester's secret lover. While standing on the scaffold, Hester sees a familiar figure on the edge of the crowd. The "stranger" is her elderly husband, Dr. Roger Prynne, who had sent Hester ahead of him from England two years earlier and had been presumed dead. The physician silently cautions her not to recognize him publicly and later, under the name of Roger Chillingworth, visits her in prison, where he demands to know the name of his wife's lover. Once again, Hester refuses to divulge his identity. Chillingworth vows to find the father of Hester's child and forces her to take an oath not to reveal to anyone that he is her husband. Shunned and ridiculed by the townsfolk, Hester lives in a lonely cottage by the seashore and supports herself and her daughter, Pearl, through her needlework. Her only companion is Pearl, a beautiful but willful and independent-minded child, who sometimes upsets her mother by the "freakish, elfish" look that comes into her eyes. Hester both loves and fears her bright, capricious child, but it is through Pearl that she demonstrates her own strength and independence, when she fights the authorities for the right to raise the child herself. She comes to see her daughter as a blessing rather than as an evil visited upon her by her sin.

Dimmesdale is unable to either confess or to accept his sin, and his health begins to fail. Tormented by guilt, he punishes himself by long night vigils, sometimes whipping himself, at other times fasting and praying for hours. Chillingworth, suspicious of Dimmesdale, moves into the reverend's house, ostensibly to provide medical assistance, but in reality to bait Dimmesdale into revealing his secret. Dimmesdale grows to fear and hate the physician, confessing as much to Hester when the two meet by chance one evening at the pillory scaffold. Later, Hester reveals Chillngworth's true identity to Dimmesdale, and the two make plans to leave Boston together with Pearl for a new life in England. However, Chillingworth books passage on the same ship, and Hester realizes that they can never escape him. After Dimmesdale gives a brilliant Election Day sermon, the crowd loudly cheers him in the marketplace. As the crowd begins to leave, Dimmesdale, by now weak and ill, ascends the scaffold with Hester's help and confesses that he is Pearl's father. He tears open his shirt and reveals a "red stigma" on his breast, which many of the townspeople later claim was a scarlet A. He then collapses on the scaffold and dies. Chillingworth, thus avenged, loses his purpose in life, and he dies within the year, leaving money and property to Pearl in England and America. Hester and Pearl leave Boston, but Hester later returns alone to the community and lives in the same small cottage by the seashore. It is thought that Pearl is happily married in Europe. Hester continues to wear the scarlet letter and work as a seamstress. Unhappy women troubled by affairs of the heart come to her for advice. After a long life, Hester dies and is buried beside Dimmesdale.

The power of *The Scarlet Letter* comes from Hawthorne's tight concentration on his four major characters—Hester, Dimmesdale, Chillingworth, and Pearl—in a series of striking tableaux that animate the novel's action and the characters' moral and psychological natures. Rather than explaining the causes of Hester's sin, Hawthorne focuses on its consequences by beginning the novel with the repentance extracted from her by the Puritan authorities. The nature of her sin is underscored by the multiple associations of the scarlet letter she is forced to wear as a public acknowledgment of her fallen nature. The scarlet letter becomes the novel's magnetic central symbol; it attracts the characters' reactions and is emblematic of each character's state of mind. For Hester, the letter is a sign of her human fallibility and her fate, which she freely chooses, acknowledges, and accepts. Ultimately, Hester, the fallen woman, is shown to be far more worthy of sympathy and respect than the narrow, intolerant Puritan community of the righteous. For Dimmesdale, the outward paragon of moral authority and saintliness, the scarlet letter is a symbol of his sinful nature and the guilty secret that he denies until the novel's climax, when he finally reveals his own "red stigma." The scarlet letter drives Chillingworth, the man of intellect and science, to hide his relationship to Hester and causes him to embark on a self-destructive pursuit of revenge, during which he is shown as more corrupt than the two lovers. The uncontrollable Pearl, who is brilliantly dressed in scarlet, is the living symbol of Hester's sin, condemned by the letter to an existence outside the human family until Dimmesdale's dying admission of his paternity.

When it was first published, *The Scarlet Letter* far surpassed any previous American novel and rivaled the greatest European works. It is the first undisputed American masterpiece, remarkable and unique for its intense moral and psychological exploration of four suffering souls in what was the dominant American culture of the early colonial era. Something of *The Scarlet Letter*'s power can be glimpsed in the reaction of Hawthorne's sensible wife after her husband finished the novel and read the last part of it to her: "It broke her heart," Hawthorne wrote.

MADAME BOVARY

by Gustave Flaubert

Subtitled *A Tale of Provincial Life*, Flaubert's masterpiece, published in book form in 1857, details the descent of his title character, desperate for sensation and deluded by romantic illusion, into tawdry affairs, finally destroyed by the conjunction of her nature and a repressive, inhospitable middle-class provincial environment. *Madame Bovary* is a must-read because it is one of the greatest and most original novels of all time and because, in Emma Bovary, Flaubert created a fascinating character whose psyche he painstakingly dissects and analyzes within the context of her constricted situation. It can also be argued that Flaubert, for the first time in fiction, presented readers with a female protagonist every bit as complex and dynamic as a central male character.

Considered a supreme example of the realistic novel, *Madame Bovary* is the artful product of a slow, meticulous writer intent on *le mot juste* and complete objectivity in telling his story. Flaubert devoted weeks to individual scenes and days to a single page; his fifty-six-month, seven-hour nightly struggle to complete *Madame Bovary* represents the birthing pains of a new kind of fictional narrative, one which earned Flaubert the accolade from Henry

James of the "novelist's novelist," and which gave the novel the respectability and seriousness in France formerly reserved for poetry, tragedy, and the epic.

Flaubert evolved his high standard for the novel, his advocacy of realism, and the novelist's strict artistic control over his material in a hard-fought struggle with his own divided temperament, which oscillated between romantic escape and the claims of a world that he often found disappointing and appalling. Flaubert's battle to shape the contradictory elements of romance and realism into an original work of art provides an interesting perspective on the dedication and craftsmanship involved in the development of what is often referred to today as a novelist's individual "voice."

Born in Rouen, Gustave Flaubert (1821–1880) came from the French bourgeois background that he analyzed so meticulously in *Madame Bovary* and found so limited and stultifying. His father was the chief surgeon at the Hôtel-Dieu hospital; his mother was the daughter of a small-town doctor. Possessing a precocious literary talent, Flaubert began writing romantic stories at the age of sixteen. His family, however, was determined that he should become a lawyer, and Flaubert spent a year at the University of Paris, where he studied little and failed his examinations. In 1844, a nervous collapse brought him back to the family estate at Croisset, near Rouen, where, after the death of his father in 1846, he lived with his solicitous mother and adoring, orphaned niece for the rest of his life, devoting his time exclusively to writing. Freed from the financial need to publish or the desire to court fame through gratifying conventional literary tastes, Flaubert began to evolve his narrative aesthetic, attempting to reconcile what he perceived was the duality of his nature: "There are in me, literally speaking, two distinct persons: one who is infatuated with bombast, lyricism, eagle flights, sonorities of phrase and lofty ideas; and another who digs and burrows into the truth as deeply as he can, who likes to treat the humble fact as respectfully as a big one, who would like to make you feel almost *physically* the things he reproduces."

Having finished an early version of what would eventually become *The Temptation of Saint Anthony* (1874) in 1849, which friends criticized mercilessly as romantically excessive, formless, and vague, Flaubert, at their suggestion, embarked upon a story of ordinary life, borrowed from the actual circumstances of the wife of one of his father's former medical students, whose love affairs and debts lead her to suicide. With a mixture of abhorrence for and fascination with this rather sordid story of provincial life, Flaubert began on St. Gustave's Day, September 9, 1851, the nearly five-year effort to penetrate imaginatively his characters and their environment. With a combination of compassion and satire, Flaubert mounted a withering indictment of his society's most cherished illusions: material satisfaction, faith in science and progress, religious consolation, and the ennobling power of love and passion. He aspired to write "a book about nothing," in which the trivial details of stultifying bourgeois life would replace the expected dramatic and romantic stimulus of other novels; it would be held together not by action but by ideas and sustained by his pursuit of *le mot juste,* in which every word, image, and scene contributed to an underlying pattern of meaning. Flaubert observed, "I am trying to be as buttoned up in this one as I was slovenly in the others and to follow a geometrically straight line. No lyricism, no commentaries, author's personality absent. It will make depressing reading. There will be atrocious things in it— wretched, sordid things." Flaubert's agonies of composition, which involved spending entire days finding the right phrase and eventually vomiting in a chamber pot after describing Emma Bovary's death by poison, suggest the novelist's attempt to subsume his entire personality in the artistic process, which more than justifies his later explanation of his protagonist's origin: "*Madame Bovary, c'est moi.*"

Emma Bovary, *née* Rouault, the character that inspired such unsettling devotion, is a convent-educated beauty with peasant roots, who has been deeply infected by the novels she has read and who dreams of the same idealized romantic fulfillment. Emotional rather than affectionate, sentimental rather than genuine, Emma is incapable of reconciling her desires and responsibilities, and becomes a martyr to her illusions, crushed when she attempts to act out her fantasies of passion and spirituality in a provincial world that only values the material, not the spiritual or the passionate that she craves. Wed to Charles Bovary, a widowed doctor of plodding mediocrity who adores her, Emma is disappointed in her marriage and unfulfilled in her expected role as wife and mother. Fueled by the stimulants of passion and the accoutrements of refinement that her limited means cannot sustain, she compensates with affairs with two men who fail her. Her first lover, Rodolphe, is a caddish libertine who exploits romantic clichés to gain Emma as his mistress but who refuses to assist her desired escape from her hateful life. Léon is Emma's pallid, timorous second lover, who seduces her not on horseback, like her previous chivalric parody, Rodolphe, but during a cab ride through the streets of Rouen. Inevitably, the prosaic, limiting reality of provincial life triumphs over her illusions and desires. Emma's life in the narrow confines of the town of Yonville is governed by the pedantic hypocrite Homais, Yonville's pharmacist, and the ineffectual parish priest, Father Bournisien, so lacking in his spiritual mission that he is incapable of recognizing even the proverbial cliché that men and women do not live by bread alone. Her dream world collapses from deceit and debt, and climaxes in suicide. In dying, Emma is finally given the ultimate opportunity of sacrificial martyrdom to become the romantic heroine that she had always aspired to be, but her death, like her life, is undermined by reality. Flaubert describes her death throes with an unflinching, clinical scrupulousness that subverts the sentimental. Emma's last vision is of a blind beggar, the novel's death's-head figure, who mirrors her own blindness and corruption, and her final dignity is undercut by those representatives of petit-bourgeois life, Homais and Bournisien, who guard her corpse. By the end, Flaubert has taken the reader simultaneously outward for a satirical portrait of mundane, provincial life that forms the environment with which Emma must contend, and inward to the formation of his protagonist's mental landscape, tracing the way in which thoughts, feelings, memories, and needs conspire to produce consciousness.

After completing *Madame Bovary* in 1856, Flaubert first brought out his novel serially in the *Revue de Paris*, reluctantly allowing some cuts to ward off the storm of controversy that promised to follow but resisting others, arguing to his editor, "You are objecting to details, whereas actually you should object to the whole. The brutal element is basic, not superficial . . . you cannot change the *blood* of a book. All you can do is weaken it." Charged with "outrage of public morals and religion" Flaubert faced a trial in which he bitterly predicted a guilty verdict, ironically finding in the trial "sweet recognition for my labors, noble encouragement to literature." Instead he was acquitted, and the novel became a notorious *succès de scandale*. He followed *Madame Bovary* with the lushly exotic *Salammbô* (1862), a historical novel set in ancient Carthage, *A Sentimental Education* (1869), in which his male protagonist develops a passion for an older married woman, the finished version of *The Temptation of Saint Anthony*, and *Three Tales* (1877), linked stories that described saints' lives. He died suddenly from a stroke, leaving unfinished the satiric novel, *Bouvard and Pécuchet*.

In writing *Madame Bovary*, Flaubert accomplished a revolution in the novel's subject matter and style. By presenting such a frank and unrelentingly realistic depiction of ordinary life, he replaced fictional idealization and falsification of character and scene with an accurate, authentic, and honest portrait of the ordinary and the ignoble. No previous novel had been so carefully designed with each part fitted into an elaborate whole; no female protagonist had been so carefully examined. A master craftsman, who insisted that the novelist should be "invisible and all-powerful: he must be everywhere felt, but never seen," Flaubert denied the reader direct, subjective narrative guidance; in doing so he raised the bar in the art of the novel by insisting that the reader play an active role in uncovering the patterns beneath the surface of things, subverting the expected fictional delights and substituting a coherent fictional universe held together by the force and clarity of the novel's vision. Flaubert's compassionate and objective penetration of human personality together with his technical skill has earned *Madame Bovary* its place as one of the most memorable and influential novels in world literature.

LITTLE WOMEN

by Louisa May Alcott

Louisa May Alcott's beloved novel of four adolescent girls growing up in nineteenth-century New England is traditionally considered a children's classic, although Alcott's sophisticated use of
language, frequent didactic narrative structure, and emphasis on
moral stricture can make it a challenging, culturally remote read
for many contemporary children—hence the adaptations published in recent years to make the story more accessible to young
readers. Some who choose to tackle *Little Women* (1868, 1869) at
an early age reexperience the novel at various times through the
years, enjoying it at different stages of their lives and intellectual
development. Originally written for young adolescent readers,
Little Women can, in fact, be appreciated as a women's novel and,
moreover, one with a feminist subtext; this is not surprising, given
that Alcott's lifelong heroine was proto-feminist writer Margaret
Fuller. Alcott's protagonists, the March sisters, and their wise,
principled mother represent five versions of nineteenth-century
womanhood, and the novel dramatizes the completeness and self-
sufficiency of their nearly all-female universe as it is eventually
joined by men who are happy to be educated in the domestic and
moral ideals of the household.

There are many telling similarities between the March family of *Little Women* and Alcott's own family. Like the spirited, literarily inclined Jo March, Louisa May Alcott (1832–1888) was the second oldest of four sisters. She would base the character of Jo on herself; the characters of Meg, Beth, and Amy March, as well as the girls' mother and father, were drawn from her sisters, Anna, Elizabeth, and Abbie May and her parents. Alcott's father, Bronson Alcott (1799–1888), one of the foremost intellectuals of his day, was variously a schoolmaster, educational innovator, school superintendent, transcendentalist, and traveling lecturer known later in his life as the celebrated "Father of Little Women." He founded the Temple School in Boston, and when that failed, he transferred his experimental educational methods to his children, teaching them at home in Concord, Massachusetts. In 1843, he founded a short-lived utopian community, Fruitlands, near Harvard, Massachusetts. The fits and starts of Bronson Alcott's career, together with his frequent absences on walking and lecturing tours, left the family in genteel poverty, which profoundly affected his children, especially Louisa, who would eventually become the family breadwinner. Louisa's mother, Abigail, known as "Abba," possessed the wisdom, strength, patience, and hopefulness necessary for marriage to an abstracted idealist who suffered from bouts of depression. When family fortunes were especially low, she worked at menial jobs to help support her family and for two years was a salaried city missionary to the poor in South Boston. Like Mrs. March, the much-loved and revered "Marmee" of *Little Women*, Abba Alcott kept the family together and exerted a powerful, steadying influence on her daughters. Louisa dedicated her books to her mother, describing her life in one inscription as "a long labor of love."

Louisa's decision to earn an income for her family was influenced in part by her desire to make life easier for her mother, "with no debts or troubles to burden her." To that end, she worked as a seamstress, domestic servant, governess, teacher, and companion, experiences she would later incorporate into her books. Beginning in 1851, with the publication of a poem in *Peterson's Magazine*, Alcott produced poems, serialized stories, and some children's tales, and was paid for her efforts. In December 1862, during the Civil War, she began service as an army nurse in Washington, D.C., but was invalided home with typhoid fever in January 1863. She recorded her nursing experiences in *Hospital Sketches*, which first appeared in the *Commonwealth* magazine in the spring of 1863, was published in book form soon afterwards, and received favorable reviews. In 1865, Alcott published her first novel, *Moods*, a romance. In his review of the novel, Henry James praised Alcott's understanding of men and women "with their every-day virtues and temptations," but felt that the author lacked an ability to "handle the great dramatic passions," and suggested that she could produce a very good novel "provided she will be satisfied to describe only that which she has seen."

In 1868, while living in Boston and working as the editor of a girls' magazine, *Merry's Museum*, Alcott was approached by Thomas Niles, Jr., of the Roberts Brothers publishing firm, with the suggestion that she use her powers of observation and sensitivity toward adolescents to write a domestic novel about young girls that would compete with the popular "Oliver Optic" series of boys' books. Using her own family as the foundation for her characters and situations, Alcott set to work on what would become the first part of *Little Women*, published in September 1868, after six weeks of writing.

Alcott incorporated into her novel the Christian moral precepts of John Bunyan's *Pilgrim's Progress*, a beloved book in the Alcott family. When *Little Women* opens, it is Christmastime and the March sisters—Meg, sixteen; Jo, fifteen; Beth, thirteen; and Amy, twelve—are in Bunyan's "Slough of Despond," lamenting the fact that they are poor (once wealthy, Mr. March lost his money "in trying to help an unfortunate friend"). Adding to the girls' sadness is the absence of their father, who is serving as a chaplain in the Civil War. The girls "played" at the story of *Pilgrim's Progress* when they were little; now Marmee suggests that they confront their own trials and tribulations, and make the pilgrim's progress toward "goodness and happiness" an actuality in their own lives: "Now, my little pilgrims, suppose you begin again, not in play, but in earnest, and see how far you can get before father comes home."

In this female-dominated household, with Marmee and Bunyan to guide them, the girls begin their journey toward maturity. Each has her particular burden: Meg, reduced to working as a governess for a rich family, longs for worldly comforts. Tall, awkward Jo, who has difficulty controlling her sharp tongue and short temper, is companion to the family's irascible Aunt March.

Jo's refuge is the attic, where she reads and writes, and cherishes dreams of literary success. Gentle Beth struggles with her painful shyness. Artistic Amy is affected and selfish.

The sisters begin their progress by resisting temptation. They use the dollar Marmee has given each of them to buy Christmas gifts for their mother, and they donate their delicious holiday breakfast to a poor German family that lives in town. On Christmas evening, after performing in a drama of Jo's devising, the girls are treated to a Christmas feast sent over to the March home by Mr. Laurence, the wealthy, somewhat gruff old gentlemen who lives in the large house next door. At a New Year's dance, Jo meets Mr. Laurence's orphaned grandson, the handsome and charming Laurie, who lives with his grandfather and has long wanted to meet the Marches. The temperamental and slightly spoiled Laurie benefits through his association with the warm, loving, principled March family and develops a close friendship with Jo.

During the course of the novel's first part, the sisters confront numerous challenges and sacrifices. Meg's vanity is tested when she spends a weekend with a wealthy school friend; Jo, in a fit of pique at her youngest sister, nearly causes Amy to drown in an icy pond; Beth must overcome her shyness to visit Mr. Laurence and play his beautiful piano; Amy disobeys at school and is humiliated by the unpleasant schoolmaster. When Mr. March becomes ill, Jo sells her beautiful long hair to help Marmee pay for the trip to Washington to nurse him. While she is away, Beth gets scarlet fever and, in one of the most affecting scenes in the novel, nearly dies. There is pleasure as well as pain: Beth recovers; Mr. March returns home on Christmas Day; and Meg falls in love with and becomes engaged to Laurie's tutor, John Brooke. Jo resents Brooke as an interloper who will take Meg away from the family, but she eventually learns to accept the situation.

Alcott ends the first part with the extended family grouped together in peaceful repose: "So grouped, the curtain falls upon Meg, Jo, Beth, and Amy. Whether it ever rises again depends upon the reception given to the first act of the domestic drama called 'Little Women.' " The novel was an immediate success, and in April 1869, after six weeks' work, Alcott published the second part of *Little Women*, called "Good Wives," which was also enormously popular. "Good Wives" contains the charm, humor, and family warmth of the first part, but it is frequently more sophisticated and serious in tone as Meg, Jo, Beth, and Amy leave their adolescence behind to confront in earnest their adult concerns. Meg marries and becomes the mother of twins. Jo is now selling stories to newspapers to supplement the family income and is mortified when Aunt March chooses the more refined Amy to accompany her to Europe. She goes to New York to develop her craft and to escape Laurie, who is in love with her. Jo becomes governess for Mrs. Kirke, who runs a boardinghouse, and befriends the kindly scholar, Professor Bhaer, one of the boarders. When she receives word of Beth's failing health, she returns home to care for her sister. Laurie proposes, but Jo refuses him, saying she does not think she will ever marry. (Alcott, who received letters from readers urging her to marry off Jo to her leading male character, wisely resisted such a simplistic plot resolution.) Beth dies, after a lingering demise portrayed in such an anti-melodramatic fashion that she almost seems to just retreat from life and fade away. Laurie and Amy fall in love and marry in Europe, and Jo, after suffering much loneliness despite her growing success as a writer and the comforting presence of her family, receives her reward in Professor Bhaer, whom she marries. When Aunt March dies, she leaves her home, Plumfield, to Jo, and the Bhaers open a school there for boys. The novel ends on Marmee's sixtieth birthday, during a jolly family apple-picking harvest. Jo, now thirty, has two sons, while Laurie and Amy have a baby daughter named Beth. The last sentiment belongs to Marmee, who, with her daughters gathered around her, "could only stretch out her arms, as if to gather children and grandchildren to herself, and say, with face and voice full of motherly love, gratitude, and humility: 'Oh, my girls, however long you may live, I never can wish you a greater happiness than this!'"

Alcott continued the story of the March family in *Little Men: Life at Plumfield With Jo's Boys* (1871) and *Jo's Boys* (1886), her last novel. The author of some 270 published works in every genre, Alcott became a celebrity on the strength of *Little Women*. Thanks to a new mass readership consisting of twelve- to sixteen-year-olds able to purchase inexpensively printed books, there was an even greater demand for Alcott fiction for young readers. Alcott obliged, producing such popular novels as *An Old-Fashioned Girl* (1870), *Eight Cousins* (1875), and *Rose in Bloom* (1876), all of which she described as "moral pap for the young." But *Little Women* in particular would not have remained as popular a book as it is today, spawned three movies and two miniseries based upon it, and prompted such critical debate over its merits and debits as a feminist novel, if it were simply a moral battering ram aimed at nineteenth-century girls. The novel may idealize the comforting coziness of nineteenth-century domestic life with, as one of the author's biographers put it, "the vividness of a Currier & Ives print," but in Meg, Jo, Beth, and Amy, Alcott created characters whose strengths and failings, struggles and triumphs are as easily recognizable to contemporary readers as they were instructive for young women marching toward a new concept called "feminism" more than one hundred years ago.

MIDDLEMARCH

by George Eliot

More than any other Victorian novelist, George Eliot (1819–1880) succeeded in transforming the novel, previously considered a lightweight form of entertainment, into a vehicle for the most subtle and profound social and psychological investigation. Insisting that the novel be the truthful and realistic examination of character, Eliot excluded from her fiction the idealization and exaggeration of other novelists, and instead offered an extensive study of culture and human behavior. Eliot's masterpiece is *Middlemarch* (1871–1872), a panoramic exploration of English society that is regarded by many critics as the greatest English novel. A detailed depiction of life in a provincial town during the 1830s, *Middlemarch* features an intriguing female protagonist of high intellect and idealism, whose dreams of defying the conventional values imposed upon her by society and attaining fulfillment in some heroic enterprise are shattered by a disastrous marriage.

George Eliot's life was anything but conventional. Born Mary Ann Evans in Warwickshire in the English Midlands, she was the youngest of five children of estate manager Robert Evans, a staunch political and Church of England conservative, who was distrustful of change and innovation. Mary Ann was a serious and studious child who read widely. While attending boarding school, she came under the influence of the charismatic, evangelical clergyman John Edmund Jones. To a precocious and thoughtful young girl like Mary Ann, Jones's dramatic preaching and message of personal salvation through faith and religious self-sacrifice struck a sympathetic chord. In 1841, she moved with her retired father to Coventry, where her family, concerned by her religious zeal, encouraged her friendship with the local progressive freethinkers Charles and Caroline Bray, hoping their influence would help moderate her almost fanatical piety. Instead, the philosophical rationalism to which she was exposed caused her to lose her religious faith entirely. In a confrontation with her family that would become a paradigm for similar scenes in her novels—conflicts between independence and duty, self and community—Mary Ann announced her refusal to attend church any longer. She eventually compromised, agreeing to go to church but refusing to give up her belief in a personal morality that was not based on the authority of religious faith.

After her father's death, in 1849, Eliot went to London, where she entered a wider circle better suited to her considerable intellectual gifts. She worked as an assistant editor of the progressive *Westminster Review*, wrote numerous book reviews, and mingled with the literary and somewhat bohemian circle surrounding the magazine. This included the critic and author George Henry Lewes, with whom Eliot fell in love and who returned her affection. The married Lewes was estranged from his wife but, under the restrictive divorce laws of the time, he could not divorce and legally remarry. The situation prompted the second and greatest personal crisis in Eliot's life. Defying convention and strong family disapproval, Eliot and Lewes established a home together, managing a happy, if secluded, life in London, ideal for their literary work. By the 1870s, Eliot was recognized as the most eminent novelist of her day and had achieved social respectability despite her unconventional life with Lewes.

It was Lewes who first encouraged Eliot to write fiction. She had always been an insightful thinker, but as she began her fiction she faced the challenge of animating her thoughts and creating believable characters and situations. She also set out to alter the basic formula of Victorian fiction—idealization and melodrama—to a careful analysis of realistic experience and diverse characters.

To avoid associating her work with other "lady novelists," whose sentimental and trivial fare ensured a lack of serious response, she chose the pseudonym George Eliot with her first fictional work, *Scenes of Clerical Life*, three stories that first appeared in *Blackwood's Magazine*. *Scenes of Clerical Life* attempted, in her words, "to do what has never yet been done in our literature . . . representing the clergy like any other class with the humours, sorrows, and troubles of other men." The book set the pattern for Eliot's subsequent novels: it insisted that ordinary life is the proper domain of fiction, showed tolerance and sympathy toward the characters, and dramatized lessons of human behavior through what she called "aesthetic teaching." Eliot's next effort was her first novel, *Adam Bede* (1859), which brought her acclaim and earned her a reputation as a major new writing talent. She quickly followed its success with two more novels, *The Mill on the Floss* (1860) and *Silas Marner* (1861).

Eliot had been drawing on her memories of Warwickshire for the settings of her first novels. When these sources began to run dry, she attempted a departure in *Romola* (1863), a historical novel set in fifteenth-century Florence. To research the novel, she traveled to Italy and studied the customs and values of that culture with the eye of a social scientist. With *Romola* Eliot learned to go beyond her memories and see an entire society as a complex whole. This experience deepened and broadened her scope as a novelist when she returned to more familiar English settings for her last three novels: *Felix Holt* (1866), *Middlemarch* (1872), and *Daniel Deronda* (1876). All three are novels in which Eliot attempted to display what she called the "invariability of sequence": the laws of social order and principles of moral conduct, including both the complex forces underlying characters' actions and the social, historical, and political climate in which her characters exist.

Eliot's original scheme for what she initially conceived of as a "novel called Middlemarch" began around 1869, and concerned a male protagonist, Tertius Lydgate, a doctor whose altruistic and scientific aspirations would be tested against the limitations of English provincial life. Eliot set his story during the period 1829–1831, the crucial years of the Catholic Emancipation, the death of George IV, the general election of 1831, and the passage of the first Reform Bill of 1832, in which traditional English authority and values were tested and out of which Eliot's contemporary world emerged. Eliot researched her subject in great detail so that she could recreate the past and gain a critical perspective on it, yet the project languished, and, in 1870, she turned to the story of another idealist, Dorothea Brooke, whose aspirations for a less constricted life would, like Lydgate's, be hampered by the demands of conventional society. Eliot decided to join her manuscript of "Miss Brooke" with the early "Middlemarch" material, and to reconstruct an entire social setting with four major plot centers: the story of Dorothea Brooke's unhappy marriage to the self-absorbed pedant Edward Casaubon, and her subsequent attraction to his relative, the artistic Will Ladislaw; Lydgate's marriage to the conventionally materialistic Rosamond Vincy and his professional life in Middlemarch; the story of Fred Vincy, a wastrel in search of a vocation, and his relationship with the sensible Mary Garth; and the circumstances surrounding the self-righteous businessman Bulstrode, whose secret and fall from grace in the Middlemarch community Eliot used to join the novel's many parts. Dorothea Brooke, Tertius Lydgate, and the rest of Eliot's wide cast of characters are all examined against a fully elaborate social hierarchy, from Middlemarch's gentry and farm families through the professional and laboring classes. All are related to a particular historical moment in which traditional values face the pressure of change in the reforming spirit of the age.

At the soul and center of *Middlemarch* are Dorothea and Lydgate. Dorothea is described as a "latter-born" Saint Theresa, "helped by no coherent social faith and order which could perform the function of knowledge for the ardently willing soul." She is a fervent neophyte and idealist in search of a great cause and the opportunity for self-expression. Instead of accepting the love of the kindly Sir James Chettam, she marries the middle-aged scholar Casaubon, whom she thinks is a kindred spirit but who, although he cares for her, fails to provide her with the expansion into the noble life of mind and spirit she seeks. The marriage falters, and the intellectually and emotionally rigid Casaubon is eventually undone by his jealousy of Dorothea and Will Ladislaw. Meanwhile, Lydgate's desire to advance medical science and to remain independent of materialistic concerns in order to do good works is similarly compromised by the petty and practical world of Middlemarch, as well as what Eliot calls his "spots of commonness"—his conceit and ambitions for social advancement that cause him to succumb to the superficial charms of the greedy Rosamond. He suffers financially and emotionally before attaining a respectable, successful career but ultimately regards himself as a failure. Dorothea finally accepts her love for Will Ladislaw in defiance of propriety, though her triumph of spirit and sense of satisfaction are muted after all that occurrs: "Certainly those determining acts of her life were not ideally beautiful. They were the mixed result of young and noble impulse struggling amidst the conditions of an imperfect social state, in which great feelings will often take the aspect of error, and great faith the aspect of illusion."

Middlemarch is a long and complex novel, which is sometimes shunned by readers seeking shorter and simpler fare. But Eliot's masterwork is well worth the time and patience for readers willing to experience what Virginia Woolf called "one of the few English novels written for grown-up people." A landmark achievement in the history of the novel, *Middlemarch,* in its subtlety and reach, provides a comprehensive and realistic vision of human nature that is as truthful today as it was in Eliot's time.

ANNA KARENINA

by Leo Tolstoy

One of the greatest novels ever written and one of the great tragic love stories in all literature, *Anna Karenina* (1877) traces the adulterous affair of the title character with the dashing Count Alexey Vronsky, which ends in Anna's destruction when she refuses to conform to the hypocritical values of upper-class morality. Providing a counterpoint to Anna's tragedy is the story of Konstantin Levin, a wealthy landowner, whose search for the meaning of his life is partially found among the peasants on his estate and through the attainment of a happy marriage. Tolstoy suggests the interconnection between his two protagonists with what has come to be one of the most famous opening sentences in literature: "All happy families are alike but an unhappy family is unhappy after its own fashion."

The quest for the significance and meaning of life, history's grip on the individual, the conflict between self-fulfillment and society, and the importance of the family are themes that Tolstoy emphasizes and explores in *Anna Karenina*, as well as in his first masterwork, *War and Peace* (1869). All are issues Tolstoy struggled with in his own life. Born in 1828 into a wealthy, noble family, Count Leo Tolstoy grew up on the family estate of Yasnaya

Polyana, south of Moscow. Both of his parents died when he was a child, and he was raised by relatives and educated by private tutors. After three years as a student at Kazan University, he returned home to manage the estate and to live an aimless and pleasure-seeking life in upper-class circles in St. Petersburg and Moscow. At the age of twenty-three, Tolstoy enlisted in the army as an artillery officer, and during the Crimean War he campaigned against the Caucasian hill tribes and helped defend Sevastopol. While in the army, he developed an addiction to gambling, as well as a determination to become a writer. His first works reflect his war experiences and his recollections of childhood. Tolstoy's early fiction, published in Russian magazines, announced the arrival of a promising new talent, part of the flowering of Russian fiction in the nineteenth century that included such literary masters as Turgenev and Dostoesvsky. Tolstoy traveled in Europe before marrying in 1862; he then settled down to raise a family of thirteen children and to reorganize his estate to reflect the principles of peasant reform, including land ownership and improved education for his serfs.

The conflicts Tolstoy explored in *War and Peace* and *Anna Karenina* sparked a personal crisis and the beginning of a quest for meaning; this led him to a renunciation of government, private property, and organized religion, and the discovery of a unique belief in primitive Christianity, together with a faith in simple peasant values that sprung from a close relationship to the land. He spent the rest of his life endeavoring to live according to his precepts, often to the consternation of his family, and writing books that embodied his philosophy. Despite his chosen role as holy man, sermonizer, and sage, Tolstoy produced some of his finest works during his later period, including "The Death of Ivan Ilyitch" and "The Kreutzer Sonata." Tolstoy's mysticism and asceticism attracted devoted followers but largely alienated him from his family. In 1910 he caught a chill and died in the house of a stationmaster while attempting to escape from his family's control during a journey to a monastery.

Tolstoy regarded *Anna Karenina*, a tightly constructed novel of deeper psychological insight than *War and Peace*, as his "first real novel." In 1870, he told his wife that he was intrigued by "a type of married woman from the highest society, but who had lost herself" and whom he intended to show as "pitiful and not guilty."

Two years later Tolstoy's core idea began to take shape after the death of a neighbor's mistress, Anna Pirogova, who had been abandoned by her lover and in despair committed suicide by throwing herself under a freight train. In 1873, armed with a first name for his protagonist and her violent end, Tolstoy began his five-year labor to finish *Anna Karenina*, with most of the novel serialized in the *Russian Messenger* between 1874 and 1877.

After *Anna Karenina*'s famous opening sentence concerning happy and unhappy families, Tolstoy begins with a disruption in the household of Anna's brother, Stiva Oblonsky, when his wife, Dolly, discovers that he has been having an affair. Anna, a warm, charming, vital woman loved and appreciated by her friends and family for her understanding and tactfulness, arrives in Moscow to restore domestic peace between her brother and his wife. From there, the novel explores the various social, psychological, and moral factors that destroy Anna's marriage to Alexey Karenin, a cold, ambitious government official by whom she has a son, and the conditions that ensure the sober, decent, and honest Levin's happiness as a husband to Dolly's sister, Kitty. Anna reconciles her brother and his wife, while her own marriage is threatened by her fateful encounter with the handsome, wealthy young cavalry officer, Count Alexey Vronsky, and the love for him that eventually consumes and dooms her. Initially, Anna and Vronsky are impediments to Kitty and Levin's marriage; at the start of the novel, Vronsky is Kitty's suitor, and he is the reason she rejects Levin's first proposal. The theme of love and marriage plays out through comparison between the two couples. Vronsky pursues Anna who tries to suppress her feelings for him and fails; she also fails in her struggle to reconcile with Karenin and to give up the man she loves. Kitty and Levin come together and marry as Anna and Vronsky, with their baby daughter, begin their version of married life in restless travel and social ostracism. Anna returns to claim her son, Seryozha, and to resolve the hopeless situation that has cut her off from society. However, her obsessive love for Vronsky has trapped her in an increasing dependency on him. Meanwhile, Kitty gives birth, and Levin witnesses a wider and richer basis for his relationship with his wife. Finally, Anna's passion, which unlike Levin's is not a means to a wider spiritual growth but exists as an end in itself, becomes the poison that destroys her. Suicide is Anna's only relief, as Levin's spiritual crisis in the face of the reality of death is resolved through the sustenance offered by family and country life; he is freed from the social and personal torments that punish Anna mercilessly.

Early drafts of *Anna Karenina* featured only the adulterous triangle of Anna, Vronsky, and Karenin, who, with his virtue besmirched because of his wife's lecherous and irresponsible passion, was marked for the tragic role. Tolstoy's uncompromising moral view concerning the sanctity of the family and the destructiveness of sexuality influenced his original decision to portray Anna as a fleshy she-devil whose lust he viewed as "terribly repulsive and disgusting." But Anna's hold on Tolstoy gradually forced a change in his view of her, which was reinforced by his incorporation of the parallel story of Levin and Kitty. The moral focus that Tolstoy derived from his own married life and spiritual struggles was deflected onto Levin, thus allowing Anna to become more than an archetype and a warning about the destructive nature of sexual passion. She emerged as a truly complex, sympathetic, and attractive character, whose deep capacity for love and defiance of convention, as well as her passion for Vronsky, is her downfall. In an upper-class social milieu that hypocritically tolerates adultery if it is discreetly pursued, Anna openly and honestly separates from her husband and goes off to live with her lover. Her society's penalty for such a breach of the rules is harsh: she is separated from her son and ostracized by her friends and acquaintances, while Vronsky retains the freedom to come and go as he pleases, just as he did before his affair. Anna is a victim of convention, trapped by the unfair divorce laws of the time, social hypocrisy, a weakness of character, and a sense of guilt, in a relationship that brings her misery rather than happiness, not because she has lost her love for Vronsky, but because that love has become her only focus. Increasingly jealous and demanding, fearful that she will inevitably lose Vronsky's love, and agonizingly torn between her lover and her son, she chooses death as her only escape. Anna Karenina would not be the first great fictional heroine to choose such a fate.

A DOLL'S HOUSE

by Henrik Ibsen

More than one literary historian has asserted that the precise moment when modern drama began was December 4, 1879, with the publication of Ibsen's *A Doll's House*; or, more dramatically, at the explosive climax of the first performance in Copenhagen on December 21, 1879, with the slamming of the door as Nora Helmer shockingly leaves her comfortable home, respectable marriage, husband, and children for an uncertain future of self-discovery. Nora's explosive exit ushered in a new dramatic era, legitimizing the exploration of key social problems as a serious concern for the modern theater, while sounding the opening blast in the modern sexual revolution. As Ibsen's biographer Michael Meyer has observed, "No play had ever before contributed so momentously to the social debate, or been so widely and furiously discussed among people who were not normally interested in theatrical or even artistic matter." A contemporary reviewer of the play declared, "When Nora slammed the door shut on her marriage, walls shook in a thousand homes."

Ibsen set in motion a transformation of drama as distinctive in the history of the theater as the one that occurred in fifth-century B.C. Athens or Elizabethan London. Like the great Athenian dramatists and Shakespeare, Ibsen fundamentally redefined the drama and set a standard that later playwrights have had to absorb or challenge. The stage that he inherited had largely ceased to function as a serious medium for the deepest consideration of human themes and values. After Ibsen, drama was restored as an important truth-telling vehicle for a comprehensive criticism of life. *A Doll's House* anatomized on stage for the first time the social, psychological, emotional, and moral truths beneath the placid surface of a conventional, respectable marriage while creating a new, psychologically complex modern heroine who still manages to shock and unsettle audiences more than a century later. *A Doll's House* is, therefore, one of the groundbreaking modern literary texts that established in fundamental ways the responsibility and cost of women's liberation and gender equality. According to critic Evert Sprinchorn, Nora is "the richest, most complex" female dramatic character since Shakespeare's heroines, and, as Kate Millett has argued in *Sexual Politics*, Ibsen was the first dramatist since the Greeks to challenge the myth of male dominance. "In Aeschylus' dramatization of the myth," Millett asserts, "one is permitted to see patriarchy confront matriarchy, confound it through the knowledge of paternity, and come off triumphant. Until Ibsen's Nora slammed the door announcing the sexual revolution, this triumph went nearly uncontested."

The momentum that propelled Ibsen's daring artistic and social revolt was sustained principally by his outsider status, as an exile both at home and abroad. His last deathbed word was "Tvertimod!" (On the contrary!), a fitting epitaph and description of his artistic and intellectual mind-set. Born in Skien, Norway, a logging town southwest of Oslo, in 1828, Ibsen endured a lonely and impoverished childhood, particularly after the bankruptcy of his businessman father when Ibsen was six. At fifteen, he was sent to Grimstad as an apothecary's apprentice, where he lived for six years in an attic room on meager pay, sustained by reading romantic poetry, sagas, and folk ballads. He later recalled feeling "on a war footing with the little community where I felt I was being suppressed by my situation and by circumstances in general." His first play, *Cataline*, was a historical drama featuring a revolutionary hero who reflects Ibsen's own alienation. "*Cataline* was written," the playwright later recalled, "in a little provincial town, where it was impossible for me to give expression to all that fermented in me except by mad, riotous pranks, which brought down upon me the ill will of all the respectable citizens who could not enter into that world which I was wrestling with alone."

Largely self-educated, Ibsen failed the university entrance examination to pursue medical training and instead pursued a career in the theater. In 1851, he began a thirteen-year stage apprenticeship in Bergen and Oslo, doing everything from sweeping the stage to directing, stage-managing, and writing mostly verse dramas based on Norwegian legends and historical subjects. The experience gave him a solid knowledge of the stage conventions of the day, particularly of the so-called "well-made play" of the popular French playwright Augustin Eugène Scribe and his many imitators, with its emphasis on a complicated, artificial plot based on secrets, suspense, and surprises. Ibsen would transform the conventions of the "well-made play" into the modern problem play, exploring controversial social and human questions that had never before been dramatized. Although his stage experience in Norway was marked chiefly by failure, Ibsen's apprenticeship was a crucial testing ground for perfecting his craft and providing Ibsen with the skills to mount the assault on theatrical conventions and moral complacency in his mature work.

In 1864, Ibsen began a self-imposed exile from Norway that would last for twenty-seven years. He traveled first to Italy, where he was joined by his wife Susannah, whom he had married in 1858, and his son. The family divided its time between Italy and Germany. The experience was liberating for Ibsen; he felt that he had "escaped from darkness into light," releasing the productive energy with which he composed the succession of plays that brought him worldwide fame. His first important works, *Brand* (1866) and *Peer Gynt* (1867), were poetic dramas very much in the romantic mode of the individual's conflict with experience and the gap between heroic assertion and accomplishment, between sobering reality and blind idealism. *Pillars of Society* (1877) shows him experimenting with ways of introducing these central themes into a play reflecting modern life, the first in a series of realistic dramas that redefined the conventions and subjects of the modern theater.

The first inklings of his next play, *A Doll's House*, are glimpsed in Ibsen's journal entry headed "Notes for a Modern Tragedy":

There are two kinds of moral laws, two kinds of conscience, one for men and one, quite different, for women. They don't understand each other; but in practical life, woman is judged by masculine law, as though she weren't a woman but a man.

The wife in the play ends by having no idea what is right and what is wrong; natural feelings on the one hand and belief in authority on the other lead her to utter distraction. . . .

Moral conflict. Weighed down and confused by her trust in authority, she loses faith in her own morality, and in her fitness to bring up her children. Bitterness. A mother in modern society, like certain insects, retires and dies once she has done her duty by propagating the race. Love of life, of home, of husband and children and family. Now and then, as women do, she shrugs off her thoughts. Suddenly anguish and fear return. Everything must be borne alone. The catastrophe approaches, mercilessly, inevitably. Despair, conflict, and defeat.

To tell his modern tragedy based on gender relations, Ibsen takes his audience on an unprecedented, intimate tour of a contemporary, respectable marriage. Set during the Christmas holidays, *A Doll's House* begins with Nora Helmer completing the finishing touches on the family's celebrations. Her husband, Torvald, has recently been named a bank manager, promising an end to the family's former straitened financial circumstances, and Nora is determined to celebrate the holiday with her husband and three children in style. Despite Torvald's disapproval of her indulgences, he relents, giving her the money she desires, softened by Nora's childish playacting that gratifies his sense of what is expected of his "lark" and "squirrel." Beneath the surface of this apparently charming domestic scene is a potentially damning and destructive secret. Seven years before, Nora had saved the life of her critically ill husband by secretly borrowing the money needed for a rest cure in Italy. Knowing that Torvald would be too proud to borrow money himself, Nora forged her dying father's name on the loan she received from Krogstad, a banking associate of Torvald.

The crisis comes when Nora's old schoolfriend Christina Linde arrives in need of a job. At Nora's urging, Torvald aids her friend by giving her Krogstad's position at the bank. Learning that he is to be dismissed, Krogstad threatens to expose Nora's forgery unless she is able to persuade Torvald to reinstate him. Nora fails to convince Torvald to relent, and, after receiving his dismissal notice, Krogstad sends Torvald a letter disclosing the details of the forgery. The incriminating letter remains in the Helmers' mailbox like a ticking time bomb as Nora tries to distract Torvald from reading it, and Christina attempts to convince Krogstad to withdraw his accusation. Torvald eventually reads the letter following the couple's return from a Christmas ball and explodes in recriminations against his wife, calling her a liar and a criminal, unfit to be his wife and his children's mother. "Now you've wrecked all my happiness—ruined my whole future," Torvald insists. "Oh, it's awful to think of. I'm in a cheap little grafter's hands; he can do anything he wants with me, ask me for anything, play with me like a puppet—and I can't breathe a word. I'll be swept down miserably into the depths on account of a featherbrained woman." Torvald's reaction reveals that his formerly expressed high moral rectitude is hypocritical and self-serving. He shows himself worried more about appearances than true morality, caring about his reputation more than his wife. However, when Krogstad's second letter arrives, in which he announces his intention of pursuing the matter no further, Torvald joyfully informs Nora that he is "saved" and that Nora should forget all that he has said, assuming that the normal relation between himself and his "frightened little songbird" can be resumed. Nora, however, shocks Torvald with her reaction.

Nora, profoundly disillusioned by Torvald's response to Krogstad's letter, bereft as it is of compassion for her heroic self-sacrifice on his behalf, orders Torvald to sit down for a serious talk, the first in their married life. She reviews their relationship. "I've been your doll-wife here, just as at home I was Papa's doll-child," Nora explains. "And in turn the children have been my dolls. I thought it was fun when you played with me, just as they thought it fun when I played with them. That's been our marriage, Torvald." Nora has acted out the nineteenth-century ideal of the submissive, unthinking, dutiful daughter and wife, and it has taken Torvald's reaction to shatter the illusion and to force an illumination. She goes on: "When the big fright was over—and it wasn't from any threat against me, only for what might damage you—when all the danger was past, for you it was just as if nothing had happened. I was exactly the same, your little lark, your doll, that you'd have to handle with double care now that I'd turned out so brittle and frail. Torvald—in that instant it dawned on me that I've been living here with a stranger . . ." Nora tells Torvald that she no longer loves him because he is not the man she thought he was, that he is incapable of heroic action on her behalf. When Torvald insists that "no man would sacrifice his honor for love," Nora replies, "Millions of women have done just that."

Nora finally resists the claims Torvald mounts in response, namely that she must honor her duties as a wife and mother, stating: "I don't believe in that anymore. I believe that, before all else, I'm a human being, no less than you—or anyway, I ought to try to become one. I know the majority thinks you're right, Torvald, and plenty of books agree with you, too. But I can't go on believing what the majority says, or what's written in books. I have to think over these things myself and try to understand them." The finality of Nora's decision to forgo her assigned role as wife and mother for the authenticity of selfhood is marked by the sound of door slamming and her exit into the wider world, leaving Torvald to survey the wreckage of their marriage.

Ibsen leaves his audience and readers to consider sobering truths: that married women are not the decorative playthings and servants of their husbands who require their submissiveness, that a man's authority in the home should not go unchallenged, and that the prime duty of anyone is to arrive at an authentic human identity, not to accept the role determined by social conventions. That Nora would be willing to sacrifice everything, even her children, to become her own person proved to be, and remains, the controversial shock of *A Doll's House*, provoking continuing debate over Nora's motivations and justifications. The first edition of 8,000 copies of the play quickly sold out, and the play was so heatedly debated in Scandanavia, in1879, that, as critic Frances Lord observes, "Many a social invitation in Stockholm during that winter bore the words, 'You are requested not to mention Ibsen's *Doll's House!*' " Ibsen was obliged to supply an alternative ending for the first German production when the famous leading lady Hedwig Niemann-Raabe refused to perform the role of Nora, stating, "I would never leave *my children!*" Ibsen provided what he would call a "barbaric outrage," an ending in which Nora's departure is halted at the doorway of her children's bedroom. The play served as a catalyst for an ongoing debate over feminism and women's rights. In 1898, Ibsen was honored by the Norwegian Society for Women's Rights and toasted as the "creator of Nora." Always the contrarian, Ibsen rejected the notion that *A Doll's House* champions the cause of women's rights:

I have been more of a poet and less of a social philosopher than people generally tend to suppose. I thank you for your toast, but must disclaim the honor of having consciously worked for women's rights. I am not even quite sure what women's rights really are. To me it has been a question of human rights. And if you read my books carefully you will realize that. Of course it is incidentally desirable to solve the problem of women; but that has not been my whole object. My task has been the portrayal of human beings.

Despite Ibsen's disclaimer that *A Doll's House* should be appreciated as more than a piece of gender propaganda—that it deals at its core with universal truths of human identity—it is nevertheless the case that Ibsen's drama is one of the milestones of the sexual revolution; it sounds themes and advances the cause of women's autonomy and liberation, echoing Mary Wollstonecraft's *A Vindication of the Rights of Women* and anticipating subsequent works such as Virginia Woolf's *A Room of One's Own* and Betty Friedan's *The Feminine Mystique*. The impact of Nora's slamming the door of her doll's house is still being felt more than a century later.

TESS OF THE D'URBERVILLES

by Thomas Hardy

Published in 1891, ten years before the end of the Victorian era, and set in Hardy's invented county of Wessex, *Tess of the D'Urbervilles* was considered controversial and unusual in its time because of its focus on rural characters and sexual frankness. The novel features one of Hardy's most compelling protagonists, Tess Durbeyfield, a young woman of beauty, strength, and passion, who is a tragic victim of her lower-class status and the double standards of Victorian morality. Critic Irving Howe observed that Tess "stands, both in the economy of the book and as a figure rising beyond its pages and into common memory, for the unconditional authority of feeling."

Thomas Hardy (1840–1928), one of English literature's longest-lived and most prodigious writers, was also one of the most influential. The last major Victorian novelist, Hardy is also the first major modern English novelist, and his work is a hybrid of nineteenth-century storytelling methods and modern ideas and concerns. He was the eldest child of Thomas and Jemima Hardy of Higher Bockhampton, Dorset, in southwest England. His father was a builder, country musician, and ballad singer who took his young son to village weddings and festivities. Through his father and his rural background, Hardy absorbed the rustic storytelling traditions he would draw upon for his novels. At eight, Hardy was sent to school in nearby Dorchester, and at sixteen he was apprenticed to an architect and church restorer. Thereafter, he would read and study on his own. In 1862, Hardy moved to London, where he was employed in an architect's office. He read Darwin and was greatly influenced by John Stuart Mill's *On Liberty*, which would become a source for his exploration of the conflict between the individual and society in his novels. Hardy also began to write poetry, which would remain his first love. He returned to Dorset in 1867, and in 1871, he produced *Desperate Remedies*, a novel that was published anonymously.

During the 1870s, Hardy published a series of conventional romances with rural settings—*Under the Greenwood Tree* (1873), *A Pair of Blue Eyes* (1874), and *The Hand of Ethelberta* (1876). He shifted from the comic to the tragic mode with *Far From the Madding Crowd* (1874) and *The Return of the Native* (1878), the first novels set in Wessex, Hardy's fictional equivalent of England's six southwest counties that formed a partly real and partly imagined landscape. By 1883, Hardy had moved permanently to Dorchester, the county seat of Dorset, and began producing his great masterpieces—*The Mayor of Casterbridge* (1886), *Tess*, and *Jude the Obscure* (1896). Thereafter, Hardy wrote poetry and produced *The Dynasts* (1904–1908), his three-part epic poem devoted to the Napoleonic era. His wife, Emma Gifford, died in 1912, and two years later he married his secretary, Florence Dugdale, who published a biography of the writer that was actually written by Hardy himself. Honored in later years for his longevity, Hardy was buried in Poet's Corner in London's Westminster Abbey, although he had designated that his heart should be interred in Emma's grave in Stinsford Churchyard in Dorset.

Hardy's decision to give up novel writing for poetry was fueled by the furor over his chosen subtitle for *Tess*—"A Pure Woman Faithfully Presented"—in which he asserted his heroine's essential virtue despite her seduction (or rape, which would have been considered just as worthy of moral condemnation), the birth of her illegitimate child, and the murder of her seducer. The novel, in fact, contained such uncomfortable truths that it effectively ended Hardy's career as a novelist. Begun in 1888, *Tess* was conceived as a full-frontal assault on Victorian hypocrisy regarding sexual matters. Hardy's subject was the fate of a ruined maiden, a popular theme of the English novel from Richardson's *Clarissa* through Scott's *Heart of Midlothian*, Dickens's *David Copperfield*, and Eliot's *Adam Bede*, as well as countless lesser works; these mainly supported the conventional view that once a seduction has occurred death or exile is the end of the matter, a climax to be avoided at all cost. Hardy would take an opposite view, arguing for interest in his heroine *after* her fall and shifting the focus from Tess's moral transgression to the circumstances that caused her fall as well as their wider implications.

In the original version published in volume form in 1891, Tess's doom is chronicled with a daring frankness and with her suffering unalloyed. Tess Durbeyfield is a young woman of humble birth and background. Dutiful and with an innate goodness and a fateful vulnerability, Tess is compelled by the economic collapse that threatens her family to claim an ancestral relationship with the well-to-do, parvenu D'Urberville family, who has, we learn, only adopted the name and has no connection to the Durbeyfields. The D'Urberville's rakish son, Alec, seduces Tess, who becomes pregnant. Ostracized by her neighbors both before and after the birth of her baby—whom she names Sorrow, and who dies after only a few months—she moves to a dairy farm many miles away from her home. Tess enjoys a brief respite at the farm, where she meets a minister's son, Angel Clare, an idealistic, supposedly progressive-thinking young man who plans to become a farmer. Tess eventually marries Angel—after the written confession of her past, slipped under his door before their marriage, goes under the carpet and is unseen. Upon listening to Angel's confession of an illicit affair in his own past, Tess, thinking she is likewise forgiven, speaks freely of Alec and her dead baby. Angel reacts with horror and abandons his wife. Despite Angel's freethinking opposition to orthodoxy, he is morally rigid and cannot accept the human, fallible Tess over the ideal figure he has created to love. Again on her own, dispossessed from the bower of bliss of the dairy, Tess finds herself in Hardy's version of the rural wasteland, condemned to grinding labor in a countryside devoid of comfort or community. Tess is again beset by Alec, now an itinerant preacher, and in despair of Angel's return to her, she finally agrees to live with Alec as his wife. Eventually a contrite Angel does return. Tess, overcome by her despair and resentment of Alec, stabs him to death. She rejoins Angel for a few days of happiness before the authorities close in on the couple, and Tess is executed for her crime.

The novel's final climactic scene at Stonehenge reflects Hardy's use of heightened effects to underscore and intensify his drama. Beyond the question of probability that these two fugitives should accidentally come upon Stonehenge on their final night together, Hardy's use of this setting seems symbolically appropriate. In a novel obsessed with the past—of past generations and actions—and natural or primitive instincts struggling against social morality, Tess's resting on a pagan altar prior to her societal sacrifice is fitting for the emblematic nature to which her drama has been raised. Yet Tess is not reduced merely to symbolic importance. Her resignation—"It is as it should be. . . . I am ready"—transcends the melodramatic extremes of sentiment and the overly expansive symbolic setting. Her humanity dominates the heavier strains of her implied martyrdom. At Stonehenge, Tess's character is not dwarfed by the monolithic stones or the cosmic symbolism, nor is it reduced by the machinations of plot. She has instead found a fit stage for her tragedy to be completed.

Hardy's tragic heroine is blighted by heredity and environment, betrayed by her lovers, and finally ground down by social laws and conventions. Yet, Hardy's provocative subtitle challenged contemporary readers to suspend conventional moral judgments in favor of the greater claims of Tess's suffering, integrity, and humanity. Hardy's defense of Tess is based on the contention that it is not circumstances but an individual's will that determines innocence or purity. Events are loaded against Tess from the start, and fate, as it is suggested through Hardy's theatrical plot, seems to conspire to ruin her. In her struggle against society's unnatural code that condemns her and the human condition that governs her, Tess is raised to the level of the heroic, the mythic, and the universal.

Hardy faced the challenge to gain an audience for his radical reinterpretation of the ruined maiden theme, and the censorship his novel eventually caused would contribute to his abandoning the novel form completely, after firing off a final vitriolic attack on Victorian complacency and hypocrisy in *Jude the Obscure*. Unwilling to forgo the lucrative market of serial publication, Hardy submitted his manuscript to two different magazine editors who contended that the book's "improper explicitness" made it unfit for family reading. Hardy eventually submitted a bowdlerized, sanitized version to a weekly newspaper—*The Graphic*—which accepted his story after Hardy had eliminated objectionable material and had rewritten sections in different colored ink so that the original version could easily be restored later. In the serial form, Tess's seduction follows a mock marriage ceremony, and no illegitimate child or its baptism are mentioned. Hardy, who eventually sought relief from censorship by abandoning the novel for poetry, bitterly and ironically contended, "If Galileo had said in verse that the world moved, the Inquisition might have let him alone." Although complaints continued about the book's indecency, and one bishop consigned the book to the flames, *Tess* was a popular and critical success in its day. It remains one of the supreme novels of the nineteenth century for its transcendent power and sheer grandiosity of vision.

"THE YELLOW WALLPAPER"
by Charlotte Perkins Gilman

Charlotte Perkins Gilman's short story, "The Yellow Wallpaper" (1892), a provocative and unsettling dramatization of a woman's despair and madness, can be described as the first feminist horror story and one of the fundamental fictions of gender studies. The most famous work of the American poet, novelist, and feminist theorist, "The Yellow Wallpaper" first appeared in the *New England Magazine* after a two-year effort to find a publisher. Editor Horace Scudder, who rejected the story for the *Atlantic Monthly*, justified his decision by declaring to the author that "I could not forgive myself if I made others as miserable as I have made myself [in reading your story]!" William Dean Howells, who would eventually include Gilman's story in his collection *Great Modern American Stories* (1920), initially regarded it as "too wholly dire" and "too terribly good to be printed." Reflecting the author's own experiences in being treated for depression, "The Yellow Wallpaper," depicting the nervous breakdown of a young wife and mother suffering what could later be diagnosed as severe postnatal depression, would be rediscovered by feminist scholars in the 1970s and proclaimed a masterpiece; it is one of the earliest and still one of the most effective psychological dramatizations of the impact of a woman's subjugation under a patriarchal system of control and repression.

Born Charlotte Perkins, in 1860, in Hartford, Connecticut, the author was the daughter of Frederick Beecher Perkins, a librarian and magazine editor who was the grandson of the noted clergyman Lyman Beecher, the father of *Uncle Tom's Cabin* author Harriet Beecher Stowe. Frederick Perkins abandoned his family when Gilman was an infant, and Gilman, her mother, and older brother depended mainly on the assistance of relatives and were forced to move to different residences at least once a year until Gilman was eighteen. Her mother attempted to toughen her daughter by showing her no signs of affection. As Gilman later observed in her autobiography, her mother, traumatized by her husband's desertion, believed that she should "deny the child all expression of affection as far as possible, so that she should not be used to it or long for it" and subsequently would not be hurt, as her mother had been. Ideas of women's empowerment and independence, however, came largely from Gilman's associations with her great-aunts, Harriet Beecher Stowe and Catharine Beecher. After home tutoring and training at the Rhode Island School of Design, Gilman worked as an art teacher, governess, and commercial artist, designing greeting cards and writing poetry. In 1884, she married artist Charles Walter Stetson, and, shortly after giving birth to their daughter, Gilman began suffering bouts of severe, debilitating depression. She eventually sought treatment from the eminent nerve specialist S. Weir Mitchell at his sanatorium in Philadelphia. Weir diagnosed Gilman with neurasthenia, or nervous exhaustion, and prescribed his "Rest Cure" of complete bed rest in total isolation, in which the patient was not allowed to read, write, talk to others, or even feed herself. After a month of this treatment, Weir sent Gilman home with the instructions to "live as domestic a life as possible. Have your child with you all the time. . . . Have but two hours' intellectual life a day. And never touch pen, brush or pencil as long as you live." As Gilman recalled in her autobiography, *The Living of Charlotte Perkins Gilman* (1935), "I went home, followed those directions rigidly for months, and came perilously near to losing my mind. The mental agony grew so unbearable that I would sit blankly moving my head from side to side—to get out from under the pain. Not physical pain, not the least 'headache' even, just mental torment, and so heavy in its nightmare gloom that it seemed real enough to dodge."

Dr. Weir's cure, particularly the limitation of her self-expression and the enforced isolation and inactivity, rather than helping Gilman recover her emotional equilibrium further exacerbated her instability and torment. She eventually took control of her own recovery and abandoned the rest cure. As Gilman observed in the essay "Why I Wrote 'The Yellow Wallpaper,' " "I cast the national specialist's advice to the winds and went to work again—work, the normal life of every human being; work, in which is joy and growth and service, without which one is a pauper and a parasite—ultimately recovering some measure of power." If inactivity was a contributing symptom of her mental anguish, Gilman self-diagnosed the root cause as her marriage. She separated from her husband, gaining a divorce in 1894, convinced that her marriage and its attendant stifling domesticity contributed to her breakdown. As Gilman recalled, "It was not a choice between going and staying, but between going, sane, and staying, insane." She described her four-year marriage as "this miserable condition of mind, this darkness, feebleness, and gloom" that threatened "utter loss." Gilman and her daughter moved to California and, as she observed, "The moment I left home I began to recover. It seemed right to give up a mistaken marriage."

Gilman supported herself by lecturing, editing, and teaching while beginning to publish the works that would gain her a reputation as one of the earliest feminist theorists and the leading intellectual in the women's movement in the United States at the turn of the century. She received her first widespread recognition for her satiric poem "Similar Cases," which argued the necessity for change in a healthy society. A collection of similarly satirical poems, *In This Our World,* appeared in 1893; many of the poems treated the restricted roles and emotional traumas suffered by women. A polemical analysis of the fate of women in America's male-oriented, capitalist society, *Women and Economics,* was published in 1898. Hailed as one of the key theoretical texts of the early women's movement, the book, which chronicles male dominance in modern society and the impact of economic dependence that made women slaves of men, would be translated into several languages. It established both Gilman's international reputation and suggested many of the central themes of her subsequent works, including *The Home: Its Work and Influence* (1903), *Human Work* (1904), *Man-Made World* (1911), and the feminist utopian novel *Herland* (1915). While these works retain a historical interest in reflecting early feminist ideas, it is the combination of the exploration of gender themes and controlled artistry that separates "The Yellow Wallpaper" from Gilman's other works and grants it a continuing relevance and significance.

Gilman would later describe her motive for writing and publishing "The Yellow Wallpaper," which appeared in book form in 1899, as a warning to others of the debilitating dangers of Dr. Weir's rest cure through a fictionalized version of her own "narrow escape." "The real purpose of the story," Gilman asserted in her autobiography, "was to reach Dr. S. Weir Mitchell, and convince him of the errors of his ways." However, the story achieves a much wider applicability, treating not just the psychological consequences of Weir's cure but the root causes for women's mental instability in the perceived connections between male dominance and female entrapment. Gilman's story, "with its embellishments and additions" to her actual circumstances—she confesses she "never had hallucinations or objections to my mural decorations"—conflates all male authority roles into the nameless narrator's physician husband, John, who supervises his wife's recovery from a nervous condition following childbirth. He has rented "ancestral halls for the summer," establishes a bedroom for his wife in the former attic nursery and playroom with bars on the windows, and prescribes complete isolation and rest in which, as the narrator reports, "I have a scheduled prescription for each hour of the day; he takes all care from me." Cautioned "not to give way to fancy in the least" but to maintain self-control, the narrator, whose "imaginative power and habit of story-making" are regarded as dangerous, is forbidden even to write; the story takes the form of secret diary fragments recording the progress of her cure, which proves to be far worse than the original complaint.

The locus of the narrator's increasing anguish and obsession in confinement is the room's decaying yellow wallpaper as it begins to mirror the narrator's condition and objectifies her increasing instability and mental deterioration. The wallpaper, with its "sprawling patterns committing every artistic sin," both intrigues and repels the narrator, forming a kind of hieroglyphic message or Rorschach test that the narrator begins to "read" and interpret. "It is dull enough to confuse the eye in following," she observes, "pronounced enough to constantly irritate and provoke study, and when you follow the lame uncertain curves for a little distance they suddenly commit suicide—plunge off at outragious angles, destroy themselves in unheard of contradictions." The wallpaper becomes a projection of the narrator's increasing feelings of desperate entrapment and alienation. Divided between an identity as her husband's good and dutiful patient and one that is increasingly suspicious of her husband's intentions and willfully defiant of his orders, the narrator sees in the pattern of wallpaper the bars of her psychological confinement, and in an emerging "sub-pattern" in the design, "a strange, provoking, formless sort of figure, that seems to skulk about behind that silly and conspicuous front design." The figure trapped within the wallpaper becomes the shape of a imprisoned woman "stooping down and creeping about behind the pattern," the narrator's double whom she tries to free: "I pulled and she shook, I shook and she pulled, and before morning we had peeled off yards of that paper." As "The Yellow Wallpaper" concludes, the narrator has become the imprisoned woman now freed from the paper, as John bursts into the locked room:

> "What is the matter?" he cried. "For God's sake, what are you doing!" . . .
> "I've got out at last," said I, "in spite of you and Jane. And I've pulled off most of the paper, so you can't put me back!"
> Now why should that man have fainted? But he did, and right across my path by the wall, so that I had to creep over him every time!

The meaning of "The Yellow Wallpaper" has intrigued readers since its initial publication. Originally interpreted as a horror story that records the stages of the narrator's descent into madness, the story has persisted as a chilling and expressive dramatization of a woman's psychosis of confinement and repression under a crippling patriarchal order. "It was not intended to drive people crazy," Gilman declared, "but to save people from being driven crazy." Gilman's therapeutic intention, to warn others of the debilitating consequences of Weir's rest cure, has been replaced in importance by the story's deeper appeal as a diagnosis of gender dynamics. Feminist critics have interpreted "The Yellow

Wallpaper" as a paradigm of male domination and female pathology and liberation. In this view, the narrator's madness becomes the means for her revenge upon and rebellion against patriarchal confinement. Beginning in total dependency and trust in her husband's judgment and power to cure her, the narrator increasingly violates his sanctions while suspecting his motives. Eventually liberating her trapped self, the narrator finds in her madness the freedom and power formerly denied her. The story, therefore, derives its considerable power by pushing gender politics to an extreme in which sanity and madness are reversed and authentic identity is reached in defiance of male authority. As Emily Dickinson, whose life was a study in female confinement and liberation, wrote:

> Much Madness is divinest Sense—
> To a discerning Eye—
> Much Sense—the starkest Madness—
> 'Tis the Majority
> In this, as All, prevail—
> Assent—and you are sane—
> Demur—you're straightway dangerous—
> And handled with a Chain.

THE AWAKENING

by Kate Chopin

Kate Chopin's frank exploration of a late nineteenth-century southern woman's quest for sexual and emotional fulfillment is a favorite text in women's studies and women's history classes. The novel, first published in 1899, was consigned to the literary oblivion reserved for women's literature until it was rediscovered in the 1950s. It received even more attention in the 1960s, when that decade brought about a new wave of feminist consciousness. Since its timely reevaluation by critics and scholars, *The Awakening* has been celebrated as an important literary document in the history of women's rights and is widely recognized as a classic of American literature.

The Awakening—arguably the last great nineteenth-century American novel and the first major novel of the twentieth century—is set in New Orleans and the resort of Grand Isle, locations Kate Chopin (1850–1904) knew well. Born Catherine O'Flaherty in St. Louis, Missouri, Chopin was the daughter of an Irish immigrant who became a successful businessman and married into a socially prominent French Creole family. When her father died suddenly in a railway accident in 1855, Chopin was raised in a matriarchal household run by her mother, her grandmother, and great-grandmother. She was educated at a Catholic girls' school, entered the fashionable world of the debutante upon graduation in 1868, and two years later married Oscar Chopin, a French Creole from New Orleans. Kate and Oscar would have five sons and a daughter, born between 1871 and 1879. The family lived in New Orleans, where Oscar worked as a cotton broker, and vacationed each summer at Grand Isle, an important setting for *The Awakening*. In 1879, to save money as a result of a poor cotton crop, the family moved to a plantation in French-speaking Cloutierville in north-central Louisiana, where Oscar ran a general store, and his wife often waited on customers, absorbing incidents and character types that she would eventually draw on in her novels and stories. Oscar died suddenly of malaria in 1882, leaving his family in debt. Chopin eventually moved her family back to St. Louis, beginning a period of self-assessment. It is during this period that Chopin declared that she "made her own acquaintance." She also studied Darwinism, and was impressed with the concept that women cannot avoid their "biological fates." At the age of thirty-nine, Chopin, who had always "scribbled," launched her writing career, motivated by her need to support her large family. She began to sell her short stories to leading periodicals, published her first novel, *At Fault,* at her own expense in 1890, and eventually brought out two well-received story collections, *Bayou Folk* (1894) and *A Night in Acadie* (1897), securing a rising reputation as a gifted and prolific writer of unsentimental southern regional life. Her work emphasized the nuances of human psychology and the various challenges faced by women. Chopin's early stories were received as "delightful sketches," but just below the surface of the southern belles and dutiful wives that comprised her characters was a rebelliousness that would become fully realized in *The Awakening*.

The Awakening, Chopin's second—and last—novel possesses a power that stems from the simplicity and economy of its story, as well as from the tragic momentum that it rapidly generates. The novel's protagonist, Edna Pontellier, is the twenty-eight-year-old wife of a wealthy, forty-year-old Creole businessman, Léonce Pontellier, and the mother of two sons. As the novel opens, Edna is vacationing with her family at a summer resort on Grand Isle in the Gulf of Mexico. Viewed conventionally, Edna's marriage is ideal. Léonce is judged by all as a model husband who has provided

Edna with a comfortable life of material ease and a place of distinction in society. For Edna, however, "a certain light was beginning to dawn" about the inadequacy of her existence. Her husband treats her as a "valuable piece of personal property"; submission to his will and sacrifice to the well-being of her children is all that is expected of her. Edna's gradual awakening is to an expanded sense of her individuality and sexuality, as well as to a corresponding need for autonomy. Experiencing an almost overwhelming aesthetic joy through music, reveling in the physical pleasure of swimming, Edna begins "to realize her position in the universe as a human being, and to recognize her relations as an individual to the world within and about her." Her recognition of herself as an individual rather than as a possession or in the role predetermined for her by her gender and class, as wife and mother, inevitably begins a process in which her relationship with Léonce deteriorates and her sympathy with the admiring Robert Lebrun grows into a passionate affection. Robert, however, is unable to cope with the implications of his feelings for Edna and flees to Mexico.

Returning to New Orleans, Edna translates her growing dissatisfaction with her life into the abandonment of her previous routine. She cultivates her aesthetic interest in painting and, in the eyes of her husband, neglects her assigned duties in his household: "Mr. Pontellier had been a rather courteous husband so long as he met a certain tacit submissiveness in his wife. But her new and unexpected line of conduct completely bewildered him. It shocked him. Then her absolute disregard of her duties as a wife angered him. When Mr. Pontellier became rude, Edna grew insolent. She had resolved never to take another step backward." Unable to comprehend or cope with the changes in his wife, Léonce follows the advice of the family doctor to bide his time, and he leaves on an extended business trip. While he is away, Edna moves out of their home into a smaller dwelling that she can finance independently, and begins an affair with the rakish Alcée Arobin. He gratifies Edna's heightened sexuality but proves to be as proprietary as her husband. When Robert suddenly returns and declares his devotion, it seems possible to Edna that she can attain both sexual desire and love; instead her hope for fulfillment is thwarted by Robert's inability to accept her autonomy. Left alone, without a satisfying role for her expanded sense of self, not as wife, mother, or lover, Edna can foresee only a succession of affairs and the scandal that will ruin her children. Instead, she acts to protect their reputation by ending her life in a way that could be viewed as accidental, by swimming out to sea and drowning.

The ending of *The Awakening* is, in the words of critic Barbara C. Ewell, "Perhaps the most ambivalent conclusion in all American literature." In it, Chopin connects Edna's self-sacrifice on behalf of her children with her desire to preserve the inviolability of her essential self that has been awakened. It is an ending that has been viewed both as a triumphant act of self-assertion, a liberation from the confines of unbearable constriction, and as a tragic failure, the self-deluded, regressive act of an individual unable to translate her desires and identity into any meaningful relationship in a world blind to the implications the novel has so effectively displayed. Chopin's novel marks out the battleground in an ongoing and escalating gender discussion, between individuality and defining roles, between self-assertion and determinism. Much of twentieth-century women's fiction will document the same or similar dilemmas and either come to the same conclusion or attempt to find a way for characters to, in a sense, regain the shore rather than feel forced to choose physical or emotional extinction.

When it appeared, *The Awakening* proved to be both the culmination of a decade of Chopin's artistic and intellectual development and the effective end of her literary career. Chopin advocates have attributed Chopin's silencing and even her early death to the hostile reaction *The Awakening* received. Many reviewers harshly attacked the novel, condemning it as vulgar, a judgment that recalls the public's reception to Flaubert's *Madame Bovary* (Willa Cather, in her review of *The Awakening*, called the novel a "Creole Bovary"). Edna Pontellier's behavior was judged immoral and her tragic end dismissed with a reassuring sense of good riddance. As one reviewer moralistically intoned, had Edna "flirted less and looked after her children more, we need not have been put to the unpleasantness of reading about her and the temptations she trumped up for herself." Libraries in St. Louis refused to carry the book, and Chopin was snubbed by a number of acquaintances. She earned few royalties from the novel. However, the novel was neither extensively banned nor uniformly condemned, as some later alleged. Chopin continued to write poems and stories up to her death, although her third collection of short stories was rejected by the firm that had published *The Awakening*. Declining health ultimately ended Chopin's career. Returning from a visit to the St. Louis World's Fair, she died of a massive cerebral hemorrhage at the age of fifty-four, in 1904.

Although never completely forgotten, Chopin's works were relegated after her death to the marginal category of the regionalist and local colorist. When her literary reputation was significantly resurrected in the 1950s and 1960s, *The Awakening* began to be reclaimed as an overlooked American masterpiece. Critics praised Chopin's considerable artistry and expressed an appreciation of her luminous, painterly style, her intricate weaving of images and symbols, and her brilliant psychological penetration. This positive critical attention secured for Chopin a place as a major literary figure and recognition for *The Awakening* as an essential American novel. The novel grew in importance as the momentum of the women's movement accelerated and gender issues prompted new literary assessments. *The Awakening* was heralded as a fundamental proto-feminist text, a powerful fictional rendering of the social, biological, and psychological dilemmas women face, as well as an exploration of the consequences of a raised consciousness. Written at the dawn of a new century in which women would struggle mightily toward freedom from gender-imposed restrictions, *The Awakening*, observed literary historian Larzer Ziff, "spoke of painful times ahead on the road to fulfillment."

THE HOUSE OF MIRTH

by *Edith Wharton*

Edith Wharton's *The House of Mirth* (1905) is, arguably, the first great novel by an American woman writer. Encouraged by her mentor Henry James to write about what she knew best—the complex web of elite New York society—Wharton, in treating the status of women in that world at the turn of the century, "emerged as a professionally serious, masterful novelist," in the words of biographer Cynthia Griffin Wolff. Her insider's tour of a "frivolous society" produced, as literary critic Diana Trilling wrote, "one of the most telling indictments of the whole of American society, of a whole social system based on the chance distribution of wealth, that has ever been put to paper." To a literary pantheon of American heroines that includes Hawthorne's Hester Prynne, James's Isabel Archer and Daisy Miller, Chopin's Edna Pontellier, and Dreiser's Carrie Meeber, Wharton added the complex and fascinating Lily Bart, whose gradual destruction in a society that knows the price of everything but the value of nothing, dramatizes cultural values, gender assumptions, and the inexorable pressures of conformity and cupidity. Drawing her title from *Ecclesiastes* 7:4, "The heart of fools is in the house of mirth," Wharton examines a uniquely American version of Bunyan's and Thackeray's

Vanity Fair, of the fashionable New York elite, whose showy brilliance conceals a moral vacuum, and whose refined manners disguise the most brutal betrayal and manipulation.

It is a world that Edith Wharton grew up in and whose values she was expected to accept and to abide by uncritically. Born in 1862, in a house near Washington Square in New York City, Edith Newbold Jones was the only daughter of socially prominent parents descended from aristocratic Old New York families. Her father's inheritance allowed the family to live, in Wharton's words, "a life of leisure and amiable hospitality." Educated by private tutors, she divided her time annually among New York, Europe, and Newport, Rhode Island. Edith delighted in reading and storytelling, and, at the age of fifteen, she secretly wrote a novella. A volume of her poetry was privately printed when she was sixteen. Her parents, fearing that their daughter was becoming unattractively bookish, rushed her debut into New York society prior to her seventeenth birthday to solidify her true vocation: to make a fashionable marriage. In 1885, she wed Edward Wharton, a wealthy Bostonian thirteen years her senior, and at the age of twenty-three she assumed her expected role as a young society hostess. The couple followed the fashionable migration according to the social seasons in New York, Newport, the Berkshires, and Europe. During her marriage to a man she discovered she had little in common, Wharton suffered periodic bouts of severe depression, culminating in a nervous breakdown, in 1898. The prescribed rest cure freed Wharton from her social obligations and allowed her to resume her creative writing. Wharton's first fiction did not appear until she was thirty, and she would later describe the experience of publishing her first collection of short stories, *The Greater Inclination*, in 1899, as an event that broke "the chains that had held me for so long in a kind of torpor. For nearly twelve years, I had tried to adjust myself to my marriage; but now I was overmastered by the longing to meet people who shared my interests." Her decision to cultivate an unfashionable artistic and intellectual life as a writer marked a decisive break with the society in which she was raised, which viewed a professional writing career for a woman as scandalous. The testing of an individual's desires and principles against a rigidly unforgiving social conventionality, reflected in Wharton's own choice to break with precedent and propriety to become a writer, would establish the central theme of her works.

Wharton's first novel, *The Valley of Decision* (1902), is a historical novel set in eighteenth-century Italy. Wharton would later dismiss it as not a novel at all but "a romantic chronicle, unrolling its episodes like the frescoed legends on the palace-walls which formed its background." Henry James urged her instead to treat what she knew intimately, to "Do New York!" even if it meant that she "must be tethered in native pastures, even if it reduces her to a backyard in New York." The challenge Wharton faced in dealing with New York's *haut monde* in *The House of Mirth* was whether she could discover in its shallowness and trivialities deeper human significance and universal meaning. As Wharton remembered in her memoir, *A Backward Glance* (1934), she asked herself, "In what aspect could a society of irresponsible pleasure-seekers be said to have, on the 'old woe of the world,' any deeper bearing than the people composing such a society could guess? The answer was that a frivolous society can acquire dramatic significance only through what its frivolity destroys. Its tragic implication lies in its power of debasing people and ideals. The answer, in short, was my heroine, Lily Bart."

To underscore its human and universal significance, *The House of Mirth* required a sacrifice to the corrupted ideals of New York society; the novel dramatizes the fate of a beautiful and exceptional young woman of inadequate means who tries to maintain her tenuous social position among the fashionable who, in turn, are incapable of recognizing any values beyond the material and are not above betrayal to assert or protect self-supremacy. By birth Lily is accepted as a member of New York's ruling social aristocracy. Orphaned, she supplements a modest inheritance with an equally modest allowance from her staid Aunt Peniston. Her income is insufficient to sustain Lily among her fashionable social set. Raised to despise the "dingy" and trained as a decorative ornament for the discriminating, Lily, at age twenty-nine, feels the pressure to make an advantageous marriage. Without a husband of means, Lily feels vulnerable and powerless, and the novel traces her maneuvering in the marriage market as well as her susceptibility as a single woman to the self-interest of her purported friends.

The reader first meets Lily waiting for a train to take her to Gus and Judy Trenor's country estate, where she hopes to catch the wealthy but priggish Percy Gryce. A chance meeting with lawyer Lawrence Selden, whose limited means causes Lily to resist his evident attraction, leads to her agreeing to accompany him to his flat for tea, an impetuous act that seals Lily's future fate. Wharton would later attribute the popularity of *The House of Mirth* to her truth telling about a materialistically driven high society and her scandalous heroine:

> This supposed picture of their little circle, secure behind its high stockade of convention, alarmed and disturbed the rulers of Old New York. . . . Here was a tale written by one of themselves, a tale deliberately slandering and defiling their most sacred institutions and some of the most deeply revered members of the clan! And what picture did the writer offer to their horrified eyes? That of a young girl of their world who rouged, smoked, ran into debt, borrowed money, gambled, and—crowning horror!—went home with a bachelor friend to take tea in his flat! And I was not only asking the outer world to believe that such creatures were tolerated in New York society, but actually presenting this unhappy specimen as my heroine!

Lily is a breakthrough American fictional heroine, a headstrong and sensitive young woman who will battle through the novel her conflicting desires for wealth and power, as well as for independence, unselfishness, and responsibility. In characterizing Lily, Wharton evades the conventional idealization of female characters into clear categories of virtue and villainy, producing one of the first believably mixed female protagonists in American fiction.

Wharton's satiric point is made clear in Lily's material descent from a position of prestige and glamour to poverty and anonymity as a victim of a society that uses her and fails to appreciate or value her true worth. At the Trenors, Lily hesitates at snaring a husband, whom she does not love, for his money. Instead, she decides against her self-interest in favor of Selden and his appeal to her better nature beyond the contingencies of class and wealth. However, to meet her gambling and dressmaking debts, Lily turns to Gus Trenor for investment advice. She later discovers that her subsequent windfall carries the cost of becoming his mistress. Once her aunt learns of her debts, she disowns Lily. Finally, Lily's fate is sealed when Bertha Dorset, to conceal her own adultery, publicly implies that Lily has been having an affair with her husband. Lily is shunned and abandoned by her fashionable friends, whose hypocrisy is underscored when it is clear that Lily is tolerated only as long as she proves useful. Lily is forced to try her luck further down the social ladder by securing the patronage of the nouveau riche, but she proves to be a liability in gaining an entrée into high society. She then tries to become a milliner, but lacks the training and stamina to keep her job.

Unemployed and ill, now living in a dingy boardinghouse, Lily is tempted to retrieve her fortune and position by using the letters she has acquired proving the affair between Bertha Dorset and Selden, and to enjoy her $10,000 legacy from her aunt rather than to pay the debt she feels she morally owes to Gus Trenor. In the end, Lily resists both temptations, destroying the letters to protect Selden and discharging the debt to Trenor, which frees her. Lily thereby achieves a moral victory of self-worth and independence, despite her shabby surroundings and her death from an overdose of chloral, which she takes seeking relief from her misery in sleep. As Wharton shows in the career of Lily Bart and her circle, residents in the house of mirth are doomed by their virtues and rewarded by their vices. By possessing the moral scruples that make her ultimately incapable of the ruthlessness and selfishness that determine supremacy in her frivolous, corrupt society Lily is fated to fail. Yet she is also a victim of that society, unable to sustain and support an independent life for herself free of her materialistic dreams and the limited roles available to women during the period. Early in the novel, Selden asks Lily, "Isn't marriage your vocation? Isn't it what you're all brought up for?" To which Lily replies resignedly, "I suppose so. What else is there?" Ultimately, Lily fails to attain her marriage goal because her evident attractions—intelligence, originality, sensitivity, and morality—are insufficiently prized by a society for whom money is all. "I have tried hard," Lily confesses to Selden at their fateful last meeting, "but life is difficult, and I am a very useless person. I can hardly be said to have an independent existence. I was just a screw or a cog in the great machine I called life, and when I dropped out of it I found I was of no use anywhere else. What can one do when one finds that one only fits into one hole? One must get back to it or be thrown into the rubbish heap—and you don't know what it's like in the rubbish heap!"

Lily's inability to survive either in the debased world of fashion or in the grim reality of diminished expectations provides a cautionary, haunting indictment of the American dream of material success and power, and its cost. As the story of a woman's "great expectations," like Dickens's masterwork, Wharton's *The House of*

Mirth is a grand reversal of fortune, a contrary Horatio Alger story—from riches to rags—in which the heroine is cast out of the "inner paradise," and her fortune is lost rather than won. In terms of the view of society that Wharton presents, it is a fortune that is well lost with Lily's final achievement, and redemption in self-understanding and selfhood a priceless though fatal compensation.

My Ántonia

by Willa Cather

In 1918, the year *My Ántonia* was published, the world was about to enter a postwar era during which the nineteenth century would be left behind for the modern clamor of the twentieth. Willa Cather would later observe that the world "broke in two in 1922 or thereabouts." Philosophically and emotionally, Cather remained with those on the side of the divide allied with America's agrarian past and unwilling to embrace its urban, industrialized future. She had already demonstrated a remarkable talent for resurrecting the past and revivifying a region in her 1913 novel, *O Pioneers!* With *My Ántonia*, her most beloved work, Cather produced the last great celebration in the American novel of the frontier past and its heroic archetypal pioneers.

Born in 1873, Cather, like Jim Burden, the novel's narrator, came to Nebraska from Virginia as a child and lived on the prairie and in the town of Red Cloud (the Black Hawk of the novel). Cather left the prairie for schooling at the university in Lincoln, and subsequently pursued her professional career in the East. She made her home in New York, but she often went back to Nebraska and wrote much of her work at her summer home in New Brunswick, Canada, and in Jaffrey, New Hampshire, where she was buried after her death in 1947. Completely absorbed in her work, Cather remained single despite opportunities for marriage.

My Ántonia, published when Willa Cather was forty-five, was the author's fourth novel, but it was the first that most completely reflected her realization that "life began for me when I ceased to admire and began to remember." Cather was fascinated by the elemental landscape of the Nebraska prairie and by the intensity and idiosyncrasies of its inhabitants, particularly the immigrants who first carved lives from the unforgiving wilderness. In 1916, on a visit to her family in Red Cloud, Cather was reunited with her childhood friend, Annie Pavelka (formerly Sadilek), a Czech immigrant, whose father's suicide was one of the earliest stories Cather recalled as a child. Annie, now middle-aged, surrounded by her children at the center of a thriving domestic world, would serve as the model for Cather's protagonist and the means for her to process her memories of her Nebraskan childhood into a mythic expression of American life and character.

The biographical elements in *My Ántonia* certainly contribute to the emotional intensity and vividness of the novel. In the introduction, the narrator (presumably Cather herself) meets a childhood friend from Nebraska, Jim Burden, now a successful New York attorney in an unhappy marriage. The two recall their mutual friend, Ántonia, who continues to exert a powerful hold on their affection and imagination. Months later, Jim delivers a manuscript of his recollections of Ántonia, apologizing that his effort "hasn't any form," and adding, "I simply wrote down pretty much all that her name recalls to me." Jim's comments alert the reader to expect a novel that is not a conventionally plotted but is instead a series of episodes or, rather, images of Ántonia that demonstrates her impact. She is "my" Ántonia in the sense that she represents for Jim Burden his attempt to clarify his feelings about the past and its role in forming his present identity and fundamental values. The novel interweaves the life of its two central protagonists—Jim and Ántonia—with the logic of memory, in which years contract and scenes expand as the past is reassessed for significance. As Jim admits, "Ántonia had always been one to leave images in the mind that did not fade—that grew stronger with time. In my memory there was a succession of such pictures, fixed there like the old wood cuts of one's first primer." Ántonia is the means by which Jim can penetrate the past and unlock its treasures.

Cather once described her unconventional method in dealing with her heroine. She had placed an apothecary jar filled with flowers on a bare table and observed that "I want my new heroine to be like this—like a rare object in the middle of a table, which one may examine from all sides. . . . I want her to stand out—like this—like this—because she is the story." At the core of the book, therefore, is the symbolic center of gravity, Ántonia, whom Jim will come to appreciate as the organizing principle to redeem his past and sustain his present.

Cather's novel is set in the late nineteenth century, close enough in time for its first readers to recognize a way of life that was already beginning to diminish. Ántonia Shimerda, a farm girl from a family of Bohemian immigrants, is first encountered when ten-year-old Jim, an orphan, comes to live on his grandparents' farm on the Nebraska prairie. There, he confronts for the first time the prairie's vastness, an elemental and featureless landscape that seems to obliterate the individual, and that will make or break all its inhabitants. "There seemed to be nothing to see," Jim recalls. "No fences, no creeks or trees, no hills or fields. If there was a road, I could not make it out in a faint starlight. There was nothing but land: not a country at all, but the material out of which countries are made." Safely sheltered on his grandparents' well-regulated farm, Jim watches the challenges faced by Ántonia's family through a seasonal cycle that will cause Ántonia's father, a sensitive former musician ill-prepared and unhardened for the poverty and grinding work they face, to commit suicide. The forces that break her father, however, strengthen Ántonia. Generous, empathetic, and vital, Ántonia meets the challenge that defeats him. His death, however, sets in motion the different courses Jim and Ántonia will take. As she remarks to her friend, "Things will be easy for you. But they will be hard for us." Deprived by her father's death of any possibility of refinement and cultivation, Ántonia is forced to take on the heaviest farm chores. She will begin to recede from Jim's view, excluded from the possibilities that education and travel open up for him. Finally, the elemental relationship between Jim and Ántonia and the land that created a kind of vivid pastoral symbiosis in the opening chapters of the novel will also be tested as the scene shifts from the prairie to the town of Black Hawk.

With Jim's grandparents too old to take care of their farm, the

Burdens move to Black Hawk, where social custom and prejudice relegate Ántonia to the lowest rung of the social ladder as one of the "hired girls," the immigrant daughters forced off the farm to work as domestics for the more established citizens of Black Hawk. As pioneer life gives way to town life, there is a confusion of assessment that undervalues as primitive those who have tamed the landscape and created the conditions out of which the prairie towns were created. Although Jim's sympathy is clearly with the hired girls whose natural, instinctive openness and vitality contrast with the pinched and dreary lot of the more respectable, supercilious townspeople, his career as a student breaks his close association with Ántonia, who is increasingly glimpsed only through occasional reports from her friends. He learns that she has been deceived by a lover and left pregnant and unmarried. Meeting her again working in the fields, Jim finds that despite all that she has suffered, Ántonia retains her sympathy with others and affection for her life. Their meeting prompts Jim's crucial statements, "The idea of you is part of my mind," and "You really are a part of me," evidence that Ántonia has secured a symbolic place in Jim's imagination that the conclusion of the novel will help to clarify.

Twenty years later Jim sees Ántonia again. She is married to Anton Cuzak, a Czech farmer, and presides, Demeter-like, over a brood of sturdy, loving children and a prosperous Nebraska farm. Now toothless and gray-haired, she is "battered but not diminished," still luminous, possessing the "fire of life" that represents the indomitable spirit of the land itself. Jim's reunion with his childhood soulmate provides a vital linkage with his past and a return to his spiritual home. The luminous Ántonia, in turn, has been grandly appreciated as a principle of fertility and goodness, steadfastly joyous, nurturing, and essentially indestructible, an archetype of the noble pioneer woman. By recovering his prairie childhood through his connection with Ántonia—the organic product of the American landscape and character—Jim makes sense of his life, offering the reader a comparable lesson in extracting what is vital and enduring in the "precious, the incommunicable past."

The American novels following *My Ántonia* would increasingly deal with the betrayal and collapse of the American dream, the nation's frontier past and heroism becoming more an absence than a vital presence. Cather's novel succeeds as one of the greatest pastoral elegies in American literature, celebrating all that is elemental and archetypal through its heroine, Ántonia, one of a core group of essential female characters in American literature.

CHÉRI

by Colette

An important figure of early twentieth-century French literature, Colette has also gained critical acceptance and a well-earned renown within the genre of women's literature for her precise, beautifully crafted writing and sophisticated, sensitive treatments of human relationships. Colette's extraordinary ability to make the reader see, feel, and sense each moment of her characters' experiences is a central feature of *Chéri* (1920), probably her best-known novel. *Chéri* has been chosen for this volume because of the delicacy, sensuality, and eloquence of Colette's writing, and because it is a masterful description of the relationship between an older woman and a younger man.

Sidonie-Gabrielle Colette (1873–1954), nicknamed in her childhood "Chéri-Minet" or "Gabri," was born in the rustic Burgundian village of Saint-Sauveur-en-Puisaye, the daughter of Jules and Sidonie ("Sido") Colette. Her father, known as "The Captain," was a former officer in the Zouaves and had won a sinecure from Napoleon III as the town tax collector. Colette described her childhood and adolescence in the memoirs *My Mother's House* and *Sido* as one of almost "edenic" happiness, although she claimed somewhat dryly, "a happy childhood is poor preparation for human contacts." She was a child of France's *Belle Époque*, a period stretching from 1871 to the start of World War I. During this time the arts and sciences flourished along with an urban cultural permissiveness that has identified the period as the era of the courtesan and the Moulin Rouge music hall, with its scandalous cancan dancers, as immortalized by the artist Henri Toulouse-Lautrec.

Beautiful, mischievous, and musically gifted, Colette received a girls-school education that stressed patriotism as well as the bourgeois notion that women should exert influence only in the domestic sphere of a solidly middle-class marriage. However, she was aware of an unconventional strain, as well as the failure of middle-class marriage, within her family: her mother had been previously and unhappily married to a wealthy landowner to whom she had twice been unfaithful, and after his death had married "The Captain," her second lover and the putative father of her first son. Colette's introverted half-sister, Juliette, thirteen years her senior, was prone to serious depression, which was made worse by an unhappy marriage to a well-to-do doctor. Juliette commited suicide in her forties. Colette's biographer Judith Thurman has observed, "One meets the shade of Juliette over and over in Colette's work. . . . She portrays depressed, abused, violent, and betrayed women—victims of their families, of their men, and of their own weakness—with an eloquence that belies her own distaste and detachment."

In 1893, the twenty-year-old Colette married the socially prominent and dissolute journalist, novelist, and music critic, Henry Gauthier-Villars, known in Parisian circles as "Willy." Fourteen years older than his country-girl bride, Willy introduced his young wife to figures of the bohemian Parisian high life and the *demimonde*. Willy's literary fame rested on putting his name to spicy novels and reviews penned by ghostwriters, and in the late 1890s, Colette joined his underground workshop with a memoir of her school days. The result was Colette's first work, *Claudine at School*, published under Willy's name, in 1900. The book, which revealed Colette's innate gift for narrative fiction, was an immediate success and led to several sequels in which Claudine grows up, marries, and, in the last of the series, *Retreat From Love* (1907), finds a much-desired independence in contented widowhood. In 1904, she produced a collection of short dialogues between a dog and a cat, *Creature Conversations*, the first of several works published under the name "Colette Willy." Colette would write about her years with Willy honing her craft in *My Apprenticeships* (1936). She separated from the unfaithful Willy in 1906 (the couple would divorce in 1910) and went on to marry the Baron Henri de Jouvenal, a politician and journalist, in 1912. She had a daughter, Colette (nicknamed "Bel-Gazou"), by Jouvenal, and divorced him, in 1925, because of his unfaithfulness and her affair with his adolescent son, Bertrand. In 1935, she embarked on her third, and happiest, marriage, to Maurice Goude-ket, a Jewish businessman and writer sixteen years her junior.

Faced with the need to earn money after her separation from Willy, Colette, while continuing to write, also pursued an adjacent career from 1906 to 1911 as a music-hall dancer and mime. This very public period of her life contributed to the notoriety for which she would become famous. She openly cohabitated with her lesbian lover, Missy de Belbeuf, the Marquise de Morny, and caused a huge citywide scandal when she and the marquise performed a love scene together in the pantomime, *Reve d'Egypte* (*Egyptian Dream*), at the Moulin Rouge in 1907. Colette's works during her music-hall years, which include *The Vagabond* (1910) and its sequel, *The Shackle* (1913), are set in the world of the popular French theater of the day and feature believable women characters who experience sexual desire and fulfillment, an uncommon ingredient in the fiction of the era. Colette left the theater after forming her liaison with the wealthy Jouvenal, and wrote news columns and reviews for the newspaper, *Le Matin*, even serving as a war correspondent during World War I.

Colette would mine her experience of the *Belle Époque*'s *demimonde* in *Gigi*, a series of five novellas, published in 1943, that would go on to become famous as a play and an Academy Award–winning musical, as well as, most notably, in *Chéri*. The novel of a young man barely out of adolescence engaged in an affair with a courtesan old enough to be his mother had its origins in eight disparate short stories Colette wrote for *Le Matin* before the war and integrated into book form in 1920. Colette drew her characters from people she had known, including her former lover and stepson, Bertrand de Jouvenal.

The action of *Chéri* begins in 1912, and concerns the six-year love affair between the forty-nine-year-old, still lovely courtesan, Léonie Vallon and the handsome twenty-five-year-old Fred Peloux, known as Chéri by his lover and his mother, also a courtesan and Léa's intimate friend. Léa and Madame Peloux have been financially successful in their chosen profession and are now able to live independent of their wealthy "benefactors." Both women, each in her own way, has been responsible for bringing up Chéri to take his place in society as a gentleman of leisure. The result is a beautiful young man who is also spoiled, childlike, irresponsible, vain, greedy, miserly, arrogant, and cruel.

The sensual, delicately nuanced quality of Colette's writing is evident in the opening pages of the novel. Having dallied together all morning, Chéri demands from Léa her glorious strand of pearls so that he can play with them. Léa hesitates—"There was no response from the enormous bed of wrought-iron and copper which shone in the shadow like a coat of mail"—but she indulges her lover and hands over the pearls. There is a suggestion that Léa does not want to call attention to the wrinkles on her neck by removing the necklace. Later in the scene, when she criticizes Chéri for "wrinkling" his nose when he laughs, he thinks, "My wrinkles, eh? Wrinkles are the last things she ought to mention." But it is Léa's age, as well as her beauty and charm, that is attractive to Chéri; she is his "nounoune," a nanny and mother, as well as a lover. By staying with her, the nearly inarticulate and puerile Chéri can remain a child. In contrast, Léa is worldly-wise, deliberate, and practical, able to identify her needs and satisfy them. She accepts with equanimity that, despite her battle against aging, their affair will eventually end.

Léa remains composed, even when she learns that a marriage of convenience has been arranged for Chéri to eighteen-year-old Edmée, a wealthy young woman of property who is pretty, quiet, and docile, with "a frightened conquered expression." Chéri promises to remain Léa's lover despite his marriage, and she submits to what is an expected and logical situation. However, after the wedding, Léa realizes that she loves Chéri with a passion stronger than any she has ever known. In despair at having to share him with a wife, Léa goes to the south of France. Mystified and discomfited by Léa's abandonment, Chéri turns on his wife, who suffers from his tantrums, accuses him of infidelity, and asks for a divorce. He refuses to divorce her and leaves home for six weeks, during which he lives with a bachelor friend and haunts Léa's vacant house in Paris. When he learns that Léa has come back to Paris, Chéri buys jewels for his wife and returns home.

In the third part of the novel the relationship between Léa and

Chéri comes full circle. Léa is aware that she has returned "a little thinner and mollified, less serene," and that, although she is still attractive, "it was necessary to drape prudently if not indeed entirely to hide her ruined throat, girdled with great wrinkles which the sunshine had not penetrated." After contemplating ways in which she can continue her profession for several more years, "an effort restored to her her common sense, filled her with lucid pride. A woman like me and not enough courage to know when to call a halt? Come, come, my fine friend, we've had our money's worth in our time." Léa is reconciled to a life of celibate independence, but a visit from Madame Peloux, who warbles on about her son and Edmée, makes her realize that she is not free of her love for Chéri. Late one evening Chéri arrives at Léa's flat, sullen and disheveled, and after quarreling for a time, the two rekindle their passion and for the first time declare their love for each other. In the morning, Léa, unknowingly watched by Chéri, makes plans for the two of them to leave Paris: "As yet unpowdered, a meager twist of hair on the nape of her neck, with double chin and ruined throat, she imprudently offered herself to the invisible eye." When Chéri rejects her plans for departure, Léa bitterly insults Edmée. The selfish Chéri rationalizes that he can no longer find in this resentful, aging woman his lovely, sophisticated, and dependable "nounoune." Léa realizes that the affair has ended, and she tenderly sends him away, granting him an adulthood in which she has no role.

In 1926, Colette published a sequel, *The Last of Chéri*, in which the title character is reunited with Léa after returning from service in World War I. He is appalled by his former mistress, now in her sixties, gray haired, matronly, and asexual, without any of her former sophisticated romantic charm. She chides Chéri for expecting life to be the same as before and adopts her earlier, maternal attitude toward him. Disillusioned with his life and in deteriorating mental and physical health, Chéri leaves his wife and takes up with Copine, another aging courtesan and a great admirer of Léa. He commits suicide in Copine's seedy apartment, which is festooned with photographs of Léa in her youth.

Chéri, which appeared at a time when Colette's penchant for the unconventional was well known, was criticized for its milieu, the world of the courtesan, and for its bad boy title character. At the same time, the novel was acclaimed for the lyrical eloquence of its prose. One of *Chéri*'s fans was novelist André Gide, who sent Colette a letter praising the work, in which he wrote, "What a wonderful subject you have taken up! And with what intelligence, mastery, and understanding of the least admitted secrets of the flesh!" But there is another important aspect of the novel. In *Chéri*, Colette dared to invert traditional gender roles by making her woman character not only older and a denizen of the *demimonde*, but also the stronger partner in their relationship. In Léa, Colette created a new female image, a sexually knowing, independent woman, who, because of her strength of character, transcends her need for her lover in order to give him the gift of liberation.

A ROOM OF ONE'S OWN

by Virginia Woolf

Woolf's powerful declaration of women's independence, autonomy, and artistry, *A Room of One's Own* is widely regarded as the first great achievement of feminist literary criticism that raised and helped to shape the central issues of the modern women's movement. As one of the groundbreaking literary modernists of the twentieth century, Virginia Woolf redefined the art of the novel, taking it from surface realism of external details to the deeper reaches of consciousness and the interior life. As an essayist and critic, Woolf demonstrated that a woman could formulate a new cultural understanding appropriate for dealing with the often neglected and misunderstood female perspective and the role woman writers ought to play in creative life. To capture the essence of Woolf's views on women, gender conflict, literary and cultural history, and the ways and means of creative criticism, *A Room of One's Own* is a foundation text, like Mary Wollstone-craft's *A Vindication of the Rights of Woman*, Simone de Beauvoir's *The Second Sex*, and Betty Friedan's *The Feminine Mystique*, works that remain powerful, compelling, and relevant.

Virginia Woolf was born in London, in 1882, the third child in a family of two boys and two girls. She was the daughter of the renowned Victorian critic, biographer, and scholar Sir Leslie Stephen, the author of the *History of English Thought in the Eighteenth Century* and the editor of the *Dictionary of National Biography*. Her mother, Julia, was a famous beauty and hostess of a distinguished literary circle that gathered at the Stephens' home. She died when Virginia was thirteen, and the loss contributed to the first of several emotional breakdowns that would recur throughout Woolf's life. In 1904, her father's death resulted in a second breakdown and a suicide attempt. When Virginia recovered, she moved with her brothers and sister to a home of their own in unfashionable Bloomsbury. There they formed the center of an eccentric and talented circle of artists, critics, and writers, including Lytton Strachey, Vita Sackville-West, E. M. Forster, and John Maynard Keynes, all of whom would become collectively famous as the Bloomsbury Group. In 1912, Virginia married Leonard Woolf, a critic and political writer. The following year she completed her first novel, *The Voyage Out,* which she had been working on for six years and which was published in 1915. Her second novel, *Night and Day,* appeared in 1919. Both are traditional in form and content; however, in the collection of stories that became *Monday or Tuesday,* Woolf began to experiment with a more daring, experimental form to render a character's stream of consciousness and the interior world of private thoughts and feelings. Her next novels, *Jacob's Room* (1922), *Mrs. Dalloway* (1925), and her masterpiece, *To the Lighthouse* (1927), are all written in Woolf's experimental style in which conventional plot is replaced by an emphasis on the inner, psychological states of her characters, and time and space reflect a deeply subjective, poetic vision. Woolf's later writing includes *Orlando* (1928), a mock biography of a character from Elizabethan times to the present in which the protagonist changes sexes to fit each age; *Flush* (1933), a biographical fantasy of the Brownings seen from the perspective of Elizabeth Barrett Browning's dog; a biography of the art critic Roger Fry (1940); and the novels *The Waves* (1931), *The Years* (1937), and *Between the Acts* (1941). During the 1920s and 1930s, Woolf also wrote several volumes of criticism, including *A Room of One's Own* (1929) and *Three Guineas* (1938), in which she expanded on her critique of artistic achievement and mounted a spirited campaign on behalf of women writers. In 1941, depressed over the outbreak of war and sensing the onset of another breakdown, Virginia Woolf drowned herself. Throughout a distinguished career as a novelist and critic, Virginia Woolf argued that the Victorian world that she was born into was obsolete, and that its patriarchal assumptions about the constricted roles women are assigned must be challenged by fresh ideas and new perspectives. None of her works better demonstrates this point than *A Room of One's Own*.

Originally entitled "Women and Fiction," *A Room of One's Own* grew out of two talks Woolf delivered at Cambridge University, in October 1928, one at Newnham College, the second at the all-women's Girton College (then the only college for women at Cambridge) before an audience, in Woolf's words, of "starved but valiant young women. . . . Intelligent, eager, poor; & destined to become school-mistresses in shoals." Woolf would later state that her motivation for her talk there was "to encourage the young women—they seem to get fearfully depressed." Mainly an argument for the financial independence and privacy necessary for female artistic achievement, backed up by a consideration of such women novelists as Jane Austen, the Brontës, and George Eliot, the talks would be expanded, in 1929, into *A Room of One's Own*. Woolf would add a fictional framework and scenes that contrast the lot of men and women at Cambridge and Oxford. She would imagine the fate of Shakespeare's sister and assert her conception of the androgynous state of mind, which she considered essential for the creation of great literature. Published by the Hogarth Press, the publishing firm Woolf ran with her husband, the essay, in which Woolf felt she would be "attacked for a feminist & hinted at for a Sapphist," is described on the dust jacket, likely composed by its author, as follows:

This essay, which is largely fictitious, is based upon the visit of an outsider to a university and expresses the thoughts suggested by a comparison between the different standards of luxury at a man's college and at a woman's. This leads to a sketch of women's circumstances in the past, and the effect of those circumstances upon their writing. The conditions that are favourable to imaginative work are discussed, including the right relation of the sexes. Finally an attempt is made to outline the present state of affairs and to forecast what effect comparative freedom and independence will have upon women's artistic work in the future.

When *A Room of One's Own* appeared, in 1929, the fight to secure women's suffrage in both Britain and America, which had dominated women's rights activists for the previous seventy-five years, had been finally won. Despite enfranchisement, women, in Woolf's view, continue to be shut out of significant cultural institutions and suffer from various economic constraints that have prevented women from achieving their potential. Woolf's essay suggests that an entrenched patriarchal system impedes and silences a distinctive female voice and perspective. In the essay, Woolf assesses the impact of this system on female literary expression, providing the first conceptualization of literary history with gender as the key determinant. It is, in the words of critic Ellen Bayuk Rosenman, also the "first concentrated attempt to create a counter-theory to Victorian sex-roles," challenging the accepted notion of women's inferiority, dependency, and marginality.

The essay begins by responding to an unheard question: "But, you may say, we asked you to speak about women and fiction— what has that got to do with a room of one's own?" Woolf's thesis is that artistic genius and the ability of women to write great fiction requires freedom: "A woman must have money and a room of one's own if she is to write fiction." Living in a male-dominated world, lacking autonomy and economic independence, women are without the essential prerequisites to create important fiction. Women, according to Woolf, must be able "to think, invent, imagine, and create as freely as men do, and with as little fear or ridicule and condescension." In Woolf's famous formulation, five hundred pounds a year and a room of one's own makes genius possible for women. With them, "Food, house and clothing are mine for ever. Therefore not merely do effort and labour cease, but also hatred and bitterness. I need not hate any man; he cannot hurt me. I need not flatter any man; he has nothing to give me."

To explore the difference between this ideal and present and past reality, Woolf contrasts the possibilities and prospects faced by men and women at Oxford and Cambridge, Britain's training ground for society's movers and shakers. The woman visitor Woolf imagines is shooed off the grass, which is reserved for the male Fellows and Scholars of the colleges. Likewise, she is barred from a college's library without a male companion or sponsorship. The luncheon she receives from the all-male college is lavish and liberating, while her dinner at the all-women's college is meager and demoralizing. Symbolically, men are shown wielding significant power, controlling the means of education and culture, while women are pushed to the margins, excluded, and circumscribed. The contrast leaves the narrator with two linked questions: why are women so poor, and why have so few women written anything to rival male authors?

To answer the first question, Woolf shifts the scene to the British Library Reading Room, where research leads her to conclude that women's impoverishment has been caused chiefly by their childbearing and childraising responsibilities, which have impeded economic independence and caused dependency on males. The second question, concerning the paucity of women's literary achievement, is also connected with women's impoverishment—in their historical limited access to wider experience, the lack of a tradition of women's artistry to draw upon, and the cultural constraints that have silenced women's voices and obliterated their history. To make her point, Woolf surmises the likely biography of an imagined sister of Shakespeare who shared her brother's genius. Frustrated at every turn by gender constraints, Judith Shakespeare ends in suicide and obscurity, with her potential crushed by a lack of education, privacy, expectations, and freedom. To further her point, Woolf surveys literary history from a perspective that focuses on the deviation from the established gender norm in the achievement of Jane Austen, the Brontës, and George Eliot, none of whom had children, but all of whom were constrained by societal pressure that limited their experiences, autonomy, and possibilities.

In contrast to the fate of Judith Shakespeare and her sisters, a contemporary woman writer, one with five hundred pounds a year and a room of one's own, has, in Woolf's view, the potential for genius to flourish as never before. Freed from a battle of the sexes that dependency ensures, the liberated and autonomous woman writer may achieve an androgynous perspective that ultimately is required for literary greatness, in Woolf's view. "If we face the fact," Woolf concludes, "that there is no arm to cling to, but that we go alone and that our relation is to the world of reality and not only to the world of men and women, then the . . . dead poet who was Shakespeare's sister will put on that body which she has so often laid down."

A Room of One's Own remains a remarkable and provocative articulation of gender issues that resists the easy self-pity of victimhood based on male oppression; instead, it challenges women to achieve their full potential. The issues Woolf raises regarding the constraints women face in a patriarchal society, and the relation between sexual identity, literary expression, and achievement, remain vital questions with which women continue to wrestle.

GONE WITH THE WIND

by Margaret Mitchell

A *New Yorker* cartoon of the late 1930s depicts a teenage girl standing in front of a full-length mirror, one shoulder bared, one hand on her breast and the other hand on her forehead. A book lies open on the floor next to her. There is an expression of rapture on the teenager's face as she passionately exclaims, "I'm not afraid of you, Rhett Butler, or of any man in shoe leather!" *New Yorker* readers would have had no trouble identifying *Gone with the Wind* as the source of the caption and the theme of the cartoon. Within a year after its publication in 1936, Margaret Mitchell's sweeping epic of the American South during the Civil War and Reconstruction had sold over a million copies and become a cultural, as well as a publishing, phenomenon. The New York *Herald Tribune* reflected the excitement generated by the novel, when it proclaimed, "*Gone with the Wind* has come to be more than a novel. It is a national event, a proverbial expression of deep instinct, a story that promises to found a kind of legend."

Despite its enormous popularity and impact (helped, in great part, by the 1939 film version of the novel), *Gone with the Wind* has received relatively little literary attention, and its author has been largely consigned to the critical netherworld of the celebrity romance writer. However, in *Gone with the Wind*, Mitchell produced more than just an iconic one-hit wonder that inserted Rhett Butler, Scarlett O'Hara, and Tara into the collective consciousness and brought forth the modern romance genre. She created an enduring woman-centered fiction that addresses important issues concerning the role of women—especially southern women—in nineteenth-century American society.

Margaret Mitchell (1900–1949) once said of her creation, "If the novel *Gone with the Wind* has a theme, the theme is that of survival." The quote fits the era in which the novel was published—the Great Depression of the 1930s—but it also reflects what Mitchell, like other southerners, learned about the Civil War and Reconstruction as a child. Born in Atlanta, a city to which she remained devoted throughout her short life, Margaret Mitchell was the daughter of Eugene Mitchell, an attorney, and Maybelle Stephens Mitchell, an active participant in the women's suffrage movement. Her mother and father had been born during the devastating aftermath of the war, and Mitchell was exposed to local history from her parents and older relatives who had experienced the conflict. Her maternal grandmother showed her where Confederate forces had dug trenches in her backyard, and Maybelle Mitchell took her daughter on tours of plantations ruined by what she called "Sherman's Sentinels" or left to slowly decay after Reconstruction brought poverty. Mitchell would later credit her mother with fixing in her imagination the image of the South uprooted by Union troops. As Mitchell recalled, "She talked about the world those people had lived in, such a secure world, and how it had exploded beneath them. And she told me that my own world was going to explode under me some day, and God help me if I didn't have some weapon to meet the new world." Mitchell's defensive weapon would become her writing, and her theme, how individuals cope in order to survive and rebuild their lives.

Mitchell's first literary efforts, begun when she was a child, were adventure stories, written mostly in the form of plays. She continued her writing through her middle teen years at Washington Seminary, a private girls' school near her home. While attending the seminary, Mitchell attempted a novel that was similar in plot to the kind of girls' series stories popular at the time. Called "The Big Four," the novel was set in a girls' boarding school, concerned the adventures of four friends, and featured a heroine named Margaret who engaged in such valiant exploits as leading her classmates through a fire. Mitchell considered the novel a failure but continued to write short fiction. She went on to Smith College, where she gained a reputation for her sense of humor and her flouting of campus rules, and fascinated her housemates with her stories of the Civil War. In the winter of 1919, Mitchell's mother died in the influenza epidemic that swept the nation, and Margaret returned home to run the household for her father and older brother, Stephens. In 1922, she married Red Upshaw, a some-time bootlegger, who raped and beat her. The couple divorced in 1924, and a year later Mitchell married the more stable and respectable John Marsh, a public relations manager.

From 1922 to 1926, Mitchell was a reporter and features writer for the *Atlanta Journal,* for which she wrote a series of articles on prominent Georgia women, and Confederate generals and their wives. In the first series, Mitchell featured women of force and power, such as Mary Musgrove, a Native American woman who was named empress of the Creek tribe despite having had three white husbands, and Lucy Mathilde Kenney, who disguised herself as a man in order to fight alongside her husband during the Civil War. Mitchell received much criticism from the paper's readers because she had favorably depicted strong women who did not fit the accepted standards of femininity. Deeply hurt by the criticism, she confined herself to writing lightweight fare for the *Journal,* including one article titled "Should Husbands Spank Their Wives?" In 1926, Mitchell gave up newspaper work, partly at the request of Marsh, who did not want her to work outside the home, and partly because she had ceased to find newspaper writing sufficiently challenging. She had also severely injured her ankle in an automobile accident and could not sit at a typewriter. She began a Jazz Age novel with a heroine named Pansy Hamilton and then completed a novella, set in the 1880s, in Clayton County, Georgia, where her ancestors had once owned a plantation (Clayton County would be the setting for much of *Gone with the Wind*). Titled "Ropa Carmagin," the novella was never published, and Mitchell later destroyed the manuscript.

While convalescing from her ankle injury, Mitchell read extensively in nineteenth-century Atlanta history. According to family legend, when few books remained at the local library that Mitchell had not read, her husband remarked, "It looks to me, Peggy, as though you'll have to write a book yourself if you're going to have anything to read." This began Mitchell's nearly ten-year labor to produce *Gone with the Wind*. She approached the project with a view toward clarifying the southern experience of the Confederate defeat, particularly from the perspective of its impact on women. It would become, of course, a romance novel as well as one author's depiction of history. Mitchell began her story with her heroine's climactic realization that would eventually appear in the book's final pages: "She had never understood either of the men she had loved and so she had lost them both." To reach this moment of insight, Mitchell centered her 1,367-page epic on the experience of her main female character, christened Scarlett, after Mitchell's publisher, Macmillan, objected to Pansy, her first choice for a name, because of its homosexual connotations.

The men Scarlett O'Hara loves and loses are Ashley Wilkes and Rhett Butler. The idealistic, dutiful, chivalric, handsome Ashley, who lives at the stately Twelve Oaks plantation, is the object of Scarlett's affections from the beginning of *Gone with the Wind*, when she is a green-eyed, sixteen-year-old spoiled and cosseted southern siren, to nearly the end of the novel, when Mitchell's heroine realizes at last that he has always been the wrong man for her. The right man is the attractive, roguish, cynical, sexually charismatic Rhett, a gambler, womanizer, and Confederate gunrunner, who nevertheless possesses a noble streak and a desire for respectability. Ashley is attracted to Scarlett but feels he is not strong enough for her; instead, he marries his female counterpart, gentle Melanie Hamilton. During the course of the novel, Scarlett will wed three times and be twice widowed. Her first husband is Melanie's brother, Charles, whom she marries to spite both Ashley and Melanie. Scarlett's second spouse is her sister's beau, shopkeeper Frank Kennedy, whom she weds for mercenary reasons. The third is, of course, Rhett, who loves her deeply. She will have a child by each of the men. Along the way, Scarlett flees burning Atlanta with Melanie and Melanie's newborn son in tow, faces poverty, disease, and death at Tara, the O'Haras' ruined plantation, kills a marauding Union soldier, and manages, with courage, fortitude, and not a little scheming, to amass a fortune and rebuild her home. By the novel's end, she has kept the fortune and the home, but has lost everything else of value to her.

Scarlett, one of the most recognizable heroines in American literature, is a morally mixed, deeply flawed protagonist, captivating and admirable in her passion and resilience, deplorable in her heartlessness and self-centeredness, and pitiable in her solipsism.

A complex mixture of modern and traditional values, and feminine and masculine traits, she is an alluring southern belle who is oblivious of people who do not contribute to her sense of entitlement. She is also an aggressive manipulator who rejects passive victimhood with a survivalist mentality that fuels her drive for mastery of her environment. Ultimately, Scarlett is doomed to exist between the conflicting poles of autonomy and dependence that Mitchell diagnosed as the central dilemma of southern women. Seen in this regard, *Gone with the Wind* offers a fascinating dramatization of gender roles and expectations, relevant not just to the period in the South before and after the Civil War, but increasingly valid to the book's first readers, struggling to survive the Great Depression while absorbing the values of the new emancipated woman of the post–World War I era.

The ambiguity of Scarlett's character is evident from the start, in the novel's memorable opening line: "Scarlett O'Hara was not beautiful, but men seldom realized it when caught by her charm as the Tarleton twins were." At once decorous and willful, Scarlett is a complex blend of her mother's carefully cultivated femininity and her father's aggressive masculinity, and the novel's events demonstrate how both are manifested in her defiance of convention and drive for independence and control. What ultimately dooms Scarlett are the traditional values of dependence on the old southern order and its definition of women that dominate here. She is pulled back from the equally iconoclastic Rhett by her obsession with Ashley, and she is stubbornly single-minded in her devotion to the antebellum values of security and protection, represented for her by Tara. She wants desperately to emulate her mother, Tara's gentle and pious chatelaine, and is distressingly aware that her turbulent character, fortified in part by the necessity to survive, forbids this. Scarlett is ultimately incapable of sustaining a meaningful role for herself beyond traditional gender expectations, yet she is unable to find contentment in independence. The failure of both the men and the women in *Gone with the Wind* to maintain the reassuring values of their formerly ordered society, however hard they may cling to these values, is the inevitable casualty of the changes brought about by the war and its disruptive aftermath.

The romance genre, and particularly historical romances, borrows much from Margaret Mitchell, particularly her survival plot in novels that endlessly test characters by circumstances and tangled relationships. Yet few characters in popular romances match the complexity of Scarlett O'Hara. In addition, most romance novels cannot resist the pleasing resolution that Mitchell's novel insistently avoids. *Gone with the Wind* features one of the most daring and unsettling conclusions in fiction. Scarlett is left alone, unsupported by Rhett, who walks out on her after uttering the immortal words, "My dear, I don't give a damn." But Scarlett refuses to give up: "With the spirit of her people who would not know defeat, even when it stared them in the face, she raised her chin. She could get Rhett back. There had never been a man she couldn't get, once she set her mind upon him." And so she falls back upon the twin consolations of Tara and the mantra that has helped to sustain her throughout the novel: "Tomorrow is another day," one of the working titles for the novel.

Despite her readers' continual pleas for a sequel to resolve the suspense over Scarlett's fate, Mitchell refused to comply and struggled to cope with "the hell on earth" that the book's popularity brought her until she was struck and killed by a taxi in Atlanta in 1949. More than fifty years after *Gone with the Wind* was first published, Alexandra Ripley, an author of historical novels and romances, took on the daunting task of continuing the saga of Scarlett and Rhett, and, in 1991, published *Scarlett*, a worthy effort, which, although it does not contain the complexity of Margaret Mitchell's novel, is recommended for its value as a sequel. In 2001, the southern stereotype set by *Gone with the Wind* was challenged in *The Wind Done Gone*, a novel by country western songwriter turned novelist, Alice Randall. Written to dispel the aura surrounding what Randall viewed as a racist cultural icon, *The Wind Done Gone* is the story of Scarlett seen through the personal diaries of Cynara, Scarlett's half-sister, the daughter of Gerald O'Hara and Mammy. It is undeniable that *Gone with the Wind* reflects the white southern point of view, and Randall deserves credit for confronting that fact. But *Gone with the Wind* nevertheless deserves its place as one of the defining popular literary expressions of the twentieth century. With Scarlett O'Hara, Margaret Mitchell offered her own unique point of view to create a riveting central female character and a view of one of America's defining historical tragedies through the lens of a female perspective that continues to express contemporary issues and concerns.

GAUDY NIGHT

by Dorothy L. Sayers

Equal parts detective novel, college novel, character study, and romance, *Gaudy Night* (1936), set at Shrewsbury, a women's college of Oxford University, is the third of four Sayers novels to feature the appealing Harriet Vane, who, like the author, is a best-selling detective novelist and an Oxford graduate. Created by Dorothy Sayers as a mate for her aristocratic, debonair sleuth, Lord Peter Wimsey, who had taken center stage in four previous detective novels and a short-story collection, Harriet is introduced in *Strong Poison* (1930), where she is on trial for the murder of her lover and is saved from the gallows by Wimsey's almost eleventh-hour apprehension of the real culprit. She next appears in *Have His Carcase* (1932), where Sayers provides her with a supporting role to Wimsey in the detection of the mystery. However, it is in *Gaudy Night* that Sayers gives Harriet the substance she deserves and demonstrates what a truly interesting character she is by placing her at the center of what is an intriguing and thought-provoking novel, as well an excellent detective story.

Dorothy L. Sayers once stated, "I am a writer and I know my craft." This was not an idle assertion. Sayers was a prodigious author, who, in addition to the mystery novels and short stories she produced during what has often been called the Golden Age of Detective Fiction, the period between the two world wars, published psychological novels, novels of manners, children's books, poetry collections, essays, literary criticism, and other nonfiction works. Sayers was also a dramatist, whose works, often with Christian themes, were produced by BBC radio, in London's West End, at festivals, and in the United States. Finally, she was a medievalist, who published translations of Dante, a twelfth-century Anglo-Norman romance, and *The Song of Roland.* This last métier was Sayers' favorite: "By instinct, preference, and training," she once declared, "I am a scholar—a medieval scholar."

Sayers began her scholarly training early. Born in 1893, in Oxford, she was the daughter of the Reverend Henry Sayers, Headmaster of Christchurch Cathedral Choir School. Her mother, Helen Mary Leigh, was the grandniece of *Punch*'s cofounder, Percy Leigh. Sayers grew up in Bluntisham-cum-Earith, a small parish in England's fen country, where her father had accepted a church living. When she was six, her father began to teach her Latin, a language in which, by the age of thirteen, she was proficient. She was tutored by a French governess and then spent two years as a boarder at the Godolphin School for Girls, where she distinguished herself academically. However, Dorothy was unhappy at the school. Tall, awkward, shy, bespectacled, and nearly bald after suffering several illnesses, including measles and pneumonia, she had few friends and threw all of her energies into academic work and preparations for obtaining a scholarship to Oxford. She won a Gilchrist scholarship and, in 1912, entered Somerville, a women's college at Oxford. Sayers flourished socially and academically at Somerville, and twenty years later described the impact of scholarly judgment and discipline she encountered there in a manner that would reflect a theme present in *Gaudy Night*: "The integrity of mind that money cannot buy; the humility in face of the facts that self-esteem cannot corrupt: these are the fruits of scholarship, without which all statement is propaganda and all argument special pleading."

In 1915, Sayers received first class honors in Modern Languages and a degree course certificate, the equivalent to women of the university's bachelor of arts degree. She would receive her master of arts in 1920, when Oxford finally granted that degree to women. After completing her studies at Oxford, she produced a small volume of poems, *OP I*, published in 1916 by Blackwell's, an Oxford publisher. After teaching at the Hull High School for Girls from 1916 to 1917, she settled in Oxford, where she pursued postgraduate studies at the university and worked for Blackwell's as a reader and editor. In 1918, she produced a second book of verse, *Catholic Tales and Christian Songs*.

Sayers' father left his parish in Bluntisham for an even poorer living in Christchurch, Wisbech, also in the fen country. Dorothy spent her vacations at the rectory there immersed in the writings of Conan Doyle, Edgar Wallace, and other authors of mystery fiction, not merely to while away pleasant hours, but also because, according to the fledgling author, "That is where the real money is!" In 1922, she moved to London, where she took a job as a copywriter at S. H. Benson, then the largest advertising agency in Great Britain. The following year, she published the first Lord Peter Wimsey detective novel, *Whose Body?*, which received favorable reviews and prompted Sayers to begin a sequel. In 1924, Sayers gave birth to a son, John Anthony, the result of an affair, probably with American writer John Cournos. The second Lord Peter mystery, *Clouds of Witness*, appeared in 1926; that same year, Sayers married Scottish-born journalist Captain Oswald Atherton Fleming. She continued to write about Lord Peter Wimsey, producing *Unnatural Death* (1927), *The Unpleasantness at the Bellona Club* (1928), and *Lord Peter Views the Body* (1928), a collection of twelve short stories.

Harriet Vane's entrance in *Strong Poison* was intended to signal the exit of Peter Wimsey as a character: Sayers planned to have him fall in love, marry, and then drop out of sight, leaving her free to develop other, more fully realized characters and social situations. But, like Sherlock Holmes, who was killed off by his creator, Arthur Conan Doyle, and then resurrected, Lord Peter proved too popular with readers to discard. Sayers also realized that it would be unconvincing for Harriet to immediately accept Wimsey's proposal of marriage. So Sayers delayed Lord Peter's exit and kept Harriet, in many ways Sayers' female alter ego, to provide an extra dimension to the series.

In the character of Peter Wimsey, Sayers created a detective who was an idealized English aristocrat-hero. The second son of the late Duke of Denver, Wimsey is rich, attractive (the late British actor Leslie Howard could have played the role to perfection), suave, elegant, sensitive, and humorous, with a quick mind and keen wit, and an abiding interest in sleuthing. He took first class honors in history at Balliol College, gained fame at Oxford as a cricketeer, is a connoisseur of food and wine, as well as a skillful amateur musician and a collector of incunabula. Wimsey served as an officer in World War I; his sergeant, Mervyn Bunter, became his valet and partner in detection.

Harriet Vane is the object of Wimsey's affection almost from the moment he first sees her in the dock. She is highly intelligent, thoughtful, fiercely independent, proud, and refreshingly forthright. Like Wimsey, she possesses a keen wit and a sense of humor. She is dark-haired and slim, with a low, attractive speaking voice. "So interesting and a really remarkable face," observes Wimsey's mother, the irrepressible Dowager Duchess, in *Strong Poison*, "though perhaps not strictly good-looking, and all the more interesting for that, because good-looking people are so often cows." In a country where class distinctions are paramount, Harriet's origins are solidly middle class. The daughter of a country doctor, Harriet was sent to Shrewsbury College, where she achieved first class honors in English. She was orphaned at twenty-three and, left penniless, was forced to earn a living and has worked hard at her chosen profession—writing detective thrillers. Described by one of Sayers' characters in the last Vane–Wimsey novel, *Busman's Honeymoon* (1937), as a "Bloomsbury bluestocking," Harriet has, like her creator, lived the London life of a post–World War I "New Woman"; her friends are bohemian, artistic, and unbound by social, sexual, and moral convention, and she has lived with a man without benefit of marriage. When she discovers that her lover, Philip Boyes, a very minor poet with a massive ego, only wanted to live with her to see if she was devoted enough to him to become his wife, she resents his dishonesty and breaks off the relationship. Harriet is then accused, tried, and acquitted of murdering Boyes with arsenic purchased while researching her latest book. She subsequently becomes a best-selling detective novelist, partly because of the notoriety she received after the trial.

By *Gaudy Night*, the thirty-one-year-old Harriet is ready to exchange the frantic existence of a best-selling London author for a celibate scholar's quiet life at her alma mater. Escape to Shrewsbury, she feels, would allow her to pursue more important work and at the same time relieve her of romantic complications—Lord Peter (now forty-five) has been assiduously but unsuccessfully wooing her for five years. Harriet is attracted to Wimsey, but she is unwilling to accept his love while she feels indebted to him for saving her life. "I could have liked him so much if I could have met him on an equal footing," she maintains. Bruised by her affair with Boyes, Harriet also doubts that a relationship based on honesty, equality, and independence can be achieved. In *Gaudy Night*, during the investigation of the mystery, Harriet attempts to resolve these emotional and intellectual issues.

Harriet has received an invitation to attend her ten-year college reunion, known as the Gaudy, at Shrewsbury College (based on Somerville). She feels intensely nostalgic for the three years she spent in pleasant and peaceful academic pursuit with schoolmates and dons, but at the same time she wonders if she can face these women after all that has happened to her. Nevertheless, she attends the Gaudy, where she is relieved to discover that both dons and classmates are only interested in her success as an author, not in her affair with Boyes nor her involvement in a sensational murder trial. She is reunited with the cheerful, kindly dean, Miss Martin, the stately warden, Dr. Baring, and several of her former tutors, including Miss Lydgate, a middle-aged English tutor of gentle aspect and great scholarly integrity, as well as the unpleasant Miss Hillyard, a bitter, contemptuous, antagonistic history don. Harriet also meets a visiting tutor, the brilliant Miss de Vine, a woman of "a penetrating shrewdness" and completely uncompromising scholarly integrity and detachment.

At the Gaudy, Harriet is heartened to find that her old friend and classmate, Phoebe Tucker, a historian wed to an archeologist, has blended career and family life in a happy marriage based on mutual respect and equality. She then encounters another schoolmate, a brilliant scholar, who has abandoned intellectual pursuits for the hardscrabble existence of a farmer's wife. The interchange between Harriet and her former schoolmate contributes to the uncertainty Harriet feels about marriage and highlights another issue explored in the novel: whether one should compromise or stifle one's natural talents and, as Miss de Vine, puts it, "persuade one's self into appropriate feelings." It also underscores the fact that, for the majority of educated women during Sayers' time, there was but one choice—marriage or a career. The Shrewsbury dons, all of whom are unmarried, illustrate this.

Harriet's enjoyable weekend is affected by two odd and discomfiting events. The first is the discovery by her of a paper blowing across the quad; when Harriet picks up the paper, she discovers a childishly rendered obscene drawing of a naked female figure "inflicting savage and humiliating outrage upon some person of indeterminable gender clad in a cap and gown." Then, during her journey back to London, she finds in the sleeve of her academic gown a crumpled paper with the scrawled message: "You Dirty Murderess, aren't you ashamed to show your face?" She has received similar letters since the trial and incorrectly assumes this one is meant for her as well.

Months later, Harriet receives a call from Miss Martin, who asks her to return to Oxford to help solve the mystery of a nocturnal college "poltergeist," who has been wantonly destroying college property and sending threatening notes to dons and students. The latest event, in many ways the most horrid from an academic viewpoint, was the destruction of manuscript sections of Miss Lydgate's monumental work-in-progress, "The History of English Prosody." Harriet goes to Shrewsbury to investigate and resides in the college under the pretext of doing research on the Victorian novelist, Sheridan LeFanu, and assisting Miss Lydate in the reconstruction of her manuscript.

During her investigation, Harriet carefully collects data, examines the alibis of everyone in college, including dons, students, and scouts (maids), keeps a detailed journal, and tries to make sense of the obscene drawings and anonymous threatening notes that mysteriously appear. The harassments and destruction of college property continue. Late one night, the mischief-maker removes the fuses in three residence halls, leaving the college in complete darkness and chaos while he or she wreaks havoc in the new library. In one bizarre occurrence, Harriet discovers swinging from the rafters in the chapel an effigy dressed in an evening gown. The dummy has been stabbed with a bread knife; under the knife is a quotation written in Latin. This points to the dons as likely suspects.

Tension and uneasiness rise among faculty, students, and staff as the harassments escalate. One Third Year student, a hardworking but emotionally fragile young women, receives thirty poison-pen letters predicting that she will fail her examinations and insinuating that she is going insane. After she attempts suicide, the dean and the warden agree with Harriet that, at this point, outside help must be obtained. At Harriet's request, Lord Peter comes to Oxford. He studies Harriet's dossier and considers the facts objectively. During a heated after-dinner discussion with the dons on the importance of intellectual integrity, Wimsey discovers that once, while teaching at another university, Miss de Vine learned that a male colleague had deliberately suppressed information that invalidated his research and the main argument of his thesis in order to obtain a professorship. When his dishonesty was exposed, the man lost his professorship and his M.A. degree, and committed suicide. Miss de Vine's story gives Wimsey a trail to follow, and he soon identifies and exposes the Shrewsbury prowler, though not before she tries her hand at outright murder.

All that remains is the resolution of the romance between Harriet and Wimsey. In the rarified atmosphere of Oxford, Harriet's attitude toward Lord Peter begins to change. The first hint of this change occurs before Wimsey arrives on the scene, when he writes to her with the caution that, despite the potential hazards of the investigation, she must not turn away from the task. Reflecting that "this was an expression of equality and she had not expected it of him," she considers, "If he conceived of marriage along these lines, then the whole problem would have to be reviewed in that new light." Later, Harriet is impressed by Wimsey's veneration of the pursuit of intellectual truth that Oxford represents and his understanding of the difficulties in reconciling scholarly and worldly values. During their time together at Oxford, he reveals his vulnerabilities as well as his strengths, his concerns, and his loyalties, and after five years, she is at last able to see him as a complete person and an equal, rather than merely a sophisticated, self-assured, imperious aristocrat. At the end of the novel, it is Miss de Vine who convinces her that with Wimsey, she "needn't be afraid of losing her independence; he will always force it back on you." She urges a still-ambivalent Harriet to "face the facts and state a conclusion. Bring a scholar's mind to the problem and have done with it." Facing the fact that she does love Lord Peter, Harriet accepts his proposal of marriage.

Sayers' skill in capturing the nuances of tone and personality is evident in *Gaudy Night*, and the novel contains several notable, sometimes humorous, characters and situations woven into the detection of mystery. There are the dons, of course, each eccentric, annoying, or endearing in her own academically ordered way; Harriet's former classmates, several of whom are comically preoccupied with their particular areas of interest and expertise (one woman is an expert in the life history of the liver fluke);

Reggie Pomfret, a Queen's student who develops a crush on Harriet; the current crop of Shrewsbury students, including the unhappy Violet Cattermole, who loses her fiancé to a seductive schoolmate after she is accused of sending one of the poison-pen letters; and Lord St. George, Wimsey's handsome, charming, and irresponsible nephew, who plays a major role in the outcome of the Vane–Wimsey romance.

Dorothy Sayers ended the Wimsey novels with *Busman's Honeymoon* (1937), subtitled "A Love Story With Detective Interruptions." In it, Harriet and Peter adjust to married life while investigating a murder in their honeymoon home. Sayers also featured the couple, along with characters from *Gaudy Night* and other Peter Wimsey novels, in a *Spectator* magazine series titled "The Wimsey Papers" (1939–1940), which dealt with issues pertaining to the newly declared world war. Author Jill Paton Walsh carried on the theme of the Wimseys' existence during the war in her mystery novel, *A Presumption of Death* (2002).

In *Gaudy Night*, the best of the Vane–Wimsey novels, Sayers felt she had come closest to producing the kind of fiction she had envisaged writing after *Strong Poison*—a "novel of manners instead of pure crossword puzzle." She succeeded in combining such a novel with the detective genre and in making a statement of paramount concern to her: the permanent value of intellectual integrity in an increasingly unstable world. *Gaudy Night* presents a fascinating glimpse of an Oxford women's college between the wars and places a winning heroine at the center of this well-ordered, often uncompromising academic universe, the better to emphasize—and resolve—her personal and professional dilemmas.

THEIR EYES WERE WATCHING GOD

by Zora Neale Hurston

College courses on African-American literature, women's litera-ture, and twentieth-century American literature inevitably in-clude what Zora Neale Hurston's biographer Robert Hemenway has called, "One of the most poetic works of fiction by a black writer in the first half of the twentieth century, and one of the most revealing treatments in modern literature of a woman's quest for a satisfying life." Hurston's remarkable novel narrating the search of Janie Crawford, the first great African-American woman protagonist, for identity in a racist and sexist society, ex-tends the concept of race beyond the range of equality and preju-dice into an expanded celebration of essential personhood that dissolves established distinctions. Hurston's lyrical, spiritualized consciousness transcends the conventional dichotomies of gen-der, race, and class, and gives the novel its power and undimin-ished capacity to unsettle and challenge.

A central figure of the Harlem Renaissance, Zora Neale Hurston was an innovator, a provocateur, and a contrarian. She was a pioneer in recording and incorporating black folktales and traditions into her work, invigorating American writing, as Mark Twain had done earlier, with the power and expressiveness of the vernacular. Hurston was born in 1891 (some sources say 1901), in Eatonville, Florida, the first incorporated all-black community in the United States. Her father, John Hurston, was the town's mayor and a Baptist preacher. The town's vibrant folk tradition with its frequent "lying" sessions of tall tales stimulated Hurston's anthropological and creative interests. When her mother died and her father remarried, Hurston was passed about from boarding school to friends and relatives. At sixteen she worked as a wardrobe girl for a traveling light-opera troupe. She quit the show in Baltimore and went to work as a maid for a white woman who arranged for her to attend high school.

From 1918 to 1924, Hurston studied part time at Howard University, in Washington, D.C., while working as a manicurist. Her first works appeared in the African-American magazine *Opportunity*, whose founder, Charles Johnson, encouraged her to come to New York City to develop her writing and to finish her college degree. While studying anthropology at Barnard College, Hurston wrote poetry, plays, articles, and stories, and, in 1925, received several awards given by *Opportunity* to promising black writers. She went on to study with the eminent cultural anthropologist Franz Boas and to conduct field research in Eatonville, Haiti, and Jamaica, which was incorporated in two important folklore collections, *Mules and Men* (1935) and *Tell My Horse* (1938). Her first novel, *Jonah's Gourd Vine*, appeared in 1934, and her masterpiece, *Their Eyes Were Watching God*, in 1937. Two final novels—*Moses, Man of the Mountain* (1939) and *Seraph on the Suwanee* (1948)—along with her autobiography, *Dust Tracks on the Road* (1942), failed to halt a declining reputation, and her later years were spent in extreme poverty and obscurity. She worked for a time as a maid, a librarian, and a columnist for the *Fort Pierce Chronicle*. She died indigent and was buried in an unmarked grave in Fort Pierce until writer Alice Walker, who was instrumental in restoring Hurston's reputation, had a headstone erected.

A complex woman, Hurston has been described by Robert Hemenway as "flamboyant yet vulnerable, self-centered yet kind, a Republican conservative and an early black nationalist." Some African-American critics reacted to her ideological independence and contrariness by complaining that the primitive, folk elements in her work were demeaning and one dimensional. Seeking acceptance by mainstream literary standards, some black writers feared that Hurston's evocation of the rural black experience marginalized African Americans and diminished wider acceptance of them. Others, like Richard Wright, author of *Native Son*, dismissed her work as outside the central protest tradition that he insisted serious black literature should embrace. In his review of *Their Eyes*, Wright ridiculed the novel as a "minstrel-show turn that makes the 'white folks' laugh." Even Ralph Ellison—in whom many subsequent critics have detected influences from Hurston in the expressionistic, folk-rich makeup of *Invisible Man*—complained about Hurston's "blight of calculated burlesque." Few initially credited Hurston's work as a major source of poetic and intellectual strength. However, as critic Judith Wilson has observed, Hurston "had figured out something that no other black author of her time seems to have known or appreciated so well— that our homespun vernacular and street-corner cosmology are as valuable as the grammar and philosophy of white, Western culture." It would take the women's movement of the 1970s, and the particular advocacy of Alice Walker, who was instrumental in reviving Hurston's reputation, to cause readers and critics to look again at *Their Eyes Were Watching God*, and to recognize it finally as a complex, groundbreaking work combining central issues of race, gender, and class in ways that had never previously been attempted in American literature.

Hurston's second novel was written in 1936, when the author was in Haiti doing fieldwork for her second folklore collection. The novel is suffused with the exoticism of the Caribbean setting, transposed to the American landscape of Hurston's youth. Hurston identified the central impetus in writing the novel as the failed love affair she had had, in 1931, with a younger West Indian student; in the novel she attempted to capture the "emotional essence of a love affair between an older woman and a younger man." Hurston's protagonist, Janie Crawford, seeks to discover her authentic self by rising above the restrictions imposed by others as well as the seemingly immutable laws of gender, economics, and race. As the novel opens, Janie has returned to her all-black Florida community after having buried her younger lover, Tea Cake Woods, and after standing trial for his murder. The black community does not know what has happened to Tea Cake, but they are affronted by forty-year-old Janie, who wears her hair swinging down her back like a much younger person, and who dresses as a man, in muddy overalls, although she is a woman of means. As far as the community is concerned, Janie is an older woman who should know better; she has undoubtedly been abandoned by her younger lover and has returned home in shame. Nothing could be further from the truth, as the reader discovers, when Janie confesses her full story to her best friend, Pheoby Watson.

Janie's story begins with her teenage sexual awakening, when she notices the organic process of bees pollinating a pear tree. The image suggests to Janie an exalted natural concept of marriage and marks the beginning of her quest for a human equivalent. "Oh to be a pear tree—*any* tree in bloom!" she exclaims. "With kissing bees singing of the beginning of the world!" Hurston writes: "She was sixteen. She had glossy leaves and bursting buds and she wanted to struggle with life but it seemed to elude her. Where were the singing bees for her?" Janie's vitality and desire for expansion will be countered by the restrictions of others with their very different concept of a woman's traditional role. Janie's poetry will be translated into prose; her sense of spirit compromised by hard, material facts. Her grandmother, a former slave, imposes on her granddaughter a marriage of security with an aging farmer, Logan Killicks, to prevent Janie becoming "de mule uh de world," the unavoidable fate of the unprotected black female. However, that is precisely what happens to Janie: as Mrs. Killicks, she exists to serve her husband's economic ambition, destined to drive a second mule and enhance his acquisitiveness. Janie runs away with the ambitious Joe "Jody" Starks, who is heading to the newly formed black community of Eatonville to make his fortune. Although Janie recognizes that Jody "did not represent sun up and pollen and blooming trees," he "spoke for far horizon," of an expansive opportunity, as compared to her restricted fate as Killicks's drudge. Jody pampers his "lady-wife" with new clothes and luxuries while restricting her direct involvement in the black community that he begins to dominate. Starks desires not a mule but a "doll-baby," a precious ornament to be admired as a sign of his distinction and power. Locked in a stagnant existence in which she "got nothing from Jody except what money could buy, and she was giving away what she didn't value," Janie's liberation comes following Starks's death, when Tea Cake Woods, eighteen years her junior, comes into her life.

Tea Cake, a musician and a gambler, is totally absorbed in the present and unfettered by social convention. Unlike Janie's first two lovers, he is also free from their class-consciousness and gender notions, uninterested in her inherited fortune from Starks and unconcerned by their age difference. Tea Cake is "a bee for her bloom," making Janie feel alive, vital, truly offering the unlimited horizon that Starks suggested but failed to provide. By loving her for what she is, neither as a mule nor a doll-baby but as an autonomous equal, he causes Janie to be reborn into a life that defies conventions of age and class. Janie, the former first lady of Eatonville, dons overalls to go "on the muck" with Tea Cake into the primitive depths of the Florida Everglades for the bean-picking season. As critic Mary Helen Washington has observed, "Here, finally, was a woman on a quest for her own identity and, unlike so many other questing figures in black literature, her journey would take her, not away from, but deeper into blackness, the descent into the Everglades with its rich black soil, wild cane, and communal life representing immersion into black traditions." But the couple's lyrical, pastoral Everglades honeymoon does not come without emotional and physical trials. Tea Cake fears that Janie will abandon him for a lighter skinned rival, and the couple is crucially tested in a hurricane. Here, Hurston suggests the significance of the novel's title—the hurricane is a sign of God's intention that must be anticipated and interpreted, an existential moment that forces self-definition. While trying to save Janie's life during the storm, Tea Cake is bitten by a rabid dog. In his subsequent derangement, his jealousy overpowers him and he tries to shoot Janie, who kills him in self-defense. As a key passage in the novel makes clear, the incident, though painful, makes a crucial spiritual point: "All gods dispense suffering without reason. Otherwise they would not be worshipped. Through indiscriminate suffering men know fear, and fear is the most divine emotion. It is the stones for altars and the beginning of wisdom. Half gods are worshipped in wine and flowers. Real gods require blood."

Janie's story now cycles back to the novel's beginning in Eatonville. As she confesses to Pheoby, "So Ah'm back home agin and Ah'm satisfied tuh be heah. Ah done been tuh de horizon and back and now Ah kin set heah in mah house and live by comparison." By embracing the intensity of experience that Tea Cake gave her, Janie Crawford has shaped a self-determined identity, one more organic, expansive, and vital than that restricted by race, gender, or class. As Janie explains in her final declaration, "It's uh known fact, Pheoby, you got tuh *go* there tuh *know* there. Yo' papa and yo' mama and nobody else can't tell yuh and show yuh. Two things everybody's got tuh do fuh themselves. They got tuh go tuh God, and they got tuh find out livin' fuh theyselves." Janie has moved from dependency to self-reliance largely through embracing experience, by not settling for the commonly imposed definition of possibility as an African American or as a woman.

Their Eyes Were Watching God is a controversial novel that has successfully resisted relegation to a narrow critical niche, whether as an exclusively feminist or culturally centered text. Janie Crawford's story, along with the techniques used in its telling, would prove to be a fountainhead for subsequent novelists such as Alice Walker, Toni Morrison, and many others who have followed Hurston's example in giving voice to the African-American experience from a long-overlooked woman's perspective.

THE DIARY OF A YOUNG GIRL

by Anne Frank

When Anne Frank began writing in the small red-and-white-checked diary, a birthday present for the new teenager, she observed that no one "will be interested in the musings of a thirteen-year-old schoolgirl." From 1942, when the Frank family and four other Jews went into hiding in the secret rooms in her father's Amsterdam business offices, until 1944, when they were discovered and sent to concentration camps, Anne used her diary to express her innermost thoughts and feelings, to grapple with the contradictory aspects of her personality, and to chronicle life inside *Het achterhuis* (the house behind), as she called their hiding place. Although she declared that, through her writing, "I want to go on living after my death!" Anne Frank could not have known that her diary would become the most influential and widely read human document to emerge from the Holocaust, one of the most enduring works of the twentieth century, and one of the most beloved autobiographies of all time. Anne Frank's death at Bergen-Belsen a month before the camp was liberated by Allied troops gives her diary an almost overpowering pathos and sadness over the waste of a life. Neither the facts of Anne Frank's fate, however, nor the particulars of her story should overwhelm an appreciation of her undeniable artistic achievement. Anne Frank crafted a great universal reflection of adolescence that expresses, as few works have done better, what the poet John Berryman has called "the conversion of a child into a person." Eleanor Roosevelt, who supplied the introduction to *The Diary of a Young Girl* when it was first published in the United States in 1952, rightly observed that the "diary tells us much about ourselves"; while critic Frederic Morton, discussing the impact of the diary on the world, has stated, "It may well be that the single most enduring thing to be born during the entire course of the Nazi nightmare was a book a young Jewish girl wrote in the occupied Holland of the early Forties." As a young woman's expression of the difficult process from childhood toward self-knowledge and maturity, Anne Frank's *The Diary of a Young Girl* is an essential and unavoidable work.

Annelies Marie Frank was born in Frankfurt, Germany, in 1929, the younger of Otto and Edith Frank's two daughters. Her father was a prosperous Jewish businessman who took his family to Amsterdam after Hitler came to power. There he managed a business selling pectin for canning and spices to Dutch housewives, leasing a warehouse and offices on the Prinsengracht, a canal/street in the old part of Amsterdam. There was little evidence to suggest that Anne was either interested in or capable of literary effort. Compared to her older sister, Margot, who was serious, well behaved, and an excellent student, Anne was recalled by a schoolmate as "interested mainly in dates, clothes, and parties." She was "a mischief maker who annoyed the neighbors with her pranks and continually was in hot water at school for her conduct." The talkative, extroverted Anne was nicknamed "Miss Chatterbox" and "Miss Quack-Quack," and her school compositions were judged by her teachers as "just ordinary, not better than average."

Anne Frank's maturity into an introspective and perceptive writer accelerated under the pressures of circumstances beginning with the German invasion of Holland and the imposition there of the same anti-Jewish laws that were in place in Germany. One of the first of her diary entries captured the growing threat felt by Holland's Jewish community: "After May 1940 good times were few and far between: first there was the war, then the capitulation and then the arrival of the Germans, which is when the trouble started for the Jews. . . . Jews were required to wear a yellow star; Jews were required to turn in their bicycles; Jews were forbidden to use streetcars; Jews were forbidden to ride in cars, even their own. . . . Jews were required to attend Jewish schools, etc. You couldn't do this and you couldn't do that, but life went on." Forbidden to own a business, Otto Frank turned over his firm to one of his employees while quietly making preparations to go into hiding. In July 1942, Margot Frank received a call-up notice from the Dutch Nazi organization, a euphemism for deportation to a labor camp. The Franks responded by making a final trek on foot from their home to their hiding place, to the so-called "Secret Annex" of Otto Frank's warehouse. Carrying luggage would have aroused suspicion, so each wore multiple layers of clothing, and Anne describes herself wearing "two vests, three pairs of pants, a dress, on top of that a skirt, jacket, summer coat, two pairs of stockings, lace-up shoes, wooly cap, scarf, and still more. . . . After we arrived at 263 Prinsengracht, Miep [Otto Frank's secretary and one of the group's protectors] quickly led us through the long hallway and up the wooden staircase to the next floor and into the Annex. She shut the door behind us, leaving us alone." For the next twenty-five months the Franks shared their cramped, secret rooms with Mr. van Pels, a coworker of Otto Frank, van Pels's wife, their teenage son, Peter (the Van Daans of the diary), and an elderly dentist, Fritz Pfeffer (Albert Dussel in the diary). Their links to the outside world were a radio and Otto Frank's loyal employees, who brought them food and supplies obtained with forged and illegally purchased ration cards, as well as news of the war and of their Jewish friends and neighbors who had been taken to concentration camps. Nearly daily roundups of Jews were observable from the windows of the Secret Annex. To avoid detection, the fugitives had to remain almost completely silent during business hours. As Anne observed, "We are as still as baby mice. Who would have guessed three months ago that quicksilver Anne would have to sit so quietly for hours on end, and what's more, that she could."

It was in this atmosphere of tense confinement and constant fear of detection that Anne experienced the first years of her adolescence. She found her refuge and future ambition to become a writer in her diary. Begun less than a month before being forced into hiding, Anne Frank's diary was initially conceived as a series of letters to an imagined friend named Kitty to whom Anne could confide her observations, thoughts, and feelings. "Writing in a diary is a really strange experience for someone like me," she noted. "Not only because I've never written anything before, but also because it seems to me that later on neither I nor anyone else will be interested in the musings of a thirteen-year-old schoolgirl. Oh well, it doesn't matter. I feel like writing, and I have an even greater need to get all kinds of things off my chest." With a growing facility and refreshing candor, Anne describes in her diary her life in hiding, her conflicts with the van Pelses and Pfeffer, her bodily changes and budding sexuality, her short-lived infatuation with Peter van Pels, her detached feelings toward her sweet but somewhat priggish older sister, her resentment of her mother, and admiration for her beloved father. Like most adolescents, Anne struggled to reconcile her "lighter, superficial self" with what she called "the deeper side of me." This self-analysis, recorded with remarkable precision and detail throughout the diary, traces Anne's development from an outgoing, vivacious child to an introspective, complex young woman. It is this introspection, and Anne's ability to objectify and to evaluate with complete honesty a young girl's feelings of longing and loneliness, that distinguishes her diary.

Throughout, Anne tries to make sense of the situation she finds herself in, alternating between feelings of despondency and hopeful idealism. In an entry from October 1943, she writes, "The atmosphere is stifling, sluggish, leaden. Outside, you don't hear a single bird, and a deathly oppressive silence hangs over the house and clings to me as if it were going to drag me into the deepest regions of the underworld. At times like these, Father, Mother and Margot don't matter to me in the least. I wander from room to room, climb up and down the stairs and feel like a songbird whose wings have been ripped off and who keeps hurling itself against the bars of its cage." Despite such despair, she often expresses a vitality and faith in her own and humanity's future. Through her writing, Anne would discover an ambition and a purpose. Inspired by a Dutch broadcast from London, in March 1944, that urged a future collection of diaries and letters to document the war experience, Anne began to revise her diary for future publication, confirming her aspirations as a writer. "I know what I want," she declared. "I have a goal, I have opinions, a religion and love. If only I can be myself, I'll be satisfied. I know that I'm a woman, a woman with inner strength and a great deal of courage! If God lets me live, I'll achieve more than Mother ever did, I'll make my voice heard, I'll go out into the world and work for mankind!" Anne's confidence in her abilities as a writer leads her to a faith in the future in the face of impending destruction, which she summarizes in the most quoted passage from her diary, written only weeks before she was taken: "It's utterly impossible for me to build my life on a foundation of chaos, suffering and death. I see the world being slowly transformed into a wilderness, I hear the approaching thunder that, one day, will destroy us too, I feel the suffering of millions. And yet, when I look up at the sky, I somehow feel that everything will change for the better, that this cruelty too shall end, that peace and tranquility will return once more. In the meantime, I must hold on to my ideals. Perhaps the day will come when I'll be able to realize them!"

Anne's last diary entry, August 1, 1944, records her ongoing struggle between hopefulness and despair: "I get cross, then sad, and finally end up turning my heart inside out, the bad part on the outside and the good part on the inside, and keep trying to find a way to become what I'd like to be and what I could be if . . . if only there were no other people in the world." On August 4, the security police raided the hideout based on information from an informant, the identity of whom has never been definitively proven. The Franks, van Pelses, and Pfeffer were transported by cattle car to Auschwitz where they were separated. A Dutch woman survivor who shared the same barracks with Edith Frank and her daughters later described Anne's courage, sensitivity, and empathy in the midst of the horror around her: "Anne was the youngest in her group, but nevertheless she was the leader of it. . . . She, too, was the one who saw to the last what was going on all around us. We had long since stopped seeing. . . . Something protected us, kept us from seeing. But Anne had no such protection, to the last. . . . She cried. And you cannot imagine how soon most of us came to the end of our tears." In the fall of 1944, as the Russians advanced on Auschwitz, Anne and Margot, along with thousands of other prisoners, were relocated to Bergen-Belsen. The following spring both died in a typhus epidemic that decimated the camp.

When Otto Frank, the group's only survivor, returned to Amsterdam, he received from Miep Gies Anne's diary, which had been discarded by the Nazis looking for valuables in the Secret Annex. He was shocked by what he read, admitting, "I never realized my little Anna was so deep." He edited and published an abridged version of his daughter's diary in 1947, called *Het achterhuis,* the title Anne herself had chosen for it. It would become a worldwide best-seller, translated into more than thirty languages and adapted into theatrical and film versions. In 1989, *The Diary of a Young Girl: The Definitive Edition* was published, which restores the portions of the diary that Otto Frank had deleted and includes the changes that Anne had edited out of the version that she made in preparation for publication after the war. It is now possible to read in full Anne Frank's extraordinary perspective as a young woman dealing with both the most natural process of adolescence and the most unnatural conditions of history, which was determined to destroy and deny the humanity that Anne Frank's diary indomitably asserts.

THE SECOND SEX

by Simone de Beauvoir

Any volume that discusses women's literature through the centuries would not be complete without the inclusion of Simone de Beauvoir's daring and controversial analysis of the role of women and the relationship between the sexes. First published in France, in 1949, and partially translated into English, in 1953, *The Second Sex* was a foundation text for the revived women's movement of the 1960s and 1970s, and remains one of the most influential works of the twentieth century. The impact of the book has been so great that the women who grew up in its wake have sometimes described themselves as "the children of Simone de Beauvoir."

Simone de Beauvoir (1908–1986) came to identify herself with feminism rather late in her life, as part of her ongoing support of a general spectrum of human rights. She once said that, when young, "feminism meant nothing to me." For her, the issue of women's equality was tied to a sense of self that was gradually extended, through intellectual and philosophical observation and discourse, to other women. Beauvoir's individualism began at a young age. She was born in Paris, the elder of two daughters of Georges and Françoise de Beauvoir, whose marriage had been arranged by Françoise's father, a wealthy banker who went bankrupt and was ultimately unable to pay his daughter's dowry. Beauvoir's father, who preferred pursuing success as an amateur actor to other pursuits, encouraged his daughter's early reading, but it was her strict Catholic mother, a person of unshakeable moral beliefs, who exerted the most influence on her and was most likely responsible for Beauvoir's lifelong interest in the questions of ethics. Early on, Beauvoir rebelled at her bourgeois upbringing and the social restrictions imposed upon her by her gender, proclaiming at the age of nineteen, "I don't want my life to obey any other will but my own." At the same time, unknown to her mother, she had rejected her religious faith, which she had once practiced intensely. Freed from the prospect of a stultifying middle-class marriage by her father's inability, because of his father-in-law's bankruptcy, to provide his daughters with a dowry, Beauvoir entered the Sorbonne, in 1928, with the intention of pursuing a career. A brilliant student, she earned her degree in philosophy at the Sorbonne, in 1929, becoming the youngest teacher of philosophy in France.

While at the Sorbonne, Beauvoir met fellow student Jean-Paul Sartre, whom she later described in the first volume of her autobiography, *Memoirs of a Dutiful Daughter* (1958), as "a soulmate in whom I found, heated to the point of incandescence, all of my passions. With him, I could always share everything." Their fifty-one-year liaison, which both viewed as essential and indestructible, precluded traditional notions of marriage, cohabitation, and children, and included a mutually agreed-upon concession for "contingent loves" of lesser importance. Beauvoir insisted that she and Sartre had "pioneered our own relationship—its freedom, intimacy, and frankness." As well known for their literary output and political commitment as they were for their unconventional relationship, Beauvoir and Sartre together formed the center of the postwar French left-wing intellectual and existential movements.

Beauvoir taught philosophy at several colleges until 1943, after which she devoted herself to writing full-time. There are signs that Beauvoir had begun to show some interest in women's issues during her year as a teacher in Rouen: she refused to spread propaganda on behalf of Marshal Pétain, France's minister of war, who wanted French women to bear more children to increase the nation's population, and she began to discuss with a teacher colleague the possibility of writing "a book about women." Before

The Second Sex, none of her books looked explicitly at the condition of women, although the three novels she had published—*She Came to Stay* (1943), *The Blood of Others* (1945), and *All Men Are Mortal* (1946)—all featured strong central female protagonists. Beauvoir seemed an unlikely spokesperson for the woman's perspective; prior to writing *The Second Sex*, she could recall no disadvantages or difficulties in her own life that she could relate to her gender. "Far from suffering from my femininity," she recalled, "I have, on the contrary, from the age of twenty on, accumulated the advantages of both sexes; after *She Came to Stay* those around me treated me both as a writer, their peer in the masculine world, and a woman; this was particularly noticeable in America: at the parties I went to, the wives all got together and talked to each other, while I talked to the men, who nevertheless behaved toward me with greater courtesy than they did toward members of their own sex."

For a period during the war, Beauvoir spent more time in the company of women, and by the war's end had observed that a great number of women suffered from the absence of men and were not willing, as she was, despite her attachment to Sartre, to seek an independent existence of their own. Beauvoir, looking for new approaches to her writing, had begun to think about issues of femininity, starting with questions pertaining to her own sense of being a woman. In her wartime journal, she wondered, "In what ways am I a woman, and what sort of woman?" After the war, when Sartre suggested she examine how being a woman had influenced her life and work so far, Beauvoir, using herself as a starting point but thinking and observing further, embarked on a study of women that, after two years' intensive research, would become *The Second Sex*.

Beauvoir divided the book into two sections. The first section, "Facts and Myths," is separated into three parts: "Destiny," exploring biological and psychological imperatives; "History," telling the story of women from the nomads through the French Revolution; and "Myths," which discusses women in the context of such authors as D.H. Lawrence, André Breton, and Stendhal. The second section, "Women's Life Today," shows how women develop during childhood and adolescence, the ways in which they have experienced different roles throughout their lives, and analyzes "The Narcissist," "The Woman in Love," and "The Mystic." Beauvoir concludes with a fourth part in "Women's Life

Today," titled "Toward Liberation," which looks toward the future and indicates how a woman can achieve independence through the establishment of an individual self.

Unmarried, childless, and free from domestic concerns and commitments, Beauvoir had experienced her independence and autonomy outside the conventional roles expected from women. Although she had little firsthand knowledge of the condition of women that she revealed in *The Second Sex*, Beauvoir's status as an outsider, assessing the relationship of the sexes from her anomalous position, provides much of the book's originality and genius. When Beauvoir began her study, she looked at the lives of women living "normal" married lives who, "in differing circumstances and with various degrees of success, had all undergone one identical experience: they had lived as 'dependent persons'. . . . I began to take stock of the difficulties, deceptive advantages, traps, and manifold obstacles that most women encounter on their path. I also felt how much they were both diminished and enriched by this experience. The problem did not concern me directly, and as yet I attributed little importance to it; but my interest had been aroused."

Beauvoir proceeded in her study, placing women's lives in the context of the existential and socialist philosophies to which she was committed, and her biological and historical research; she arrived at a central thesis that would come to resonate deeply with a generation of women ready to initiate and carry out a revived women's movement:

> Women lack concrete means for organizing themselves into a unit which can stand face to face with the correlative unit. They have no past, no history, no religion of their own; and they have no solidarity of work and interest as that of the proletariat. . . . The bond that unites [a woman] to her oppressors is not comparable to any other. The division of the sexes is a biological fact, not an event of human history. Male and female stand oppressed within a primordial *Mitsein*, and woman has not broken it. The couple is a fundamental unity with two halves riveted together, and the cleavage of society along the lines of sex is impossible. Here is to be found the basic trait of woman: she is the Other in a totality of which the two components are necessary to one another.

In Beauvoir's analysis, women accept their subordination and objectification for certain privileges and advantages bestowed on them as females but which are an evasion of full, adult, moral responsibility. For Beauvoir, the way out of this trap is for women to reject the feminine, the various modes that dictate dependence and subservience, and to choose an autonomous and independent life as a free and active person. As Beauvoir insists, "One is not born, but rather becomes, a woman. No biological, psychological, or economic fate determines the figure that the human female presents to society; it is civilization as a whole that produces this creature, intermediate between male and eunuch, which is described as feminine." She argues, "The emancipated woman wants to be active and refuses the passivity man means to impose on her. The 'modern' woman accepts masculine values: she prides herself on thinking, taking action, working, creating on the same terms as men." For Beauvoir, two keys to the safeguarding of women's freedom are paid work and contraception.

Beauvoir's solution to the objectification and subordination of women in *The Second Sex* can be seen as somewhat problematic in that the author's liberated woman who has left behind any traces of the feminine is in danger of resembling the free and independent male oppressor. Beauvoir also rejects any positives to be found in the experience of motherhood and marriage. However, the significance of *The Second Sex* rests more in its diagnosis of the problem rather than in its solution. As women's studies professor Mary Evans observed in her study of the author's works, *Simone de Beauvoir: Feminist Mandarin*: "Whether we agree or disagree with the conclusions of the book, its significance lies in de Beauvoir's success in placing on the intellectual agenda three crucial questions about the nature of relations between the sexes, namely, the problem of the origin of sexual difference, the nature and elaboration of sexual inequality and difference, and the issue of how men and women should live. These issues still dominate feminist discussion, and form an important part of debates in a number of academic disciplines and in psychoanalysis."

The Second Sex produced a firestorm of controversy upon its publication in France, and the book was both praised and excoriated. Beauvoir recalled that "some professors threw the book across their offices because they couldn't bear to read it." She was not surprised when the Catholic novelist, François Mauriac, attacked the book, but she was disappointed by the hostile reaction of her close friend, the novelist Albert Camus, who complained that Beauvoir had "made a laughing-stock of the French male."

By the time *The Second Sex* was published in its English translation, opinion was more temperate. Anthropologist Margaret Mead, writing about the book in the *Saturday Review of Literature*, held that "the book violates every canon of science and disinterested scholarship in its partisan selectivity," but praised the work's imaginative originality and granted that Beauvoir "provides a rare, exasperating, but unfailingly interesting experience." Philip Wylie, in the same magazine, wrote, "No one can leave her book unread and still be considered intellectually up-to-date. It makes a fresh contribution to awareness that cannot be missed any more than the contribution of Freud, say, or Einstein or Darwin—without the onset of a private cultural lag."

If *The Second Sex* provoked horrified gasps from traditionalists, it also generated the impassioned gratitude of women who had finally found in Beauvoir the first true explicator of their condition. In *Simone de Beauvoir on Women*, Jean Leighton observes that Beauvoir's "analysis of the subtle and insinuating way women are molded by society to accept their inferior role is masterful and devastating. Her perception of how the male-dominated culture tries to transform women into an 'object' who exists primarily to please men has had profound reverberations." *The Second Sex* ranks with Mary Wollstonecraft's *A Vindication of the Rights of Woman*, and Betty Friedan's *The Feminine Mystique* as one of the crucial documents on women's emancipation. Betty Friedan has called Simone de Beauvoir "an authentic heroine in the history of womanhood." Friedan's own groundbreaking work, which can be said to have launched the modern women's movement in America, would been inconceivable without the courageous examination of the status of women provided by Simone de Beauvoir in *The Second Sex*.

CENTURY OF STRUGGLE:
THE WOMEN'S RIGHTS MOVEMENT
IN THE UNITED STATES

by Eleanor Flexner

In 1959, during the so-called social doldrums before the acceleration of the second wave of the women's movement (the same year Barbie debuted), Eleanor Flexner produced a now-classic documentary history of the women's rights movement, *Century of Struggle*, that still serves as the best single-volume account of the struggle to win the right to vote in the United States. Writing in 1967 of her book, Flexner states:

> Ask students who invented the steamboat or the cotton gin, explored the sources of the Mississippi River, led the Populist Movement or the Progressive Party—and if they do not remember they will look for the answers in their history books. Ask them who founded the early women's college, who led the seventy-five-year campaign for their right to vote, who pioneered in protective legislation for working mothers, who developed the concept of settlement houses and social work among the underprivileged—ask them to identify Mary Lyon, Elizabeth Blackwell, Leonora Barry, Elizabeth Cady Stanton, Lillian Wald, Florence Kelley—and they will have to head for the nearest library.

Century of Struggle served then and now to dramatize a crucially important chapter of American history and to highlight the contributions of American women who have often been neglected or ignored. Progress by contemporary women toward equality and empowerment owe so much to these women, as Flexner rightly argues: "The history of women in this century continues to be relevant because even today almost every woman who seeks to widen her sphere of activity beyond her home encounters conflict." Compared to today, however, the crusading women of a Flexner's study "had to prove to others and to themselves as well, that a woman's brain was capable of the same kind of intellectual activity as a man's. They had to combat not only public prejudice but their own fears of being unladylike, of becoming unsexed creatures if they tried to be doctors or mathematicians. . . . No one really knew whether they might not sicken and die if they were exposed to logarithms—or physical education. It had to be proved, not once but over and over again, that they would survive—until these things were finally taken for granted." *Century of Struggle* supplies a detailed account of how far women had to go to secure equality, as well as the challenges that remain.

Born in 1908, in New York City, Flexner graduated from Swarthmore College in 1930, and did postgraduate work at Oxford. Her first book, *American Playwrights, 1918–38: The Theatre Retreats from Reality* (1938), reflects her theatrical activity during the Depression. Trade-union membership stimulated her interest in working conditions for American women that eventually led to *Century of Struggle*. A contributor to *Notable American Women, 1609–1950*, Flexner also wrote a 1972 biography of Mary Wollstonecraft. She died in 1995.

Century of Struggle, which concentrates on the nearly one-hundred-year effort to secure the vote for women in America, begins with a survey of the status of American women prior to 1800, to demonstrate the considerable gender obstacles women faced. As Flexner summarizes: "Married women could not sign contracts; they had no title to their own earnings, to property even when it was their own by inheritance or dower, or to their children in case of legal separation. Divorce, when granted at all by the courts or by legislative action, was given only for the most flagrant abuses." Moreover, women were restricted from educational opportunities to expand their possibilities beyond home and childcare. "It was almost universally believed," Flexner points out, "that a woman's brain was smaller in capacity and therefore inferior in quality to that of a man." Flexner locates the beginning of the women's movement to early educational reformers, such as Emma Willard, Frances Wright, Catharine Beecher, Mary Lyon, and Prudence Crandall, who challenged these restrictions and opened the door of educational opportunities for women. A second important factor in stimulating a women's movement in the United States, in Flexner's view, was the burgeoning antislavery campaigns of the 1820s and 1830s. "It was in the abolition movement," Flexner asserts, "that women first learned to organize, to hold public meetings, to conduct petition campaigns. As abolitionists they first won the right to speak in public, and began to evolve a philosophy of their place in society and of their basic rights. For a quarter of a century the two movements, to free the slave and liberate the woman, nourished and strengthened one another." Flexner celebrates contributions to both causes by such women as Sarah and Angelina Grimké, and labor activists such as Sarah Bagley of the Lowell, Massachusetts, mill workers who created the first women's trade unions.

The breakthrough came when Lucretia Mott and Elizabeth Cady Stanton, disappointed that women were excluded from the 1840 World Anti-Slavery Convention in London, began to conceive of a Women's Rights Convention. Announced for July 19, 1848, at the Wesleyan chapel in Seneca Falls, New York, the convention drew some three hundred participants who passed the Declaration of Principles asserting property and marriage rights for women, as well as the controversial, and by no means unanimous, claim that "it is the duty of the women of this country to secure to themselves their sacred right to elective franchise." The culmination of almost half a century of reform efforts, the Seneca Falls convention became the milestone and launching ground of the movement of women's rights in America. As Flexner declares, "Beginning in 1848 it was possible for women who rebelled against the circumstances of their lives, to know that they were not alone. . . . A movement had been launched which they could either join, or ignore, that would leave its imprint on the lives of their daughters and of women throughout the world."

Flexner goes on to chronicle the powerful alliance between Elizabeth Cady Stanton and Susan B. Anthony in directing the women's rights movement through the rest of the nineteenth century, as well as the intellectual progress of women, the growth of women's social organizations, and women in trade unions during the period as a context for considering the advancement of the suffrage movement following the Civil War. Flexner ably summarizes the dissension that widened the gap between the interests of African-Americans and women over the passage of the Fourteenth Amendment to the Constitution to enfranchise black males, which introduced the phrase "male citizens" for the first time in the Constitution, and thereby raised "the issue of whether women were actually citizens of the United States." *Century of Struggle* documents the hard-fought, state-by-state battle for voting rights for women and the seemingly impossible lobbying for a constitutional amendment.

Between 1896 and 1910, the period Flexner identifies as the "doldrums," no new woman suffrage states were won, and only six states even held referenda on suffrage, all of which were lost. The federal woman suffrage amendment, which had been introduced into Congress in 1878, and perfunctorily considered and dismissed annually ever since, seemed moribund. The aging Susan B. Anthony stepped down as president of the National American Woman Suffrage Association in 1900, and was replaced by Carrie Chapman Catt, a brilliant tactician who set out to organize grassroots suffrage support. Others, like Harriet Stanton Blatch, the daughter of Elizabeth Cady Stanton, and the militant Alice Paul increased the pressure for suffrage by marches and demonstrations. During World War I, Paul's Women's Party began daily, around-the-clock picketing of the White House, with banners referring to "Kaiser Wilson" and proclaiming "Democracy should begin at home." Arrests of picketers led to hunger strikes and force-feeding. Meanwhile, Catt and the NAWSA actively supported the war to demonstrate women's loyalty, while keeping pressure on states to consider suffrage referenda and supporting the federal amendment.

By the end of the war, NAWSA's painstaking work and the Women's Party's dramatic demonstrations had created a public climate favorable to passage of the federal suffrage amendment. On January 10, 1918, Jeanette Rankin of Montana, the first woman elected to Congress, introduced the suffrage amendment onto the floor of the House. As Flexner observes, "Endless lobbying and tallying by both suffrage groups had shown that the vote would be painfully close and that no one could foretell the outcome. It was with real anguish that the women keeping their tallies up in the galleries saw the hair-line finish and their supporters rounding up every possible vote." Four congressmen with determining votes came to the House from their sickbeds; one came from the deathbed of his suffragist wife. The final tally was 274 in favor of suffrage and 136 against. The amendment passed with only one vote more than the required two thirds.

It would take another year and a half to win over the Senate, which passed the Nineteenth Amendment on June 5, 1919. Flexner is particularly insightful in her chapter "Who Opposed Woman Suffrage" and in her account of the further delays obstructing ratification by the "antis," including southern white supremacists, liquor interests, anti-Bolsheviks, northern political bosses, and a National Women's Organization to Oppose Suffrage. On August 18, 1920, however, Harry Burn of Tennessee cast the deciding vote in favor of ratification, and the amendment carried 49 to 47, thus enfranchising twenty-six million American women after seventy-two years of struggle from the Seneca Falls convention. As Flexner points out, ninety-one-year-old Charlotte Woodward, the only surviving participant of the Seneca Falls convention, voted in the 1920 presidential election.

Having detailed the eventual triumph of women's suffrage in America, Flexner concludes with some sobering reflections. "Almost forty years after adoption of the Nineteenth Amendment," she observes, "a number of promised or threatened events have failed to materialize. The millennium has not arrived, but neither has the country's social fabric been destroyed." Flexner reminds her readers that the tireless campaigner for the vote Carrie Chapman Catt, in 1920, "warned suffragists that the franchise was only an entering wedge, that they would have to force their way through the 'locked door' to the place where real political decisions are made." From the perspective of 1959, Flexner sees scant evidence that the break-in and breakthrough has taken place. She points out that most working women remain at the bottom of the professional ladder, and political representation by women lags considerably behind the percentage of women in the population. Although improved and improving, women's progress to equality and power remains unfinished, with major obstacles still to be faced. The encouragement that Flexner offered her readers, in 1959, is no less needed today. "Whatever its hazards," Flexner concludes, "it is doubtful if the world which women face today can appear to them any more hostile or bewildering than that which confronted the early nineteenth century woman with aspirations. . . . Perhaps in learning more of the long journey these, and hundreds more, made into our present time, we can face our own future with more courage and wisdom, and greater hope."

THE LITTLE DISTURBANCES OF MAN

by Grace Paley

"In a world where women's voices have been routinely silenced," Jacqueline Taylor, in her critical study *Grace Paley: Illuminating the Dark Lives,* asserts, "Grace Paley dares to create a voice that is boldly female. In her three volumes of short stories, Paley manifests a willingness to speak the unspeakable. . . . Paley is an innovator, and her innovations often occur in relationship to the particularly female consciousness she articulates. . . . Written in colloquial language, her stories are deceptively simple; they seem at first glance to be uncomplicated and even unadorned tales, but closer inspection reveals their careful craft." Paley's friend and fellow short fiction innovator Donald Barthelme declared her "a wonderful writer and troublemaker. We are fortunate to have her in our country."

A first-generation Jewish American and a New Yorker, Paley derives her power as a writer by mining the rich core of her characters' ethnic and racial backgrounds, their idiomatic speech, and the telling details of their unexceptional but instructive lives. She has given voice to those who are often assumed to have little to say and has investigated aspects of our world that, but for her, would have gone beyond our notice. Although Paley's oeuvre is thus far relatively small—three volumes of short stories, three collections of poetry, and a volume of essays—she is considered one of the most distinctive and important contemporary American writers. The world of her fiction is centered almost exclusively on the areas in New York City where she grew up and in Manhattan's Greenwich Village, where she raised her family and began her association with the various political groups that have directed her activism ever since. Yet there is little about her work that strikes the reader as narrow or dated. Paley has distilled significance from the local to reveal a complex, demanding world that resonates with universal human meaning. There is no better entrée to that world than Paley's first collection, *The Little Disturbances of Man* (1959), which established her reputation as a distinctive fictional voice.

The volume, like all of Paley's work, rests on a solid foundation of her own experiences and observations of the world around her. Born Grace Goodside in the Bronx, New York, in 1922, she was youngest child of Russian-Jewish immigrants. Her parents were Ukrainian socialists who immigrated to America after both had been arrested for participating in workers' demonstrations and after her father's brother had been killed by the czarist police. The family worked at menial jobs to allow Paley's father to attend medical school; after he became a physician, he set up a practice in the family's Bronx home. Paley grew up in a multi-language neighborhood in which Russian, Yiddish, and English blended together; the cadences of these languages would later inform her work.

To the great disappointment of her family, Paley showed little academic ambition. "I was a very good student up to the age of ten," she has recalled, "then my mind began to wander." She spent a year at Hunter College, another at New York University, and studied briefly at the New School for Social Research, taking a course in poetry with W. H. Auden. After reading her poetry, Auden urged her to abandon the artificiality of language she had derived from her reading for the more authentic vernacular that she knew firsthand. It would be a lesson she would take to heart when she began to write her stories more than a decade later.

In 1942, at the age of nineteen, Paley dropped out of college to marry Jess Paley, a motion picture cameraman, with whom she had two children. She devoted her time to her family and took occasional jobs as a clerical worker. On her many trips to Washington

Square Park near her Greenwich Village home with her children, Paley listened to other mothers talking about their lives. It struck her that no one was attempting to tell their stories. She began to write while immersed in her homemaking responsibilities. As her daughter later recalled, "She should have had a door to close and be behind it—but none of that happened; it wasn't like that. I don't know when she got the time, how she did it. She must have done it sometime—maybe it was while we were in day care. . . . It's not like my father took us to the park so she could work—none of *that* was going yet." As Paley recalled, "In 1954 or '55 I needed to speak in some inventive way about our female and male lives in those years." She began writing fiction because she was "thinking an awful lot about women's lives" and "wasn't able to get it into poems."

Paley's first story, "Goodbye and Good Luck," was inspired by a chance remark heard from her husband's aunt on a visit to the Paleys. The aunt said, "I was popular in certain circles, and I wasn't no thinner then," and Paley used both the comment and its cadences to reveal the life of the irrepressible Rose Lieber, who becomes involved with a married actor in New York's Yiddish theater. Rose manages to accept all the many compromises and disappointments that life imposes with a grace and joy that redeem her experiences. The story became the first work for *The Little Disturbances of Man,* a collection focused on the lives of ordinary characters who are shown confronting the unexceptional but testing moments of experience. The title of the volume refers to those seemingly trivial and insignificant incidents that shape a life. The story, "An Interest in Life," from which the collection's title is drawn, concerns a husband's desertion of his wife and four children and opens with the matter-of-fact but chilling perspective of the wife: "My husband gave me a broom one Christmas. This wasn't right. No one can tell me it was meant kindly." The story traces the wife's attempt to cope with her situation and place it into a context that will allow her to face her future. "The Loudest Voice," which draws on the Jewish immigrant experience and the challenge of assimilation, tells the story of a Jewish child who is recruited to play a prominent part in the school's Christmas pageant. The comically treated situation expands into a far-reaching and profound exploration of culture, identity, and compromises in a multiethnic community. In the two companion stories, "The Used-Boy Raisers" and "A Subject of Childhood," which are grouped under the title "Two Short Sad Stories from a Long and Happy Life," Paley introduces Faith Darwin, a recurring protagonist, who contrasts her identity as a wife, mother, and lover with the assumptions of the men in her life. It is one of the earliest dramatizations of the complicated emotional and psychological dilemma women faced in the pre-liberation era, balancing traditional gender roles and desired independence and autonomy. As Paley recalled, "I was a woman writing at the early moment when small drops of worried resentment and noble rage were secretly, slowly building into the second wave of the women's movement." What is most striking about *The Little Disturbances of Man* is Paley's articulation of those resentments and rages in the voice of characters whose voices had previously been silent or ignored.

In writing about Paley's work, novelist Jamaica Kincaid has observed, "Her prose is deceptively comforting. You are wired into the most simple, everyday language, just enjoying it, and then you find yourself in the middle of enormous questions or strange territory." The British novelist A.S. Byatt has commented that "we have had a great many artists, more of them women than not, recording the tragedies of repetition, frequency, weariness and little disturbances. What distinguishes Grace Paley from the mass of these is the interest, and even more, the inventiveness which she brings to her small world."

The Little Disturbances of Man heralded the arrival of a major writing talent, but it would be fifteen years until her next collection appeared. A contributing reason for the delay was Paley's increasing political activities during the 1960s and 1970s. She protested the Vietnam War as a founding member and later secretary of the War Resisters League, and campaigned in favor of draft resistance. In addition, she helped organize an artists' and writers' venture called Vietnamese Life, the goal of which was to share Vietnamese music, art, and culture with her Greenwich Village community. In 1969, she was part of a delegation that traveled to North Vietnam with the goal of bringing back three American pilots who had been shot down. Other issues that claimed Paley's attention were nuclear proliferation, women's rights, and human rights. As one of the White House Eleven arrested in December 1978, for displaying an antinuclear banner on the White House lawn, she was fined and given a suspended sentence. In 1980, Paley was awarded the Peace Award from the

War Resisters League for her activism. "I believe in the stubbornness of civil disobedience, and I'm not afraid of it," she has said.

Paley's political concerns, first introduced in *The Little Disturbances of Man*, become more central in *Enormous Changes at the Last Minute* (1974), her second collection. The collection brings backs characters from *The Little Disturbances of Man*, but it also employs a more open-ended experimental fictional technique and offers a darker vision of life. In one of her most anthologized stories, "A Conversation with My Father," Paley comments on her literary method. An ailing father requests from his daughter a simple story, "the kind de Maupassant wrote, or Chekhov, the kind you used to write." She wishes to please her father but cannot give him the straightforward, easily resolved story he desires. She reveals that she has avoided plot, "the absolute line between two points," in her writing, "not for literary reasons, but because it takes all hope away. Everyone real or invented deserves the open destiny of life."

Paley's third collection, *Later the Same Day* (1985), reintroduces characters from her earlier collections, such as Faith Darwin, who, in "Dreamer in a Dead Language," visits her parents in a nursing home only to discover that they are considering divorce. One of her strongest stories, "Zagrowsky Tells," concerns a bigoted Jewish pharmacist whose daughter gives birth to a child by an African-American father. Zagrowsky assumes responsibility for the care of his grandson, and his love for the child transforms him. It is one of the most hopeful stories in Paley's canon, with its affirmation firmly built on the actual world of mixed motives and ambiguous, complex individuals.

Throughout her life, Grace Paley has consistently chosen to explore complex issues, whether in her politics or in her writing. She has persistently insisted that both writing and action can produce the "little disturbances" and "enormous changes" she records in her stories. As she has observed, we all "have to remember, the world still has to be saved—every day." As her political activism attests, Paley has lived her life according to her conscience. She brings to her life and work the consciousness of herself as a Jew, a woman, a writer, and a citizen of the world. Nowhere is this consciousness more evident than in the voices of her characters—especially her women. They meet their challenges, from playground politics to global conflicts, with determination, wit, humor, and love. Paley has said, "People will sometimes ask, 'Why don't you write more politics?' and I have to explain to them that writing the lives of women is politics." *The Little Disturbances of Man* and Paley's subsequent collections make clear the truism that all politics is local, and that the opportunities for both revolution and reform come unexpectedly during the ordinary moments of one's life.

THE GOLDEN NOTEBOOK

by Doris Lessing

The Golden Notebook (1962) is one of the most influential and intense works of fiction to come out of the 1960s. It is not an easy novel to experience—divided into five sections, four of which contain subsections called "The Notebooks," it demands from the reader both an objective consideration of its construction and a visceral response to each of its parts. A profound and complex examination of a women's psyche, Lessing's masterpiece was published in 1962, just before the decade gave birth to a second wave of feminism (the following year saw publication of Betty Friedan's *The Feminine Mystique*), and has been read as a successor to the work of Simone de Beauvoir. At once a self-reflective text, a feminist manifesto, and an exploration of contemporary and British colonial culture, *The Golden Notebook* explores, as a *New Statesmen* reviewer observed, what it means to be "free and responsible, a woman in relation to men and other women, and to struggle to come to terms with one's self about these things and about writing and politics."

The fragmented style of *The Golden Notebook* and its humanistic vision reflects the circumstances in which Lessing grew up and how she has lived, as well as the way she has approached her writing. She was born in 1919, in what is now Iran, the elder of two children of a bank clerk who had lost a leg as a result of a wound suffered in the battle of Passchendaele during World War I. Lessing's father, Alfred Tayler, moved his family to an isolated area of Southern Rhodesia (now Zimbabwe), then a British colony. There, Tayler tried his hand at farming, at which he was unsuccessful, and the family lived in poverty for some twenty years. Lessing was educated at the Dominican convent school in Salisbury (now Harare) until she developed eye trouble at twelve or thirteen and returned home. From the age of sixteen until she went to London, in 1949, Lessing did secretarial work for, among others, the Southern Rhodesian Parliament and a Capetown newspaper. Lessing's first husband, Frank Wisdom, to whom she was married from 1939 to 1943 and by whom she had two children, held a civil service position in Salisbury. Lessing became involved in radical politics and, in 1945, married Gottfried Lessing, a German communist, with whom she had a son. After moving to London, Lessing was declared a Prohibited Immigrant and barred from Rhodesia until the advent of black majority rule, in 1980. Gottfried Lessing, who had immigrated to East Germany, where he became the commissar of trade and ambassador to Uganda, was accidentally killed, in 1979, during the revolt against Idi Amin. Lessing never remarried and, since 1949, she has lived with her son Peter Lessing in various residences in London.

Lessing had published four novels prior to *The Golden Notebook*. The first, *The Grass Is Singing* (1950), is set in Rhodesia and is the story of a white farmer's wife and her black servant, and the violent conclusion of their relationship. A candid presentation of apartheid, the novel presages the psychological insight, and political and social consciousness, Lessing would bring to her later works. She followed *The Grass Is Singing* with the first three novels that would become the "Children of Violence" series, a quintet published between 1952 and 1969, that traces the history of Martha Quest from her childhood in Rhodesia through postwar Britain to the year 2000. Critics found autobiographical parallels in the series, especially with the first novel, *Martha Quest*, an observation Lessing disputed, preferring to characterize "Child-ren of Violence" objectively as a "study of the individual conscience in its relations with the collective."

Lessing similarly objected to *The Golden Notebook* being read as an autobiographical confession, as well as a chronicle of contemporary "sex wars." Instead, she insisted that the novel be seen in the context of the great European works of the nineteenth century that attempted to synthesize the intellectual and moral climate of their times. "For me the highest point of literature," Lessing declared, "was the novel of the nineteenth century, the work of Tolstoy, Stendhal, Dostoevsky, Balzac, Turgenev, Chekhov." But Lessing was writing about a modern world dominated by fragmentation and chaos that resists such a straightforward synthesis and what D.H. Lawrence called "the old stable *ego* of the character." Lessing's solution was to turn the novel inside out, breaking up and realigning its component parts, shattering chronology and narrative sequence, and rendering her protagonist in multiple narrative voices and alter egos. For Lessing, *The Golden Notebook*'s "meaning is in the shape," and in her introduction, written in 1971, Lessing explains the plan of the novel:

> There is a skeleton, or frame, called *Free Women*, which is a conventional short novel, about 60,000 words long, and which could stand by itself. But it is divided into five sections and separated by stages of the four Notebooks, Black, Red, Yellow and Blue. The Notebooks are kept by Anna Wulf, a central character of *Free Women*. She keeps four, and not one because, as she recognises, she had to separate things off from each other, out of fear of chaos, of formlessness—of breakdown. Pressures, inner and outer, end the Notebooks; a heavy black line is drawn across the page of one after another. But now that they are finished, from the fragments can come something new, *The Golden Notebook*.

The Golden Notebook breaks up a conventional narrative describing Anna Wulf and her friend Molly Jacobs, set in London during the 1950s, with the intense interior views recorded in Anna's four notebooks, each concerned with a different aspect of her life (or its projection), so that a section of *Free Women* is followed by an excerpt from Anna's black, red, blue, and yellow notebooks. This pattern is repeated four times. A fifth "Golden Notebook" follows, recording Anna's breakdown and recovery, in which it is learned that she has been given the first line of *Free Women*—"The two women were alone in the London flat"—by her lover Saul Green. By the end of the novel, the reader reaches the present moment of the embedded novel's beginning, which is then concluded; it reaches, as well, the protagonist's developmental state that has allowed her to write the novel we have just read. The novel encompasses the widest possible exploration of its sexual, political, psychological, and authorial themes, depicting a protagonist in the multidimensional role of lover, mother, writer, individual, and political activist. "It is a novel about certain political and sexual attitudes that have force now," Lessing observed. "It is an attempt to explain them, to objectivize them, to set them in relation with each other. So in a way it is a social novel, written by someone whose training—or at least whose habit of mind—is to see things socially, not personally." Anna Wulf's inner crisis, her search for wholeness, mirrors a world in chaos in which identity is co-opted and undermined by various personal and social forces. The novel, within its unconventional style, articulates these points of pressure on its central protagonist and the process by which they operate and can be managed.

In the initial segment of "Free Women," Anna Freeman Wulf is a blocked writer visiting her friend Molly Jacobs. Both are technically "free women," since they are in between relationships, but beneath the surface they are both prisoners of forces that they cannot control. For Anna, her dilemma of balancing emotional and sexual fulfillment while retaining personal autonomy in the face of a world that seems bent on destruction has paralyzed her. As she tells her friend, "As far as I can see, everything's cracking up." The "Free Women" segment introduces simplified versions of the experiences and aspects of Anna's psychic distress that her notebooks will treat in complex detail. In order to cope with her existential crisis as a woman, intellectual, and activist, Anna compartmentalizes her life and reflections into her four color-coded notebooks. Lessing would explain that she divided Anna's reflections and different narrative forms into "four parts to express a split person. I felt that if the artist's sensibility is to be equated with the sensibility of the educated person, then it is logical to use different styles to express different kinds of people." When asked by Molly why she bothers with her notebooks, Anna responds, "Chaos, that's the point," meaning that collectively her experiences are spinning out of control and that keeping formlessness at bay by managing the parts might enable her to discover the whole truth about herself and her life, its purpose and point.

Anna's black notebook records her transactions with film and television agents who want to adapt her novel, *Frontiers of War*.

This prompts her to consider the experiences on which her novel was based: her own past in Rhodesia and her relationships with a group of communist intellectuals there during the war. These formative experiences, which she has converted into her successful first novel, now seem to her a distortion and a simplification of her past. What she perceives as an indulgence in nostalgia for death and destruction leads her to despair about the ability of writing ever to deliver the truth, which is the cause of her current writer's block. The red notebook treats Anna's disillusionment with the British Communist Party, based on the inability of either ideology or activism to cope with the conflicts Anna feels as an individual and a woman, and the moral collapse of the party as the news of the Stalinist purges come to light. If writing distorts the truth, political solutions equally fail to respond to personal and private imperatives or to halt violence and chaos; and the notebook breaks down into a series of newspaper clippings about such events as the execution of the Rosenbergs and the hydrogen bomb tests.

The yellow notebook shows Anna's response to her experiences in a narrative about a women's magazine writer named Ella, Anna's fictionalized alter ego, and her unsatisfying relationship with Paul Tanner, a married psychologist. It is an attempt to put Anna's public and private selves into fictional perspective. Ella is, therefore, a projection of Anna, whose self-destructive tendencies and emotional dependency on her lover, mirror her creation's dilemmas. The narrative eventually unravels into a series of story ideas, exploring various possible relationship scenarios. The blue notebook is a diarylike, more straightforward record of daily events, including Anna's psychotherapy sessions with her Jungian analyst, Mrs. Marks, who provides the basis of Anna's eventual recovery by having her relive her experiences. It also records her affair with the American writer Saul Green, which leads to the breakdown and recovery recorded in the final Golden Notebook. The reader now has the interior view and context to understand the character "Anna Wulf" introduced in the novel's opening pages. Alienated from her past, from her former political convictions, from those she has loved, Anna is unable to write or unify her world that has shattered into parts that do not cohere.

To achieve some psychic unity Anna and her lover go through a cathartic experience that expands the normal limitations of "individuality." She confronts the various selves that she has kept carefully separated in her notebooks, and, by risking madness, by recognizing a central principle that "we must not divide things off, must not compartmentalize," Anna moves from destruction toward control, from fragmentation to unity, encouraged by her lover to face their demons and confront their fears. "They 'break down,' " Lessing explains, "into each other, into other people, break through the false patterns and formulas they have made to shore up themselves and each other, dissolve." If the individual notebooks represent a defeat of integration and unity, the inner "Golden Notebook" shows the various elements of Anna's past and psyche reassembled. Anna refuses the role of victim (in love, politics, and art) and accepts the conditions of her past and present circumstances, breaking the spell that has incapacitated and silenced her. She provides the first sentence for Saul Green's next novel, and he provides the first line of hers, the initial sentence of the "Free Women" and *The Golden Notebook*. "Free Women," therefore, is a demonstration of what her experiences have taught Anna, converted into the simplified outline of her conventional novel. In it Molly deals with the pressures of her ex-husband and the suicide attempt of her son by remarrying. She urges her friend to begin writing again, but Anna opts instead for a life of service as "a matrimonial welfare worker." Anna, the author of "Free Women," has gained a foothold for her character and herself in the world of experience, and a tenuous control and victory over the forces of destruction and madness. Similarly, the pieces of Lessing's remarkable multidimensional responses to dissolution manage to cohere as "The Golden Notebook" gives way to *The Golden Notebook*.

The novel's contradictions and multiplicity, its evasion of simple categories and responses are central sources of its power, influence, and still vital relevance. One of the most ingenious, thorough, and honest explorations of identity, society, politics, and gender issues in literature, *The Golden Notebook* is acknowledged as a twentieth-century classic.

THE FEMININE MYSTIQUE

by Betty Friedan

An influential treatise on the status of women in post–World War II American society, *The Feminine Mystique*, published in 1963, is a must-read on anyone's short list of women's nonfiction. No other work in the history of feminist thought called for change in the position of women with as much reverberating success as Friedan's analysis of a postwar society that subordinated women and repressed their desires for greater opportunity and fulfillment beyond their expected roles as wives, mothers, and homemakers. *The Feminine Mystique* resonated deeply with American women and sparked a revolution that would result in the revitalized women's movement of the 1960s and 1970s.

The Feminine Mystique was born out of a postwar climate in which Americans, feeling a sense of displacement resulting from the upheavals of war and an awareness of a frightening new phenomenon called the "cold war," sought cultural stability and found it in idealized domesticity; in it men went to work, while most women, after either marrying right out of high school or college, or leaving careers to marry, put all their energies into rearing their children, keeping their husbands contented, and making sure their homes were tidy and attractive. However, despite the unprecedented economic progress that had purchased the American dream in suburban households with two-car garages and shiny new appliances, many women in the 1950s were beginning to experience a discontent so profound it could not be articulated.

One of these women was Betty Friedan, a freelance writer, wife, and mother of three children. Born Betty Naomi Goldstein in Peoria, Illinois, in 1921, Friedan was the oldest daughter in a family of two daughters and a son. Her parents had immigrated to the United States to escape the pogroms of Eastern Europe. Her father, Harry Goldstein, was a jeweler; her mother, Miriam Horowitz Goldstein, worked as a journalist after attending college but gave up her career when she married. Friedan was a gifted student who founded a literary magazine in high school, won a dramatic award (for a time she aspired to become an actress), and graduated as valedictorian of her class. She went on to Smith College, where she studied psychology and, after graduating summa cum laude, in 1942, won two research fellowships to the University of California at Berkeley. Unwilling to commit to a doctorate and a career as a psychologist, Friedan left Berkeley for New York City. The labor shortage caused by men who had left to fight in World War II gave Friedan the opportunity to find work there as a journalist, first for the Federated Press, a news agency for labor unions and liberal and radical newspapers, and then for the *U.E. News*, the official publication of the United Electrical Workers. In 1947, she married Carl Friedan, and a year later gave birth to the first of the couple's three children. The couple divorced in 1969.

In the 1950s, Friedan lost her job as a newspaper reporter after requesting her second maternity leave. She continued to write, however, submitting articles to women's magazines, whose messages of domestic fulfillment for women she would later use as sources for her assessment of a "feminine mystique." Dissatisfied with her primary role as wife and mother, Friedan began to explore the causes of her discontent. Her research revealed that women's magazines urged deference to men, the repression of ambition outside the home, and concealment of intellectual ability, while glorifying domesticity, so that women could become, as one *Ladies' Home Journal* article preached, "The fragile, feminine, dependent, but priceless creature every man wants his wife to be." Concurrent with this media viewpoint was the popular notion that the educational system was not adequately preparing women for their proper domestic roles. To that end, some colleges and universities featured a required course called "Marriage and Family Life Education," in which, Freidan would later observe in *The Feminine Mystique*, "the old role became a new science."

Friedan found disturbing the overriding message that women's contentment lay solely in domestic accomplishments. At the same time, she began to wonder whether other women shared her dissatisfaction with domesticity. In 1957, she sent out questionnaires to two hundred of her former Smith College classmates. The answers she received convinced her that she was not alone in suffering from a psychic distress she would come to define as "the problem that has no name." When Friedan and her Smith classmates met to discuss the questionnaire results during their 1957 college reunion, they canvassed Smith seniors about their aspirations. As Friedan later observed, "Try as we might, we couldn't get these fifties seniors to admit they had become interested in *anything*, at that great college, except their future husbands and children, and suburban homes. . . . It was as if something was making these girls defensive, inoculating them against the larger interests, dreams and passions, really good higher education can lead to."

Friedan next submitted an article to *McCall's* titled "Are Women Wasting Their Time in College?" in which she suggested that "maybe it wasn't higher education making American women frustrated in their role as women, but the current definition of the role of women." *McCall's* and *Redbook* rejected the article, and Friedan refused to allow the *Ladies' Home Journal* to print it after she saw that it had been rewritten to support the opposite viewpoint of her findings. She continued to research her subject, interviewing professional women and housewives on what she described as "the strange discrepancy between the reality of our lives as women and the image to which we were trying to conform." She then decided to expand the article into a book, which was published by W.W. Norton five years after Friedan signed her contract with them.

In *The Feminine Mystique*, Friedan aimed to heighten awareness about a woman's powerlessness within the family and in society, her limited opportunities for self-expression and fulfillment, and the negative stereotyping and discrimination career-minded women faced, as well as the unequal salaries earned by women who did work outside the home. Drawing her conclusions from her own experience and observations, and from the letters, interviews, and questionnaires she compiled from educated middle-class housewives who were struggling to find some meaning in their domestically ordered lives, Friedan diagnosed the anxiety and aimlessness experienced by American women as the product of a fantasy of postwar happy suburban female domesticity created and reinforced by educators, sociologists, psychologists, and the media. In the booming, if inflationary, postwar economic climate, advertisers in particular required a large class of consumers, and women, considered America's hyper-consumers, were encouraged in their roles as sex objects and domestic guardians whose longings could be fulfilled by buying the home and beauty products companies sold. According to Friedan, women accepted their social and sexual subordination in exchange for the material and psychological pleasures their passive femininity and protective, maternal roles as wives and mothers afforded them—but at the cost of feeling imprisoned and dehumanized in gilded suburban palaces.

After identifying and analyzing the dilemma of women trapped in the feminine mystique, Friedan called for a reassertion of female identity beyond that of domestic icon, consumer, helpmate, and caregiver. It was a call to activism that rejected the characterization of women as helpless victims and asserted the need for increased education and opportunities that would allow women to grow to their full potential. In her famous conclusion, Friedan writes somewhat prophetically: "Who knows what women can be when they are finally free to become themselves? Who knows what women's intelligence will contribute when it can be nourished without denying love? Who knows of the possibilities of love when men and women share not only their children, home, and garden, not only the fulfillment of their biological roles, but the responsibilities and passions of the work that creates the human future and the full human knowledge of what they are? It has barely begun, the search of women for themselves. But the time is at hand when the voices of the feminine mystique can no longer drown out the inner voice that is driving women on to become complete."

The Feminine Mystique was brought out in a modest first printing of two thousand copies. Over the next ten years it sold three million hardcover copies and many more in paperback, and has never gone out of print. Friedan received numerous letters from women who wrote that they had no idea, until they read her book, that other women shared their feelings. Women were not the only buyers of Friedan's book. As she recalls in her autobiography, *Life So Far*, "Many men whose wives had made those feminine mystique renunciations had bought the book for their wives, and encouraged them to go back to school or work." *The Feminine Mystique* also received a positive reception from such veterans of the first women's movement as historian and Women's Party member Alma Lutz, who declared that the book offered "a glimmer of hope that some of the younger generation are waking up."

Although the book was seen as a new unifying force in a second wave of twentieth-century feminism, it drew criticism, as well, for its focus on well-educated, middle-class and upper-middle-class white women, especially during the early 1970s, as the women's liberation movement was taking shape and the voices of African-American, working-class, and lesbian women began to be heard. However, the call for reform that *The Feminine Mystique* articulated and the movement that followed the book provided a flashpoint for debate on the status of all women, not just Friedan's target audience. Along with Simone de Beauvoir's *The Second Sex*, and such later feminist works as Germaine Greer's *The Female Eunuch* and Kate Millett's *Sexual Politics*, *The Feminine Mystique* is one of the most influential early texts on feminism, as well as a landmark work in the history of twentieth-century women's literature.

THE BELL JAR

by Sylvia Plath

The Bell Jar, Sylvia Plath's harrowing and mordantly funny account of a college woman's breakdown, suicide attempt, and recovery, was initially published in England, in 1963, just two weeks before Plath's suicide. Recognized as one of the most influential and powerful poets of the twentieth century and a writer who put at the center of her work the demands and limitations of being a woman—daughter, wife, career woman, and mother—Plath has been both mourned as a casualty in the pre-liberation gender wars and revered as an harbinger and early voice of the modern women's movement. Ellen Moers wrote in *Literary Women* (1976), "No writer has meant more to the current feminist movement," and Plath's life, death, and works continue to reverberate and fascinate. *The Bell Jar* has consequently assumed a central importance in helping to understand and interpret one of the most debated and controversial modern writers. However, it also deserves to be appreciated as more than an important autobiographical key to a literary and feminist icon. Critic Tony Tanner has called the novel, "Perhaps the most compelling and controlled account of a mental breakdown to have appeared in American fiction"; while other critics have commended Plath's ability to set intensely personal trauma within a wider social and cultural context. The book is a brilliant dramatization of the problems of growing up female in the United States during the 1940s and 1950s, a fictionalized version of the dilemma faced by women of the period, as anatomized by Betty Friedan in her groundbreaking study, *The Feminine Mystique,* which also appeared in 1963. *The Bell Jar* is one of the earliest novels to express rebellion against the conventional roles assigned to women, a forerunner of such later works as Erica Jong's *Fear of Flying* (1973) and Marilyn French's *The Women's Room* (1977). According to Charles Newman in *The Art of Sylvia Plath, The Bell Jar* is "one of the few American novels to treat adolescence from a mature point of view. . . . It gives us one of the few sympathetic portraits of what happens to one who has genuinely feminist aspirations in our society, of a girl who refuses to be an *event* in anyone's life." Newman goes on to assert that Sylvia Plath "remains among the few woman writers in recent memory to link the grand theme of womanhood with the destiny of modern civilization." Compared with other post–World War II American expressions of alienation and psychological crisis, such as J.D. Salinger's *The Catcher in the Rye* (1951), Ken Kesey's *One Flew Over the Cuckoo's Nest* (1962), Saul Bellow's *Herzog* (1964), and Philip Roth's *Portnoy's Complaint* (1969), *The Bell Jar* is the only one of these novels with a woman protagonist and one of the earliest modern novels of growth and development from a female perspective. Anchored by a satirical impulse to characterize the gender assumptions that blighted a young woman's aspirations in mid-century America and intimately informed by Plath's own experiences and traumas, *The Bell Jar* is a still-powerful, instructive, and universally relevant *Portrait of the Artist as a Young Woman.*

Described by its author as "an autobiographical apprentice work which I had to write in order to free myself from the past," *The Bell Jar,* initially published under the pseudonym Victoria Lucas to protect the identity and feelings of her family and friends, and withheld from publication in the United States until 1971, draws extensively on the details of Plath's background and biography. Born in 1932, in Jamaica Plain, Massachusetts, Plath was the eldest child of Otto and Aurelia Schoeber Plath. Her father had emigrated from Germany at the age of sixteen, earned a doctorate in entomology from Harvard, and had met her mother, an Austrian immigrant, while he was teaching at Boston University. Otto

Plath died suddenly, in 1940, when Plath was eight years old, and the trauma of his death would become a central theme in Plath's poetry and fiction. Many have speculated that Plath's determined assault on academic and artistic achievement became a way of gaining symbolic approval from her missing father. Plath began publishing poetry while a high school student and won a scholarship to the prestigious women's college, Smith, in 1950. During her junior year, she was selected as one of twenty coed guest editors for the college issue of *Mademoiselle* magazine. After returning home following a month in New York City, depressed over being rejected from a creative writing seminar at Harvard, Plath attempted suicide by taking an overdose of sleeping pills in the crawl space beneath her house. Found barely alive two days later, Plath became a patient in a mental hospital and began the therapy that eventually allowed her to return to Smith, in 1954. The circumstances leading up to and following her breakdown and suicide attempt would provide the narrative material for *The Bell Jar.*

Plath graduated *summa cum laude,* in 1955, and won a Fulbright fellowship to study at Cambridge University. There she met the aspiring English poet Ted Hughes, and they were married, in 1956. After living in Massachusetts, where Plath taught at Smith and worked as a secretary in the psychiatric division of Massachusetts General Hospital, the couple returned to England, in 1959. Her first volume of poetry, *The Colossus,* appeared in 1960, the same year she gave birth to a daughter, Frieda. In 1961, she began work on *The Bell Jar,* confiding to a friend that she had "been wanting to do this for ten years but had a terrible block about Writing A Novel. Then suddenly . . . the dykes broke." Plath labored to complete her novel while living in an isolated village in rural Devon, through her pregancy that resulted in the birth of a son, Nicholas, in 1962, and the breakup of her marriage when she learned that Hughes was having an affair. Despite ill-health, exhaustion from caring for her two infant children, and disillusionment over the collapse of her marriage, Plath managed to finish her novel—which she described to her brother as "a pot-boiler" that "no one must read"—began a second, and managed to write many of her greatest poems that later appeared in the posthumous collection *Ariel* (1965). Moving to a London flat in December 1962, Plath would write a final letter to her mother stating that "I have been feeling a bit grim—the upheaval over, I am seeing the finality of it all, and being catapulted from the cow-like happiness of maternity into loneliness and grim problems is no fun." On February 11, 1963, Plath committed suicide.

The issues that Plath struggled with throughout her life in the conflict between her artistic aspirations and the gender limitations imposed on her as a daughter, wife, and mother form the dramatic core of *The Bell Jar,* the story of approximately eight months in the life of nineteen-year-old Esther Greenwood, the novel's narrator. The plot of *The Bell Jar* closely follows the events of Plath's own life during 1953 to 1954, divided into three parts: reflecting her experiences living in New York City as a guest editor for a fashion magazine; her breakdown upon her return home that culminates in her suicide attempt; and her hospitalization, therapy, and eventual recovery. Like Plath (who wrote during this period of her life, "I am afraid of getting older, I am afraid of getting married. Spare me from cooking three meals a day—spare me from the relentless cage of routine and rote. I want to be free—free to know people and their backgrounds—free to move to different parts of the world"), Esther struggles with her aspiration to live an independent, fulfilling life as a writer and the shallow, restrictive reality she faces as a women of her time. It is her inability to integrate her experiences—with sex, work, and her relationships—with her sense of self and the gender role she is expected to accept that eventually leads to her breakdown.

Living in a New York City women's hotel and exposed to the glamorous lifestyle of editors of a popular fashion magazine, Esther finds herself feeling "very still and very empty, the way the eye of a tornado must feel, moving dully along in the middle of the surrounding hullabaloo." She is both attracted to the sophisticated adult world she is introduced to and repulsed by its tawdry shallowness. Esther is similarly divided between admiration for the sexually sophisticated Doreen and the simple innocence of the Kansan coed Betsy, whom Doreen dismisses as "Pollyanna Cowgirl." Esther finds herself torn between her desires for chastity and sex, feelings as seemingly mutually exclusive as her aspiration to become a poet and the expectations that surround her to become a dutiful wife, mother, and homemaker. On her last night in New York, after a series of disastrous encounters with men and disappointment over her future prospects, Esther climbs to the roof of her hotel and throws away her recently acquired fashionable wardrobe, symbolically rejecting the artificial identity imposed by her New York experience and underscoring her disillusionment and disorientation.

Returning to her surburban Boston home, Esther feels similarly trapped, limited to the world of "white, shining, identical clapboard houses . . . one bar after another in a large but escape-proof cage." Amid confused attempts to establish her career goals, sorting out her relationship with Buddy Willard and the double standard that allows males to explore their sexuality while females are expected to preserve their virginity, and a botched treatment of electroshock therapy, Esther grows increasingly dislocated and despairing. With her artistic dreams stymied, Esther finds the alternative route as a traditional wife and mother a life sentence of drudgery and subservience: "I saw the years of my life speed along a road in the form of telephone poles threaded together by wires. I counted one, two, three . . . nineteen telephone poles, and then the wires dangled into space, and try as I would, I couldn't see a single pole beyond the nineteenth." Esther imagines her despondency as a gigantic bell jar that descends upon her, suffocating her, imprisoning her, isolating her from others, and distorting her view of the world. "To the person in the bell jar," Esther observes, "blanked and stopped as a dead baby, the world itself is the bad dream." Her only way out is suicide, and after a series of often comic explorations of the means of self-destruction, Esther almost succeeds with an overdose of sleeping pills.

The final section of the book records Esther's painful recovery after surviving her suicide attempt. First placed in the psychiatric ward of a city hospital, she resists all efforts to help her. However, after she is moved to a private mental hospital, Esther makes progress in self-awareness under the care of an empathetic woman psychiatrist, who helps her come to terms with her feelings about her mother, her aspirations, and attitudes toward sexuality and self-worth. When allowed to leave the hospital for short excursions into Boston, she obtains a diaphragm and loses her virginity, an unpleasant experience with disastrous consequences. Esther survives that disillusionment, however, as well as the suicide of her friend Joan, and is finally brought to the point of expectantly awaiting her release from the asylum—"patched, retreaded and approved for the road." Central to Esther's recovery is her facing down and rejecting the identities imposed on her, accepting an imperfect but authentic self that allows her to break out of her disorienting, tortured confinement. "I felt surprisingly at peace," Esther realizes. "The bell jar hung, suspended, a few feet above my head. I was open to the circulating air." Although the novel ends with hope, with a sense of rebirth and engagement, Esther's future remains unsure, with the ominous threat of another breakdown still haunting her: "How did I know that someday—at college, in Europe, somewhere, anywhere—the bell jar, with its stifling distortions, wouldn't descend again?"

Plath, who in her own life was unable to prevent another descent of the bell jar, manages in her novel to present brilliantly the trauma of growing up female in pre-liberated America and the universal and timeless struggle of self-discovery.

WIDE SARGASSO SEA

by Jean Rhys

Wide Sargasso Sea (1966), Jean Rhys's final novel, published when
she was in her seventies and twenty-seven years after her previous
book, rescued a major twentieth-century author from obscurity
and gained Rhys deserved international recognition. The author
of five novels, three collections of short stories, and an unfinished
autobiography, Rhys would be heralded by critic A. Alvarez as
"one of the finest British writers of this century." Continuing her
exploration of the alienated lives of isolated and marginalized
women who dominate her works, *Wide Sargasso Sea* intensely and
poetically explores cultural and gender alienation through an
imaginative addendum to Charlotte Brontë's 1847 novel *Jane
Eyre,* giving voice and understanding to the earlier novel's speechless and raving madwoman in the attic. Rhys shifts the emphasis
of *Jane Eyre* from the identity and romantic struggles of the plain
governess Jane and her Byronic employer, Edward Rochester, to
his marriage to the mad Bertha, a West Indian heiress whom he
has secretly confined to the attic of Thornfield Hall. Bertha's
identity and existence are the sensational secrets of Brontë's novel
and the gothic stimulus of the novel's plot and resolution. The
revelation of Rochester's bigamy at the altar during Jane and

Rochester's wedding separates the lovers and provides a seemingly insurmountable obstacle to their desires. Jane and Rochester are finally reunited and reconciled only after Bertha burns down Thornfield and dies, eliminating Rochester's marital impediment and causing his penitential but redemptive injury, the physical disfigurement that allows Jane to return to him and to confess: "Reader, I married him." As brilliant and compelling as Charlotte Brontë's novel is in its interior view of one of the first great fictional heroines, Jane Eyre's story also crowds from center stage an equally fascinating character whose motives and identity are subsumed by the monster's role Bertha is made to play in *Jane Eyre*. Rhys's *Wide Sargasso Sea* supplies what is missing from Brontë's novel: a biography of the first Mrs. Rochester and an account of the events that led up to her confinement in the attic rooms of Thornfield Hall. Rhys's novel, which she described as her "dream book which has often been a nightmare to me," becomes an encapsulated history of the West Indies and an intense critique of patriarchy and cultural imperialism from a female colonial sensibility.

Jean Rhys once observed that the only truth she knew was herself, and her life and works are thereby closely intertwined. Her background and heritage help to explain her fascination with outsiders, with alienated women protagonists caught between cultures, struggling to formulate a sustaining identity, as well as coping with the consequence of independence and autonomy. Rhys was born Ellen Gwendolyn Rees Williams, in 1890, on the Caribbean island of Dominica. Her Welsh father was a ship's doctor who had settled in Dominica toward the end of the nineteenth century. Rhys's mother was a third-generation Dominican Creole whose slaveholding family had experienced the hostility of their former slaves after emancipation when an estate house was burned down in the 1830s—the same experience suffered by the family of her protagonist, Antoinette Cosway, in *Wide Sargasso Sea*. The fourth of five children, Rhys was tall and thin, with fair hair and, in her words, "huge staring eyes of no particular colour." All of her brothers and sisters had brown eyes and brown hair, and her sense of physical alienation was exacerbated by her mother's declaration that black babies were prettier than white ones. Rhys recalled that she "prayed so ardently to be black." Like Antoinette in *Wide Sargasso Sea*, Rhys attended a convent school and gained her knowledge of the black culture of the islanders from servants.

At the age of sixteen, Rhys left Dominica for England and the start of a lifelong exile from her Caribbean home, returning only for a short visit, in 1936. Rhys attended a strict all-girls school in Cambridge and experienced the cultural shock of English public school life. A talented singer, Rhys passed the entrance examination for the Academy of Dramatic Art in London, but her family disapproved of her acting aspirations, and her financial support from her family came to an end, in 1910, with her father's death. She took a job in the chorus of a musical comedy and toured with a theatrical troupe for two years. She also posed as an artist's model, and her face was once used for a Pear's soap advertisement. Rhys began to write, in 1914, as a form of therapy to help her cope with a painful love affair as the mistress of a London stockbroker twenty years her senior.

In 1919, Rhys married the half-French, half-Dutch journalist Jean Lenglet, and the couple settled in Paris. Her writing came to the attention of English novelist and editor Ford Madox Ford who suggested "Jean Rhys" as her pen name. In 1922, Lenglet was arrested and imprisoned for fraud, leaving Rhys destitute. She managed to publish her first book, *The Left Bank, and Other Stories,* in 1927, and settled in England where she met literary agent Leslie Tilden Smith, whom she was to marry after divorcing Lenglet, in 1932. Her first novel, *Quartet,* appeared in 1928, to be followed by three more, *After Leaving Mr. Mackenzie* (1931), *Voyage in the Dark* (1934), and *Good Morning, Midnight* (1939). Reflecting her experiences in London, Paris, and Vienna, these novels all focus on the economic and emotional struggles of women protagonists in destructive relationships. Appreciated by a small cadre of fellow writers and reviewers for their understated, ironic, controlled artistry and candor in capturing female consciousness, her novels, however, failed to find a popular audience. During World War II, Rhys disappeared from the literary scene. Her books went out of print, and the few who had read and admired her work assumed she had died. Rhys's rediscovery began when actress Selma Vaz Dias solicited contact with the author through a magazine advertisement to get approval for a dramatic adaptation of *Good Morning, Midnight.* Rhys, who was living in Kent after the death of Smith in 1945, answered the ad, and cleared the way for *Good Morning, Midnight* to be performed as a dramatic monologue, in 1949. The actress' interest in her work became the impetus for Rhys to resume her writing career. She told Dias, "You've already lifted the numb hopeless feeling that stopped me writing for so long." Dias's adaptation would be subsequently broadcast on the BBC, in 1957, the year Rhys visited London to have dinner with the actress and talked about her plans for *Wide Sargasso Sea*. Rhys suffered a heart attack just before that novel was finished, and publication was delayed until 1966.

Taking its title from the huge mass of seaweed in the mid-Atlantic that tricks and traps ocean travelers with the appearance of solid land, *Wide Sargasso Sea* explores the stagnation and suspended animation that besets Antoinette Cosway, beginning with her childhood as the daughter of a West Indian plantation owner who has recently died, leaving his young wife and two children destitute on the isolated, decaying island estate of Coulibri. To save her family, Antoinette's mother attracts by her beauty a wealthy Englishman, Mr. Mason, whom she marries. Mason tries to revive Coulibri by importing cheap off-island labor, angering the estate's former slaves, and a mob burns down Coulibri, resulting in the death of Antoinette's feeble brother and the madness of her mother.

Following Antoinette's education at a convent school and the death of her mother and stepfather, Richard Mason, her stepfather's son by a previous marriage, arranges a match between Antoinette and an English gentleman, a younger son sent to the West Indies to help restore the family's fortune by an advantageous marriage. Although never named, the Englishman is identifiable by his circumstances as Edward Rochester. The second narrative section of *Wide Sargasso Sea* shifts from Antoinette's perspective, in part one, to Rochester's account of the couple's honeymoon on the isolated, seductive, but ultimately alien and terrifying island retreat of Grandbois. Here, Rochester's sexual repression and patriarchal gender assumptions, which reveal his will to dominate and punish, corrode his relationship with his bride. The dramatized conflict between reason and passion, order and chaos, English respectability and West Indian exoticism destroys the potential idyll of bride and groom, and sets in motion the events that will lead to Antoinette's confinement. Like the exotic natural beauty that surrounds them, both attracting and repelling Rochester by its excess, the passionate Antoinette profoundly unsettles the young Englishman, underscoring the guilt he experiences from his sexual desires and his fear of losing control. To try to win back her husband's affections, Antoinette solicits from her old black nurse, Christophine, a potion that succeeds both in enflaming Rochester's passions and exacerbating his abhorrence of his bride and her "primitive" island culture. To punish Antoinette, he has sex with a black servant so that his wife cannot fail to overhear them, and accepts the false accusations made by Daniel Cosway, a jealous and vindictive mulatto who claims to be Antoinette's half-brother, that Antoinette was sexually active before her marriage and that through her mother she is hereditarily insane.

Renaming Antoinette Bertha, after her mad mother, Rochester takes his wife to his English estate, and the narrative perspective returns to Antoinette's disoriented and confused mind as she attempts to understand her confinement in her attic room, attended by the servant Grace Poole, whose identity is the first clear indication that the narrative has joined the story of Brontë's *Jane Eyre*. As told in *Wide Sargasso Sea*, Antoinette's story contradicts Rochester's version as told to Jane Eyre. She, not Rochester, has married against her will in a conspiracy to gain her fortune. Deprived of her Christian name, exiled, and entrapped, Antoinette is a double victim of patriarchy and imperialism. Antoinette dreams of escape, comforted by a red dress that reminds her of her island home and her destiny, which she associates with the flames that destroyed that home. *Wide Sargasso Sea* ends, anticipating Antoinette's defiant act of setting the house afire that will claim her life. The novel concludes ambiguously, with Antoinette's suicide either a final defeat at the hands of a repressive society or a pyrric victory of self-assertion and vengeance on a victimizing ethos.

By filling in the gaps of Charlotte Brontë's novel and exposing its gender and cultural assumptions, *Wide Sargasso Sea* makes it impossible ever to read *Jane Eyre* in the same way again. Antoinette is revealed as a compelling, dark double to Jane Eyre. Like Jane, Antoinette is an orphan figure, neglected at home and abused by other children. Both are sensitive individuals who seek the consolation of love in their isolation and misery. However, unlike Jane, Antoinette is not rescued by a caring man with means but enslaved by him, and punished for her passion and identity as a cultural alien and sexual threat. Rhys's novel makes clear that Jane Eyre's ultimate victory at the expense of another woman should not stand unconsidered. Nor should the gender assumptions that drive the conventional romantic hero to enslavement and bigamy be so easily dismissed in the wish fulfillment of Brontë's happy ending. Rhys thoughtfully and poetically reopens consideration of a classic feminist text and forces a reassessment that unsettles and enriches by exploring an overlooked and neglected female consciousness.

SEXUAL POLITICS

by Kate Millett

Kate Millett's *Sexual Politics* (1970) is the rarest of all publishing phenomena: an erudite work of cultural and literary criticism that became a best-seller. Millett's Columbia University doctoral thesis examining gender politics in history and literature was the first scholarly justification for the modern women's liberation movement and became the manifesto of the movement as well as one of the seminal works of feminist criticism. As critic Maureen Freely observed, *Sexual Politics* "attacked the very people credited as authors of sexual liberation—Freud, D.H. Lawrence, Henry Miller, Jean Genet—and gave emerging 70s feminists the sexual metaphor that went on to define their politics for years to come." Selling more than 80,000 copies in its first year, *Sexual Politics* transformed its author from an anonymous artist and teacher to a feminist icon and media target who was hailed *and* reviled as the "Karl Marx of New Feminism" and the "Mao Tse-tung of Women's Liberation." *Time* magazine, which featured Millett on its cover, claimed that prior to *Sexual Politics* "the movement had no coherent theory to buttress its intuitive passions, no ideologue to provide chapter and verse for its assault on patriarchy"; while *Life* asserted that *Sexual Politics* was "to Women's Liberation what *Das Kapital* was to Marxism." In *Sexual Politics*, Millett set the boundaries and terms for subsequent feminist criticism and paved the way for the proliferaton of feminist scholarship worldwide.

Kate Millett was born in St. Paul, Minnesota, in 1934. After her father, a civil engineer, abandoned his family when Millett was fourteen, she and her two sisters were supported by their mother, who struggled to make ends meet selling insurance on commission, having been denied a guaranteed salary reserved for male salesmen. Millett earned her B.A. degree from the University of Minnesota, in 1956, and studied Victorian literature at Oxford University, becoming the first American woman there to receive a postgraduate degree with first class honors, in 1958. After teaching college English in North Carolina and to young children in Harlem, Millett moved to Japan, in 1961, to concentrate on sculpture. First becoming interested in gender issues after reading Simone de Beauvoir's *Second Sex* at Oxford, Millett would later credit this period of her life, experiencing Japan's extreme gender inequalities, with raising her consciousness as a woman. Millett met and married fellow sculptor Fumio Yoshimura, to whom *Sexual Politics* is dedicated, and returned with him to the United States to resume her teaching and artistic career. While a doctoral candidate at Columbia University, Millett taught part-time at Barnard College and increasingly began to get involved in social reform causes.

Her direct involvement with the emerging American women's movement was stimulated after attending a lecture during the winter of 1964 to 1965 titled "Are Women Emancipated?" Millett became a founding member of the New York chapter of the National Organization of Women (NOW), in 1965, and served as the chair of its education committee, from 1966 to 1970, producing the radical pamphlet, *Token Learning: A Study of Women's Higher Education in America*, in 1968. During the 1968 student strike at Columbia, Millett actively joined the protest on the student side and was fired from her teaching position at Barnard, an experience Millett would later say inspired *Sexual Politics*. Growing out of a paper Millett delivered at Cornell, her doctoral study was directed by Victorian literature scholar Stephen Marcus, whom Millett credits with supplying the necessary guidance to produce a rigorous academic argument. "I was trying for a combination of English critical writing, . . . and then threw in a bit of American plain talk too," Millett later recalled. Millett's work-in-progress was also criticized by her fellow members of the Downtown Radical Women, described by Millett as "a long-vanished . . . debating society where each detail of the theory of patriarchy was hatched, rehearsed, and refined upon again." The dissertation was awarded distinction, and it appeared to considerable media attention, in 1970, as *Sexual Politics,* having been accepted in a rough draft by Doubleday editor Betty Prashker.

Sexual Politics has been described by critic Muriel Hayes as "an impressively informed, controlled polemic against the patriarchal order, launched in dead seriousness and high spirits, the expression of a young radical sensibility, nurtured by intellectual and social developments that could barely be glimpsed even twenty years ago." In it, Millett shows her break with the dominant critical practices of the time, which eschewed extrinsic literary issues over the intrinsic qualities of a literary text; she chose instead to explore the cultural context in which literary works are conceived and produced. *Sexual Politics* begins by exploring the patriarchal assumptions underpinning the works of writers Henry Miller, Norman Mailer, and Jean Genet. Her explication of sexual descriptions in excerpts from each author's work reveals "notions of ascendancy and power played within them." Dominating Millett's interpretation is the radical notion that sexual relationships are expressions of political and "power-structured relationships, arrangements whereby one group of persons is controlled by another." Buttressing her analysis is a theory of sexual politics presented in the book's second chapter, which introduces her central thesis: "When one group rules another, the relationship between the two is political. When such an arrangement is carried out over a long period of time it develops an ideology (feudalism, racism, etc.). All historical civilizations are patriarchies: their ideology is male supremacy." The chapter goes on to outline the "techniques of control"—biological, sociological, psychological, economic, educational, and others—by which patriarchal values have been enforced and sexual relationships have been defined by male dominance and female subordination. Millett's theory of sexual politics formulates a useful set of analytical categories by which history and literature might be read in gender terms, while establishing key tenets of contemporary feminist literary criticism.

Having asserted a theory of sexual politics, Millett goes on in the third and fourth chapters to provide an historical analysis of the sexual revolution, during the period 1830 to 1930, in which patriarchal values were challenged, and the subsequent period Millett calls the "Counterrevolution," from 1930 to 1960, when patriarchal ideology reasserted its dominance and control. Arguing that a successful sexual revolution should accomplish complete economic independence for women and a redefinition of traditional family structures, Millett sees in the gains made by women in education, politics, and employment reform rather than revolution, while she shows how the objectification and subordination of women have continued through the institution of marriage and modern conceptions of romantic love. In the reactionary policies of Nazi Germany and the Soviet Union, Millett demonstrates how women have been coerced to serve the ends of the state, while she convincingly shows how patriarchal institutions and ideology affect the private lives of individuals. Dealing with the ideological forces opposing gender revolution, Millett harshly rejects Sigmund Freud's psychoanalytical theory as gender bias masquerading as science: "Although generally accepted as a prototype of the liberal urge toward sexual freedom, and a signal contributor toward softening traditional puritanical inhibitions upon sexuality, the effect of Freud's work, that of his followers, and still more that of his popularizers, was to rationalize the invidious relationship between the sexes, to ratify trational roles, and to validate temperamental differences." *Sexual Politics* establishes, therefore, a theoretical, historical, and psychological framework for an understanding of the working of a patriarchal ideology in modern civilization.

Sexual Politics concludes with chapters on the "counterrevolutionary sexual politicians"—D.H. Lawrence, Henry Miller, and Norman Mailer—writers, who, "after the usual manner of cultural agents, both reflected and actually shaped attitudes." Millett's critique of these writers, along with Jean Genet, who is treated for his "homosexual analysis of sexual politics," serves as a tour-de-force model of feminist criticism in which gender assumptions and bias are deciphered in each writer's works. Lawrence, in Millett's view, sentimentally celebrates virility and female passivity; while Miller and Mailer, both prisoners "of the virility cult" Lawrence promulgated, are indicted as misogynists who degrade women. Throughout this section of the book, Millett reveals her daring, iconoclastic interpretive and rhetorical skills that have made *Sexual Politics* a feminist classic.

Sexual Politics concludes with a postscript in which Millett optimistically forecasts the possibility of the revolution to overthrow the forces of patriarchy and social repression:

> As the largest alienated element in our society, and because of their numbers, passion, and length of oppression, its largest revolutionary base, women might come to play a leadership part in social revolution, quite unknown before in history. The changes in fundamental values such a coalition of expropriated groups—blacks, youth, women, the poor—would seek are especially pertinent to realizing not only sexual revolution but a gathering impetus toward freedom from rank or prescriptive role, sexual or otherwise. For to actually change the quality of life is to transform personality, and this cannot be done without freeing humanity from the tyranny of sexual-social category and conformity to sexual stereotype—as well as abolishing racial caste and economic class.
>
> It may be that a second wave of the sexual revolution might at last accomplish its aim of freeing half the race from its immemorial subordination—and in the process bring us all a great deal closer to humanity. It may be that we shall even be able to retire sex from the harsh realities of politics, but not until we have created a world we can bear out of the desert we inhabit.

An indictment and a rallying cry, *Sexual Politics* provoked a strong reaction from critics, both positive and negative, including a rebuttal from Norman Mailer in *The Prisoner of Sex* (1971). Millett would chronicle her attempts to cope with the pressure of her celebrity in *Flying* (1974), the first in a series of autobiographical books that include *Sita* (1977), *The Loony-Bin Trip* (1990), *A.D.: A Memoir* (1995), and *Mother Millett* (2001), which deal candidly with her loves, drug dependency, and family relations. Her other nonfiction works include *The Basement: Meditations on Human Sacrifice* (1980), *Going to Iran* (1981), and *The Politics of Cruelty: An Essay on the Literature of Political Imprisonment* (1994). As in *Sexual Politics,* all of Millett's subsequent work shows her interest in the relationship between the personal and the political, and the ways in which history, culture, and ideology shape human destiny. Candid, quirky, with a single-mindedness that characterizes the polemicist, Millett blazes trails and enables further exploration. Critic Martha Bridegam, in reviewing *Mother Millett*, offers useful advice that is equally relevant to *Sexual Politics* and all of Millett's writing: "Warts and all, this book belongs in your brain. You'll argue with Kate Millett as you read, but the important part is, you'll think."

SISTERHOOD IS POWERFUL: AN ANTHOLOGY OF WRITINGS FROM THE WOMEN'S LIBERATION MOVEMENT

Compiled and edited by Robin Morgan

There is perhaps no better time capsule for an understanding of the commitment and rage that fueled the second wave of the modern women's movement, during the 1960s and 1970s, than Robin Morgan's now-classic anthology of feminist manifestos, critiques, and position papers, *Sisterhood Is Powerful* (1970). Morgan, described by Alicia Ostriker as "one of the most honestly angry women since Antigone," masterminded what has been described by Kathleen Wiegner as "one of the first of the good anthologies of the women's movement" that, in the words of Paul Robinson, "profoundly affected the way that many of us think about women and the relations between the sexes." Although there is a strong hint of the mimeographed in the collection, hastily printed slogans, incitements, and morale boosts to be rushed to the frontline of a battle in progress, Morgan's feminist reader also includes several carefully considered justifications for the radical agenda that these committed feminists advocated. Its principal value today rests in its ability to reflect the sense of urgency and importance of a gender revolution that set out to rewrite the rules of gender etiquette and women's possibilities. Lacking a time machine with which to experience firsthand the turbulent gender conflicts of the 1960s, a reader is particularly well served by this anthology, both to help explain the past and to measure the losses and gains in the gender wars ever since.

Although "conceived, written, edited, copy-edited, proofread, designed, and illustrated by women," *Sisterhood Is Powerful* seems dominated by the shaping presence of one woman—its flamboyant editor, Robin Morgan, whose own feminist conversion and activist career typify much about her era. Born in 1941, Morgan grew up in Mount Vernon, New York, where she aspired to be a doctor and a poet. "The male-supremacist society destroyed the first ambition," she has observed, "but couldn't dent the second." Morgan had become a celebrity at an early age when she hosted her own radio program in the 1940s, "The Little Robin Morgan Show," and later, when she acted in the role of Dagmar on the popular 1950s television series *I Remember Mama.* Graduating from the Wetter School in Mount Vernon at the age of fifteen, Morgan was privately tutored in the United States and Europe, from 1956 to 1959, before attending Columbia University to cultivate her skills as a poet. During the early 1960s, she began publishing her poetry while working as a literary agent and freelance editor in New York City. Much of her focus began to be dominated by radical political activities centered around civil rights and opposition to the war in Vietnam. She contributed articles and poems to such underground journals as *Liberation, Rat, Win,* and *The Guardian.* In 1962, Morgan married Kenneth Pitchford, a poet and openly homosexual cofounder of the Gay Liberation Front. In 1968, Morgan came out publicly as a lesbian in *The New York Times,* but she and her husband had a son in 1969, and remained married until 1983.

Morgan's involvement with feminism was spurred by her disenchantment with the sexism she encountered among the radical left. As Morgan recalled in her memoir, *Going Too Far: The Personal Chronicle of a Feminist* (1977):

There were the years in the New Left—the civil-rights movement, the student movement, the peace movement, and their more "militant" offspring groups—until my inescapably intensifying women's consciousness led me, along with thousands of other women, to become a refugee from what I came to call "the male-dominated Left" and what I now refer to as "the boys' movement." And it wasn't merely the mass epidemic of bursitis (from the continual cranking of mimeograph machines) which drove us all out, but the serious, ceaseless, degrading and pervasive sexism we encountered there, in each man's attitude and in every group's structure and in the narrow political emphases and manhood-proving tactical styles themselves. We were used to such an approach from the Establishment, but here, too?

Morgan would include in *Sisterhood Is Powerful* a section entitled "Know Your Enemy: A Sampling of Sexist Quotes," with the following examples of the sexism of the New Left:

The only position for women in SNCC is prone—Stokeley Carmichael, 1966.

The only alliance I would make with the Women's Liberation Movement is in bed—Abbie Hoffman.

Active as a member of the New York Radical Women, Morgan participated with Kate Millet and others in developing much of the theoretical formulations of the contemporary women's movement. She became publicly identified as a radical feminist during the 1968 protest of the Miss America pageant, which many regard as the catalyzing event of the second feminist wave. Other public demonstrations sponsored by WITCH (Women's International Terrorist Conspiracy from Hell), the guerrilla theater, action-oriented group she founded, included protesting the New York Bridal Fair and "hexing" Wall Street. For Morgan sexual oppression became the core source for all gender, racial, and class inequity. "I believe that sexism is the root oppression," Morgan would assert, "the one which, until and unless we *uproot* it, will continue to put forth the branches of racism, class hatred, ageism, competition, ecological disaster, and economic exploitation."

Evidence of the widespread and interconnected social oppression of sexism in contemporary culture is evident in the various articles in *Sisterhood Is Powerful*, which join the issues of class, ethnicity, race, and social equality to the persistence of gender subordination. To combat it, Morgan, in her introduction, rejects the reformist feminist views of such groups as the National Organization for Woman (NOW), which she calls a "bourgeois feminist movement that never quite dared enough, never questioned enough, never really reached beyond its own class and race," for the revolutionary change fully implied by women's liberation. Less a coherent political or social philosophy, women's liberation, in Morgan's formulation, is an internal transformation that the anthology is intended to stimulate. "I hope this book means something to you," Morgan addresses her readers, "makes some real change in your heart and head . . . because *you* are women's liberation. This is not a movement one 'joins.' There are no rigid structures or membership cards . . . . It exists in your mind, and in the political and personal insights that you can contribute to change and shape and help its growth."

Morgan comments in her introduction about the origin and nature of *Sisterhood Is Powerful*. Its original title was to have been *The Hand that Cradles the Rock,* an "at-least triple entendre" referring to William Ross Wallace's 1865 poem, "What Rules the World," with its famous lines: "The hand that rocks the cradle / Is the hand that rules the world." However, that title had been previously used by humorist S. J. Perelman, who threatened an injunction if Morgan appropriated it. "So, we were forced to change the title," Morgan declares. "Not that I now mind, having convinced myself that Sisterhood must be *very* Powerful for us to have even survived, let alone finished this damned book." She lists the "reprisals" taken on the articles' authors and the setbacks encountered: "five personal relationships were severed, two couples were divorced and one separated, one woman was forced to withdraw her article, by the man she lived with; another's husband kept rewriting the piece until it was unrecognizable as her own; many of the articles were late, and the deadline kept being pushed further ahead, because the authors had so many other pressures on them—from housework to child care to jobs. More than one woman had trouble finishing her piece because it was so personally painful to commit her gut feelings to paper. We were also delayed by occurrences that would not have been of even peripheral importance to an anthology written by men: three pregnancies, one miscarriage, and one birth—plus one abortion and one hysterectomy." The format as well as the production of *Sisterhood Is Powerful* was affected by the gender of its creators. Morgan explains, "There is also a blessedly uneven quality noticeable in the book" that is markedly different from the "linear, tight, dry, boring, male super-consistency that we are beginning to reject. That's why this collection combines all sorts of articles, poems, graphics, and sundry papers. There are the well-documented, statistically solid pieces and the intensely personal experiences." As Morgan observes, "Women's liberation is the first radical movement to base its politics—in fact, create its politics—out of concrete personal experiences." It is "also the first movement that has the potential of cutting across all class, race, age, economic, and geographical barriers—since women in every group must play essentially the same role, albeit with different sets and costumes: the multiple role of wife, mother, sexual object, baby-producer, "supplementary-income statistic," helpmate, nurturer, hostess, etc. To reflect this potential, contributors from those different groups speak in this book—and frequently disagree with each other."

Arranged into six major divisions, *Sisterhood Is Powerful* begins with a documentary look at the status of contemporary women as wives, mothers, and workers, with articles on women in medicine, publishing, in the media, academia, factories, and offices. At every level, the writers find considerable evidence of gender oppression. If the first section looks at results, the second section, "The Invisible Woman: Psychological and Sexual Repression," examines causes, with articles such as "The Politics of Orgasm," by Susan Lydon, a section from Kate Millet's *Sexual Politics,* and the now classic essay by Naomi Weisstein, " 'Kinde, Kuche, Kirche' As Scientific Law: Psychology Constructs the Female." Included is Morgan's own "Barbarous Rituals," an itemization of a lifetime of conventional gender attitudes, values, and circumstances that defines being a women, from "kicking strongly in your mother's womb, upon which she is told, 'It must be a boy, if it's so active!' " to "getting older, getting lonelier, getting ready to die—and knowing it wouldn't have had to be this way, after all."

The third section of *Sisterhood Is Powerful* widens the focus to consider the perspectives of African Americans, high school students, and "colonized women"—Chicanas in the United States and the women of China. The fourth section collects ideological responses to sexism, including articles on the politics of housework by Pat Mainardi and "Female Liberation as the Basis for Social Revolution" by Roxanne Dunbar. The anthology closes with a collection of poetry by such writers as Marge Piercy, Rita Mae Brown, and Sylvia Plath, and a compilation of historical documents, including the NOW Bill of Rights and excerpts from the infamous SCUM (Society for Cutting Up Men) Manifesto, by Valerie Solanis. An appendix provides a bibliography, a listing of Women's Liberation Movement contacts, abortion counseling information, recommended "consciousness-raising" films, and a "Drop Dead List of Books to Watch Out For."

As much as there is a quaint obsolescence about a good deal of *Sisterhood Is Powerful*, with many of its positions and poses as defunct today as the listed phone numbers of its suggested women's liberation contacts, the spirit and force of the anthology still resonate. The apocalypse forecast by the overturning of sexism that is valiantly urged here may not have materialized, and the issues of feminism more than thirty years later may have grown too complex for such easy sloganeering, but what the second wave of the feminist movement set out to accomplish remains vitally compelling in the pages of *Sisterhood Is Powerful*. The truths that Robin Morgan and her earnest sisters expose and explore still provoke and still claim consideration.

THE FEMALE EUNUCH

by Germaine Greer

Of the books that defined and fueled the second wave of the women's movement in the 1960s and 1970s, such as Betty Friedan's *The Feminine Mystique* and Kate Millett's *Sexual Politics,* Germaine Greer's *The Female Eunuch* (1970 in England; 1971 in the United States) is perhaps the most rambunctiously iconoclastic. Witty, erudite, and irreverent, *The Female Eunuch* challenged conventional wisdom about feminism and gender assumptions. If her fellow feminist commentators and critics emphasized women as victims of male repression and culturally conditioned subordination, Greer, in surveying the problems of women's sexuality, psychological development, relationship with men, as well as their social and cultural history, identified "the castration of our true female personality" as "not the fault of men, but our own, and history's." Women, Greer argued, are complicit in their powerlessness by subscribing to a conception of female identity and sexuality that has been "misrepresented by being identified as passivity." Explaining the significance of her book's title, Greer, in her introduction, summarizes her thesis that women have been raised to endorse and live up to a stereotype of the "Eternal Feminine" that shares the characteristics associated with the castrate—

"timidity, plumpness, languor, delicacy and preciosity." Women, Greer declared, have abandoned their autonomy and considerable innate powers and accepted a contrary definition of femininity that has emphasized submissiveness and helplessness. The result is dependence, resentment, and lack of sexual pleasure and life fulfillment. *The Female Eunuch,* with an unprecedented frankness and candor about women's sexuality and desires, and an irreverent and contrarian stance that leaves few truisms held by either men or women unchallenged, served as a rallying cry and incitement for women to take back control of their bodies, their pleasures, their lives, and their relationships.

The author and her book broke the mold of what was expected of a feminist and a feminist text. When many feminists were characterized as dour manhaters, Greer provided a counter persona: feisty, vital, and unapologetically libidinous. *The Female Eunuch,* less a solemn argument than a string of explosive provocations, very much revitalized the gender debate. It was described as "women's liberation's most realistic and least anti-male manifesto," and its author was touted as a "dazzling combination of erudition, eccentricity and eroticism." Christopher Lehmann-Haupt, in a 1971 *New York Times* review titled "The Best Feminist Book So Far," contrasted it favorably to Kate Millett's *Sexual Politics,* calling *The Female Eunuch* "a book with personality, a book that knows the distinction between the self and the other, a book that combines the best of masculinity *and* femininity." *The Female Eunuch* became a much talked-about best-seller, and Greer, then a thirty-one-year-old Australian professor of literature at England's Warwick University, became an international media celebrity and feminist icon, gracing the cover of *Life* magazine along with the headline: "Saucy Feminist that Even Men Like." Despite such a superficial claim to importance, Germaine Greer and *The Female Eunuch* remains one of the defining works of the women's liberation movement and a still volatile polemic that rewrites the rules of female empowerment and women's identity.

Greer's take-no-prisoners style and maverick opinions that equally shocked the feminist faithful as well as the chauvinist opposition can be traced from her background, her involvement in the 1960s counterculture, and her somewhat late and accidental interest in feminism. Born in 1939, near Melbourne, Greer was educated at a convent school and completed an honors arts degree at Melbourne University, in 1959, before doing graduate work in Sydney. Greer's antiauthoritarian ideas were shaped by a group of freewheeling intellectuals who met for discussions at the Royal George Hotel. "When I first came to Sydney," Greer recalled, "what I fell in love with was not the harbour or the gardens or anything else but a pub called The Royal George, or, more particularly, with a group of people who used to go there every night . . . and sit there and talk." Greer earned a master's degree at Sydney University, in 1962, before going as a Commonwealth scholar to Newnham College, Cambridge, where she earned a doctorate, in 1967, writing her thesis on Shakespeare's early comedies. Richard Neville, editor of the underground magazine *Oz*, for which Greer would write, described her during her Oxford days as a "militant anti-authoritarian, trained in Australia" in which a "regular diet of reasoned anarchy, sexual precocity and Toohey's Bitter helped mould her unique shock style." Between 1967 and 1972, Greer lectured in English literature at the University of Warwick, was a self-styled "super-groupie" to jazz and rock musicians, and frequently contributed to a number of underground newspapers and magazines on themes of sexual liberation and anticensorship.

Greer came to her involvement in women's issues by chance, late in her intellectual development. Greer credits the genesis of *The Female Eunuch* to her agent, who urged her to develop a book marking the fiftieth anniversary of female suffrage. " 'You should write a book why female suffrage failed,' " Greer recalled her agent suggesting. "I remember losing my temper. I thought, 'What are we talking about! Women didn't get the vote until there was nothing left worth voting for. And what do you think the vote accomplishes anyway?' " A few days later, Greer had lunch with publisher Sonny Mehta, a friend from Cambridge, who wanted to pick her brain for prospective book ideas. Greer told him what her "dumb agent" had suggested and launched into a rant attacking the idea. When she had finished, Mehta told her, "That's the book I want," and despite Greer's conviction that such a book would never sell, they returned to Mehta's office where they agreed to a contract. She would spend much of 1969 in the Reading Room of the British Museum working on the book. "I showed the first chapters to Sonny and he said nothing," Greer recalled. "And I knew I hadn't done it. One day, I suddenly realized it had to be written in short chapters; otherwise nobody would read it because women don't have spare time and their concentration span is generally brief. So I began writing short chapters." When she showed what she had done to Mehta this time, he was "speechless as usual. But I could tell by the look in his eyes that I was doing the right thing now. It was only a matter of weeks after that and it was finished." Greer, who had up to then showed little evidence of having considered women's issues other than from her own perspective as a woman in the debate over sexual liberation, had produced one of the landmark books in the debate over women's identity and empowerment. With the 1970 publication of *The Female Eunuch* Greer would be hailed as "the high priestess of women's liberation in Britain," and her reputation would be further enhanced, in 1971, on a book tour of the United States that featured a highly publicized onstage debate in New York City with Norman Mailer.

The Female Eunuch is less a coherent, sequential argument than variations and multiple perspectives on Greer's central thesis of the denial and misrepresentation of female sexuality. Called by its author "part of the second feminist wave," *The Female Eunuch* differs in its mission and approach from the work of "old suffragettes" who, after gaining the vote, allowed their energy to be "filtered away in post-war retrenchments and the revival of frills, corsets and femininity after the permissive twenties, through the sexual sell of the fifties, ever dwindling, ever more respectable." Instead of reform and accommodation to accepted gender roles and rules, Greer argues for revolution. Criticizing Betty Friedan's National Organization for Women and other "organized liberationists," Greer charges that the liberation they promise is vacuous: "At worst it is defined by the condition of men, themselves unfree, and at best it is left undefined in a world of limited possibilities." Instead, Greer asserts that a woman who desires real and radical change should "begin not by changing the world, but by reassessing herself." *The Female Eunuch* offers such a reassessment.

The book is arranged into five major sections—*Body, Soul, Love, Hate,* and *Revolution*—that consider the physical and psychological conceptions of the female and a concluding series of provocative challenges to gender assumptions once the notion of passive femininity is rejected. In *Body* Greer anatomizes "the degree of inferiority or natural dependence which is unalterably female," as well as the ways in which women's physicality has been objectified with an emphasis on the passive, producing the stereotype of the feminine that Greer considers in *Soul*. Greer describes the stereotype she calls the "Eternal Feminine," as "the Sexual Object sought by all men, and by all women. She is of neither sex, for she has herself no sex at all. Her value is solely attested by the demand she excites in others. All she must contribute is her existence. She need achieve nothing, for she is the reward for achievement. She need never give positive evidence of her moral character because virtue is assumed from her loveliness, and her passivity." Greer goes on to trace the development of this stereotype from infancy and its conditioning. The castration of women leads to the distortion of the concept of *Love*, and this section surveys the ways in which the notion of the passive female is embedded in literature, marriage, and the nuclear family. In *Hate* Greer treats the consequences of the castrated female in sections on "Loathing and Disgust," "Abuse," "Misery," "Resentment," and "Rebellion."

The Female Eunuch concludes with a call for revolution and radical alternatives to the repression of the passive female. Violence in society is attributed to displaced male virility, and women are urged to "humanize the penis, take the steel out of it and make it flesh again. What most 'liberated' women do is taunt the penis for its misrepresentation of itself, mock men for their overestimation of their virility, instead of seeing how the mistake originated and what effects it has had upon themselves. Men are tired of having all the responsibility for sex; it is time they were relieved of it." Greer asserts that if women are "to effect a significant amelioration in their conditions it seems obvious that they must refuse to marry. No worker can be required to sign on for life: if he did, his employer could disregard all his attempts to gain better pay and conditions." Women must also "reject their role as principal consumers in the capitalist state," and Greer offers alternative cooperative models to undermine capitalism's competitiveness: women "could form household cooperatives, sharing their work about, and liberating each other for days on end." However, Greer argues, "The chief means of liberating women is the replacing of compulsiveness and compulsion by the pleasure principle." By reestablishing the preeminence of spontaneity and desire, woman, in Greer's view, can break the bonds of the female castrate and achieve a transformation in gender identity and women's prospects:

> To be emancipated from helplessness and need and walk freely upon the earth that is your birthright. To refuse hobbles and defor-

mity and take possession of your body and glory in its power, accepting its own laws of loveliness. To have something to desire, something to make, something to achieve, and at last something genuine to give. To be freed from guilt and shame and the tireless self-discipline of women. To stop pretending and dissembling, cajoling and manipulating, and begin to control and sympathize. To claim the masculine virtues of magnanimity and generosity and courage.

Greer's daring challenges to the status quo energize *The Female Eunuch.* If her solutions at times veer toward the outrageous and unrealistic, her framing of essential questions about the ways women are seen and see themselves remain on point and relevant. Provocation is in fact the point of *The Female Eunuch,* as Greer states at the outset: "This book represents only another contribution to a continuing dialogue between the wondering woman and the world. No questions have been answered but perhaps some have been asked in a more proper way than heretofore. If it is not ridiculed or reviled, it will have failed of its intention."

BLACK WOMEN IN WHITE AMERICA: A DOCUMENTARY HISTORY

Compiled and edited by Gerda Lerner

Concurrent with the revived women's movement of the 1960s and 1970s was a new sense of what came to be called "black pride," fostered in the wake of the civil rights movement and the turbulent sociopolitical climate of the late 1960s. At the same time, there was a new awareness of women's cultural experience that would result in the implementation of women's studies and women's history courses in American colleges. Gerda Lerner, now a professor emeritus at the University of Wisconsin, provided the framework for the development of women's history as a recognized field of study. In the mid-1960s, Lerner, a published author then in her forties and a graduate student in history at Columbia University, wrote her dissertation on women's history, a highly unusual choice at a time when the women's movement was still in its infancy. In 1968, a year after receiving her doctorate, Lerner began a twelve-year academic career at Sarah Lawrence College, where she began and directed the first program to offer a graduate degree in women's history. She would go on to organize programs designed to train future feminist historians and to earn a reputation as one of the world's foremost scholars in her field. Lerner published books and articles that would advance the concept that class and race were central to an understanding of the role gender had played in historical events and, in 1972, she produced *Black Women in White America*, a remarkable collection of writings, lectures, and speeches of African-American women from the time of slavery to the early 1970s.

In her preface, Lerner writes, "Seeing women cast only in subordinate and inferior positions throughout history and seldom, if ever, learning about female heroines and women of achievement, American girls are conditioned to limit their own life goals and self-esteem. Black women have been doubly victimized by scholarly neglect and racist assumptions. Belonging as they do to two groups which have traditionally been treated as inferiors by American society—Blacks and women—they have been doubly invisible. Their records lie buried, unread, infrequently noticed and even more seldom interpreted." In *Black Women in White America* Lerner helps to make amends for this lack of inclusion in the historical canon by chronicling the black experience from the perspective of African-American women through a variety of documents, including diaries, slave narratives, letters, and newspaper articles, over a period stretching from 1811 to 1971.

The voices in Lerner's compilation range from unknown slaves and well-known former slaves, such as Harriet Tubman and Sojourner Truth, to school founders like Mary Macleod Bethune, Lucy Laney, Charlotte Hawkins Brown, and Nannie Burroughs; the antilynching activist and suffragist Ida B. Wells Barnett; educator, suffragist, and first president of the National Association of Colored Women Mary Church Terrell; voting rights activist Septima Clark; civil rights leaders Fannie Lou Hamer and Ella Baker; congresswoman Shirley Chisolm; and many more women who may be less familiar but whose presence provides us with equally eloquent and important revelations concerning the African-American experience. Lerner has divided the book into ten chapters, with a general introduction for each and subsections that categorize the type of document and feature separate introductions where appropriate. These introductions furnish the essential historical and biographical context necessary for a complete understanding of the documents included in the volume.

Lerner begins her documentation with the voices of women slaves. She reminds readers that slavery was a "mutually reinforcing interplay of racism and economic motivation," which became increasingly oppressive over time. The essence of this institution "was that the slave was legally a chattel, a piece of property to be bought and sold and disposed of at the master's will." Lerner includes examples of bills of sale, as well as accounts of one women sold away from her children and another who shammed illness to stay with her husband. One moving account, taken from a slave narrative dated 1844, tells the story of Moses Grandy, a slave who witnessed his wife walking by him in chains. Although it is not told from a woman's viewpoint, it illustrates the cruelty of separation that was so devastating to both wives and husbands:

> Mr. Rogerson was with them on his horse, armed with pistols. I said to him, 'For God's sake, have you bought my wife?' He said he had; when I asked him what she had done, he said she had done nothing, but that her master wanted money. He drew out a pistol and said that if I went near the wagon in which she was, he would shoot me. I asked for leave to shake hands with her which he refused, but said I might stand at a distance and talk with her. My heart was so full that I could say very little. . . . I have never seen or heard from her from that day to this. I loved her as I love my life.

Also documented are accounts of the daily lives of women slaves and how they survived, the treatment of women under slavery, and stories of escapes to freedom, which include a narrative detailing an escape "conducted" by Harriet Tubman. Also included is a harrowing journal account by Frances Kemble, a distinguished British actress who had married a Georgia plantation owner, which narrates the frustration she feels at her inability to convince her husband to allow their female slaves the customary four weeks of rest after giving birth.

Once emancipation was achieved, education for African Americans became of paramount importance. Lerner's introduction to her second chapter, "The Struggle for Education," provides a history of this struggle and gives examples of black women who were the first to excel in the arts and the professions, such as the physicians Rebecca Cole and Susan M. McKenny Steward, attorney Lutie M. Little, sculptor Edmonia Lewis, and poet Phillis Wheatley. Lerner also points out that nineteenth-century black (and white) women "took up teaching, not as an avocation, but because it was, for a woman, the only respectable means of earning a living." The documents contained in the chapter highlight the efforts of black women teachers and school founders during Reconstruction and afterwards as they endeavored to teach the freedmen and to find innovative methods of instruction, worked to keep the schools they founded from failing through fundraising initiatives and considerable frugality, and faced the challenge of teaching in the "underfinanced, poorly equipped, and overcrowded" schools in the south during the Jim Crow era, a time of institutionalized racial segregation.

Teaching was not the only way in which African-American women earned a living. Lerner offers examples of twentieth-century women engaged in domestic work (Lerner names a figure of some 1,017,000), which includes accounts that reveal the exploitation of black domestics by white families—the poor wages paid to these workers and the punishing hours experienced by them—as well as pieces on the union organization of domestic workers in Atlanta and the Domestic Workers' Union. The writings and speeches of black women factory workers show that they fared little better, usually working longer hours and earning less than white women. Except for the southern tobacco and textile industries, where they were considered unskilled labor, African- American women were denied access to factory work until World War I. During World War II, writes Lerner, "black women worked in the war industries, entered the automobile, textile, electrical and transportation industries in large numbers, and worked in hospitals, schools and other institutional occupations. But the temporary gains of the war periods were quickly eroded in the postwar years, when black women were the first to be fired from wartime jobs and through economic need were forced back into domestic and other service jobs." Still, postwar union activity was present, primarily in the south, as examples of articles concerning rank-and-file workers and union organizers show. "The nation won't ever be free," asserted factory worker Luannna Cooper, in a speech given at a Progressive Party Conference in 1949, "unless people learn the truth. Speeches is all right but you might as well be asleep if you just have speeches. I tell you, black and white, we can't survive without the other. We got to organize."

In "A Woman's Lot," Lerner gives examples of what she calls "the special victimization," chiefly sexual, of African-American women, in documents dating from the nineteenth century through 1959. She describes the abusive treatment, including rape, of black women as "essential" to "the functioning and perpetuation" of an institutionalized racist system. In one account given to the national newspaper, *The Independent*, by "A Southern Colored Woman," in 1912, a black nurse asserts that she and other black women are little more than slaves, as well as the objects of lust: "On the one hand, we are assailed by white men, and, on the other hand, we are assailed by black men, who should be our natural protectors; and whether in the cook kitchen, at the washtub, over the sewing machine, behind the baby carriage, or at the ironing board, we are but little more than pack horses, beasts of burden, slaves!" (The theme of black women during the nineteenth and early twentieth centuries as little more than slaves despite emancipation is reiterated throughout the book.) Lerner also addresses and provides documentation of what she calls "the myth of the 'bad' black woman," sustained by a racism that mythologized the sexual potency of African Americans, both men and women. By this wayward definition, writes Lerner, "Every black woman was . . . a slut . . . therefore to assault her and exploit her sexually was not reprehensible and carried with it none of the normal communal sanctions against such behavior." Lerner advances this mythology to include the practice of lynching and highlights the efforts of antilynching activists, which includes an illuminating example from Ida B. Wells Barnett's celebrated *A Red Record*, her statistical survey of lynching.

The black family unit was a crucial component of survival for African-American women in a white-dominated society. In "Survival is a Form of Resistance," Lerner writes, "The black family established its own form of existence in response to the environment. Theirs was not the small and vulnerable nuclear family of white America, but the extended kinship system of rural folk and of the poor who cooperate that each child may live and survive. . . . Black women stood beside and with their men, doing their share and more, taking over when there was a need, seeing to it that the race survived." The struggles of black families are documented here. The chapter also includes a letter from Mrs. Henry Weddington, written to President Franklin Roosevelt, in 1941, in which she addresses the terrible labor situation among African Americans and writes in part:

> Why must our men fight and die for their country when it won't even give them a job that they are fitted for? They would much rather fight and die for their families or race. Before it is over many of them might. We did not ask to be brought here as slaves, nor did

we ask to be born black. We are real citizens of this land and must and *will* be recognized as such! . . . If you are a real Christian you can not stand by and let these conditions exist.

The last half of Lerner's compilation documents the experiences of African-American women in politics and government, benevolent societies and the national club movement, the Herculean struggle to deal with and overcome prejudice and racism before and during the years of Jim Crow, the battle to achieve integration, the fostering of black pride, and issues concerning black women and womanhood, which includes a 1970 *Washington Post* column by journalist Renee Ferguson on the subject of women's liberation and its meaning for black women. Regarding the entry of black women into political life, Lerner cites examples of clubwomen who were suffragists and the increased political activity of African-American women after passage of the nineteenth amendment. One of these post-suffrage women was Mrs. Robert M. Patterson, who ran as a Socialist candidate for the Philadelphia Assembly in 1922. In an article printed in *Women's Voice*, Mrs. Patterson called for greater opportunity for black women in public service: "In these times of unrest we need women of the type of Harriet Tubman and Sojourner Truth. Women of mental ripeness, courage and clearness of purpose and a burning spirit to dare and to do. . . ." Examples of calls for racial pride are given in documents dating from 1833 to a 1970 assertion of the necessity for black nationalism by Dara Abubakari (Virginia E. Y. Collins), a New Orleans grassroots com-munity leader and voting rights activist who gave up hope, writes Lerner, "that working from within the establishment can benefit black people." In a taped interview with Lerner, Abuba-kari compares the experience of African Americans to that of the Jews who achieved statehood with the creation of Israel and insists, "Black people have to get freedom for themselves; it cannot be given to them. . . . The only thing you can aspire to is nationhood."

The last voice in *Black Women in White America* belongs to Fannie Lou Hamer, who, in a 1971 speech given at the NAACP Legal Defense Fund Institute, speaks of the "special plight and role of black women" as a 350-year-old condition ripe for change:

We have a job as black women, to support whatever is right, and to bring justice where we've had so much injustice. . . . You see now, baby, whether you have a Ph.D., D.D., or no D, we're in this bag together. And whether you're from Morehouse or Nohouse, we're still in this bag together. Not to try to fight to try to liberate ourselves from the men—this is another trick to get us fighting among ourselves—but to work together with the black man, then we will have a better chance to just act as human beings and to be treated as human beings in our sick society.

Black Women in White America is essential reading for those interested in both black history and women's history. What makes the collection unique and so comprehensive is the presence of African-American women in an inspiring union of race, class, and gender. The voices in Lerner's extraordinary compilation speak to us with a directness that demands our empathy and our respect, and allows us to achieve an understanding of the struggles, the strength, the pride, and the sense of community that has historically defined the experience of African-American women in white America.

FROM REVERENCE TO RAPE:
THE TREATMENT OF WOMEN
IN THE MOVIES

by Molly Haskell

First published in 1973, Molly Haskell's pioneering discourse on the treatment of women in film arrived at a time when the revived women's movement, sparked by Betty Friedan's *The Feminine Mystique* and launched during the second half of the 1960s, had gained momentum, and literature examining the status of women began to proliferate. The era saw the burgeoning of women's studies as an academic discipline and the emergence of feminist film theory, which had its beginnings with *From Reverence to Rape: The Treatment of Women in the Movies*—since the 1970s a studied text in college film and women's studies courses.

Born in 1939, in Charlotte, North Carolina, Molly Haskell received her undergraduate degree from Sweet Briar College and then studied at the University of London and the Sorbonne. Before turning to film criticism, she worked as a public relations associate and at the French Film Office in New York. Haskell has reviewed movies for the prestigious film journals *Film Comment* and *Film Heritage*, for the *Village Voice*, *Vogue*, and *New York Magazine*, and has been a regular film reviewer for National Public Radio, as well as a member of the selection committee of the New York Film Festival and an associate professor at Barnard College. She has also written the "New Yorker" diary column for *The New York Observer* and taught writing at Marymount Manhattan College. Haskell's other books include *Love and Other Infectious Diseases: A Memoir* (1990), which chronicles her relationship with her husband, noted film critic Andrew Sarris, during Sarris's life-threatening bout with encephalitis, and *Holding My Own in No Man's Land: Women and Men, Film, and Criticism* (1997).

In *From Reverence to Rape* Haskell analyzes traditions of different types of women portrayed in American and European films. She explores the images of women created in film, the stars who filled those images or defied them, and the attitudes of their directors. Her focus is on the screen's heterosexual relationships, although, addressing the broader social context of the real world, she does ask, as have some questioning feminists since the beginning of the women's movement, "Is the separatism advocated by the lesbians and the manhaters (and which serves, like much movement rhetoric, to exalt rather than diminish men's power) the answer?" Nevertheless, Haskell's main argument in *From Reverence to Rape* is that heterosexual film relationships degenerated from reciprocal partnerships based on mutual growth and respect to unequal couplings in which women are portrayed as sex objects. Women viewers have accepted these relationships because, as Haskell suggests in her introduction, "Like recollections of old love affairs, the images of stars that stay with us are the triumphs rather than the disappointments. We remember them not for the humiliations and compromises they endured in conforming to stereotypes, but for the incandescent moments in which their uniqueness made mockery of the stereotypes."

For Haskell, literary heroines have fared little better than those on the screen; the majority of female central characters created by the world's most celebrated male and female novelists were socialized, as Virginia Woolf famously put it, to serve "as looking glasses possessing the magic and delicious power of reflecting the figure of man at twice its natural size." Traditional heroines were forced to use beauty, wit, charm, and, all too often, gentle passivity, to attain their main goal of experiencing love and marriage, not necessarily in that order. Haskell acknowledges the presence of strong, interesting heroines in fiction and movies, but at the same time she cites a prevailing nineteenth-century literary romantic sensibility and stereotyping in film, which, during the 1970s, deserved to be challenged in a new feminist climate. "Women," she writes, "have grounds for protest, and film is a rich field for the mining of female stereotypes." After asserting that the "big lie perpetrated by Western society is the idea of women's inferiority" and delving into the psychology that supports and challenges this notion in the context of male and female film roles, Haskell deconstructs movies and women's place within them by decade, from the 1920s to the 1980s (in the 1987 revised edition).

In her discussion of the movies of the 1920s, the last decade of silent films, Haskell acknowledges that the era is difficult to decipher because the prevailing cinema art form of the time has been largely lost to us. Cineastes have come to appreciate the silent comedy of Charlie Chaplin, Buster Keaton, and Harold Lloyd, and the epic morality films of Cecil B. DeMille, but, as Haskell observes, our historical view of women on screen during the 1920s has been shaped in great part by "the crystallized images posterity has given them, a sense of the archetypal forms without the variations," primarily the sexually predatory "vamps" (the exotic and sultry Pola Negri, "party girl" Joan Crawford, Clara Bow, who radiated a playful sexuality as the "It Girl," and even the early Greta Garbo) and the "virgins" (longstanding screen child-woman Mary Pickford, sweet-faced Lillian Gish, and gamin Janet Gaynor). A hallmark of the silent screen, with its reliance on the telling gesture, was the Victorian romantic and melodramatic tradition, in which love and marriage became the virgins' reward and the vamps' redemption.

The post–World War I, post-suffrage "new woman" became more evident in the films of the 1930s—an era that Haskell, as well as other film historians, have characterized as separated by the years before and after the Hays Office of the Motion Picture Producers and Distributors of America (MPPDA) created the Motion Picture Production Code, and the movie studios implemented what came to be known as the Hays Code in 1934, in an effort to impose standards of "good taste" in American films and to soften the stars' images after the sex and murder scandals of the 1920s. The female stars of the precode era, such as Greta Garbo, Marlene Dietrich, Mae West, Jean Harlow, Claudette Colbert, and Carole Lombard, brought a liberated, "salutary" sexuality to the screen, which the Hays Office, writes Haskell, "having assumed the mantle of our national superego," suppressed.

The dramas and comedies of the mid-1930s into the 1940s

featured professional and working-class heroines, played by such stars as Katharine Hepburn, Ginger Rogers, Rosalind Russell, Jean Arthur, and Barbara Stanwyck, "who were always doing something," observes Haskell, "whether it was running a business or running just to keep from standing still. But their mythic destiny, like that of all women, was to find love and cast off the 'veneer' of independence." In writing on Katharine Hepburn, that paragon of female screen independence and individuality, Haskell cites her feminist character in the 1936 flop *A Woman Rebels* as the role that labeled her "box office poison" until 1940 and her comeback in *The Philadelphia Story*; she points out that, although she played an influential and powerful political commentator romantically and complementarily paired with Spencer Tracy's earthy sportswriter in 1942's *Woman of the Year* (the couple's first film together), her character is ultimately castigated for her professional drive and lack of interest in home and family.

Haskell refers to Hepburn again, in concert with such leading ladies as Bette Davis, Joan Fontaine, Joan Crawford, and Gene Tierney, in a chapter devoted to the so-called "woman's film"—a genre that, like "women's fiction," observes Haskell, implies "a generically shared world of misery and masochism the individual work is designed to indulge." It is not a concept found in Europe, where, Haskell writes, "affairs of the heart are of importance to both men and women and are the stuff of literature." This matinee genre, with its weepy, soap-opera-like emphasis on romantic fantasy and sacrifice, "pays tribute at its best (and at its worst) to the power of the imagination, to the mind's ability to picture a perfect love triumphing over the mortal and conditional."

During the 1940s, the decade that ushered in the genre of *film noir* in the American cinema, "Woman," writes Haskell, "came down from her pedestal and she didn't stop when she reached the ground. She kept going—down . . . to the depths of the criminal world, the *enfer* of *film noir*—and then compelled her lover to glance back and betray himself." These characters were either treacherous, two-faced women (Mary Astor in *The Maltese Falcon*, Barbara Stanwyck in *Double Indemnity*) or morally ambiguous but essentially decent (Veronica Lake in *The Blue Dahlia*, Lauren Bacall in *The Big Sleep*). The *film noir* woman "was, in fact, a male fantasy. She was playing a man's game in a man's world of crime and carnal innuendo, where her long hair was the equivalent of a gun, where sex was the equivalent of evil. . . . She is to her thirties counterpart as night—or dusk—is to day." In addition to her discussion on *film noir* antiheroines, the war dramas featuring women nurses, and the screwball and pinup beauty-queen comedies of the 1940s, Haskell mentions examples of such "superwoman" characters as Rosalind Russell's Hildy Parks in Howard Hawks's *His Girl Friday* and what she calls "perfectly balanced" couples— Lauren Bacall and Humphrey Bogart in *To Have and Have Not,* and Hepburn and Tracy in *Adam's Rib.*

The postwar 1950s was marked by the demise of the Hollywood studio system and the emergence of television as a major influence. Haskell discusses the voluptuous, technicolor *femmes fatales* (Marilyn Monroe, Jane Russell, Ava Gardner, Kim Novak), the breathtaking beauties (Elizabeth Taylor, Grace Kelly), the musical comedy stars (Debbie Reynolds, Jane Powell, the early Doris Day, and Judy Garland), the "serious-artist actresses in black and white" (Anne Bancroft, Julie Harris, Patricia Neal, and Shelley Winters), as well as the ambiguous sexuality of plays by Inge and Williams on film, and the social realism and passive female sexuality in the films of directors like Elia Kazan. Of the fifties' "dumb" blond portrayers, Haskell spends time on Monroe but also singles out the "glowing" Judy Holliday, who, she writes, "stretches the stereotype . . . into her own doughy shape." She presents the dilemma of the aging female star in the context of fifty-three-year-old Gloria Swanson in *Sunset Boulevard* and the forty-year-old Bette Davis character in *All About Eve,* observing that the director (in the above cases, Billy Wilder and Joseph Mankiewicz, both in their forties) projects onto these women "the narcissism, the vanity, the fear of growing old which he is horrified to find festering within himself."

Haskell next takes on the European cinema, about which she suggests that, because of "centuries of tradition and all the forces of culture," the "myths and inventions made by man" is even more prevalent than it is in American film. "In America," she interestingly observes, "men and women are not so closely and inextricably, emotionally and ideologically, bound. A woman can more easily invent herself . . . and she is proportionately less venerated." The product of such male artist-directors as Ingmar Bergman, Federico Fellini, Bernardo Bertolucci, Luis Buñuel, Francois Truffaut, Roger Vadim, Jean-Luc Godard, and Jean Renoir, the actress in European films comes across "as the result of the 'higher' sensibility projected onto her by her director." In

contrast to the heroines in American movies, the female characters in European film, even at their most archetypical—"the waif,
the rebel, the discreet bourgeoisie, the older woman, and the
whore—seem to emanate not from their own desires, but from
those of the men who both worship and fear them."

Even while citing female stereotyping in American movies produced from the 1920s to the 1960s, Haskell acknowledges and
praises the mutual support and camaraderie that existed between
the spirited heroines of these films, relationships lost during the
"swinging sixties." (These virtues would be revived in the late
1980s and throughout the 1990s in one form, as a postfeminist
"sisters" genre—or, as some have called it, a "chick flick"—exemplified by such films as *Beaches*, *Steel Magnolias*, and *Thelma and
Louise*.) Haskell characterizes the years between 1962 and 1973
as "the most disheartening in screen history." The collapse of the
star system meant that women lost the economic leverage they
once had and, in a climate of increased sexual freedom and the
loss of a phony glamour imposed upon them by the studios, were
easily exploited. "The growing strength and demands of women
in real life spearheaded by women's liberation," writes Haskell,
"obviously provoked a backlash in commercial film: a redoubling
of Godfather-like machismo to beef up man's eroding virility
or, alternatively, an escape into the all-male world of the buddy
film. . . . With the substitution of violence and sexuality (a poor
second) for romance, there was less need for exciting and interesting women. . . ." Haskell cites the presence of a handful of "illustrious" women involved in the creative end of filmmaking
during this decade, but asks, "Where are the women to create
new fictions, to go beyond the inner space—as women are doing
every day in real life—into the outer world of invention, action,
imagination?"

When Haskell revised *From Reverence to Rape*, she added a
chapter entitled "The Age of Ambivalence," in which she explored women in film from 1974 to 1987. It was a period that reflected the ambivalence women were beginning to feel, having
pursued and won a certain level of equality, and now finding it a
challenge to balance work and career—"having it all." Movies of
this era tended to feature the "superwoman" or the "crazy
woman," observing that the latter included "neurotics, murder-
ers, *femmes fatales*, vamps, punks, misfits, and free-floating loonies
whose very existence was an affront, not only to the old, sexist de-

finitions of pliant women . . . but also to the upbeat rhetoric of the women's movement." These characters were "postfeminist types whose moves were orchestrated less by male needs than by some mysterious promptings of their own." Women moviegoers of the 1980s no longer expected films to reflect their lives, "no longer expected them to, nor looked for heroines who worked, married, divorced, thrashed out the conflicts between home and career." According to Haskell, the feminism served up in mainstream films was "shallow and formulaic"; during the eighties, television was the medium that responded best to the day-to-day working and family lives of women. Haskell ends the chapter with a catalog of women filmmakers whose diversity of experience and sensibility has affected the roles women play on screen—"their very diversity a guarantee against stereotype." For Haskell, women "want nothing less, on or off, the screen, than the wide variety and dazzling diversity of male options."

When *From Reverence to Rape* first appeared, Haskell was taken to task by hard-core cineastes who felt uneasy with the concept of movies as a social indicator and by feminists who thought that she had not been ideological enough. Some reviewers felt that she had been *too* ideological. But the significance of Haskell's comprehensive study cannot be disputed. It is still relevant today as film criticism and as social criticism. As a historical document, *From Reverence to Rape* joins *Sexual Politics* (1970), *Sisterhood is Powerful* (1970), and the iconoclastic *The Female Eunuch* (1970, 1971) as an example of the powerful, now classic literature on women published during the watershed years of the women's liberation movement.

FEAR OF FLYING

by Erica Jong

Perhaps no novel by a woman has generated more notoriety than Erica Jong's iconoclastic *Fear of Flying* (1973). Not since Chaucer's Wife of Bath, DeFoe's Moll Flanders, or Joyce's Molly Bloom had a heroine—this time the creation of a woman—spoken out so frankly and candidly about her sexual appetites, fantasies, and hangups while taking control of her life in ways that defied previous gender assumptions and the roles traditionally assigned to women. *Fear of Flying,* which Jong called her "emancipation proclamation," opened the floodgate for women writers to deal honestly with sex and gender anxieties. Isadora Wing's picaresque adventures in search of sexual fulfillment and self-definition became one of the biggest selling novels of the 1970s. During the women's liberation era, Isadora and Erica, who became synonomous, served as the poster kin for the movement. Both were either admired as feminist icons or reviled and dismissed as sex-obsessed and vulgar gender transgressors. Jong would later recall the cultural moment out of which *Fear of Flying* was created by stating that "something new was beginning to happen. Women were starting to write about their lives as if their lives were as important as men's. This took great courage. It meant going against all the parental and cultural admonitions of the time. I wrote *Fear of Flying* with heart in throat, terrified by my own candor." It is the novel's candor on such formerly taboo topics such as women's sexual fantasies that both electrified and outraged its audience.

Before *Fear of Flying* had even been published, shocked typesetters refused to work on the book; meanwhile galleys were quickly disappearing from editorial offices, being passed excitedly from friend to friend, everyone wanting to get an early look at the book that would eventually become a cultural phenomenon. When Jong wrote the novel, she was a young published poet and a graduate student studying eighteenth-century English literature. Despite the prepublication buzz, her publisher did little to promote her first novel. The initial reviews were tentative, and sales were sluggish. However, the book began to sell and get talked about after John Updike's review in the *New Yorker* compared it to a female *Portnoy's Complaint* and *Catcher in the Rye.* Updike applauded the book's "cheerful, sexual frankness," calling it "the most uninhibited, delicious, erotic novel a woman ever wrote." Henry Miller would subsequently praise Jong as "more forthright, more daring than most male writers," and predicted that *Fear of Flying* "will make literary history, that because of it women are going to find their own voice and give us great sagas of sex, life, joy, and adventure." By the end of 1974, when the book appeared in paperback, sales had reached three million copies in the United States alone, and few people were unaware of Erica Jong or the novel that *Time* magazine had dubbed "an ICBM in the war between the sexes."

The identification between Isadora Wing and Erica Jong, and the autobiographical basis of *Fear of Flying,* are unmistakable and contribute to the novel's daring intimacy. Jong was born, in 1942, on Manhattan's Upper West Side. Her father was a Broadway musician who became "a traveling salesman of tchotchkes," and her mother was a painter whose artistic aspirations were sacrificed as a homemaker. "What I remember most about my mother," Jong recalled, "was that she was always angry," and that "my mother's frustrations powered both my femininism and my writing." Her mother's warning to her daughter, that fulfillment as an artist and a woman were contradictory, sets the underlying tension of *Fear of Flying.* It caused Jong to observe, "Womanhood was a trap. If I was too much like her, I'd be trapped as she was. But if I rejected her example, I'd be a traitor to her love. I feld a fraud no matter which way I turned. I had to find a way to be like her and unlike her at the same time. I had to find a way to be both a girl and a boy." Jong, like Isadora, attended Barnard College as an undergraduate and did doctoral work at Columbia in eighteenth-century English literature before concentrating on poetry. Also, like her protagonist, Jong's first marriage to a fellow graduate student ended in divorce, and both subsequently married Chinese-American psychiatrists, accompanying them to Germany during their military service. Jong's first book of poetry, *Fruits & Vegetables,* appeared to critical acclaim, in 1971. "I started with poetry," she recalled, "because it was direct, immediate and short. . . . I went on to fiction because fiction can contain satire and social comment and still tell stories." As Jong summarized in her memoir, *Fear of Fifty,* these stories have dealt with sexual matters, societal hypocrisies and taboos, as well as her own life, including the subsequent divorces of her second and third husbands, a volatile combination that marked her as an easy target:

> I have lived as I chose, married, divorced, remarried, divorced, re-married and divorced again—and, still worse, dared to write about my ex-husbands! This is the most heinous of my sins—not having done these things, but having confessed to them in print. It is for this that I am considered beyond the pale. No PR can fix this! It's nothing more or less than the fate of rebellious women. They used to stone us in the marketplace. In a way, they still do.

Fear of Flying picks up the threads of Jong's autobiography, refracted through the lens of Isadora Wing, when her marriage to her steady but uncommunicative and predictable psychoanalyst husband, Bennett Wing, has grown stale, and marital sex has turned as bland as Velveeta cheese: "filling, fattening even, but no thrill to the taste buds, no bittersweet edge, no danger. And you longed for an overripe Camembert, a rare goat cheese: luscious, creamy, cloven-hoofed." As Isadora accompanies her husband to a psychiatrists' convention in Vienna, her phobia about flying serves as a metaphor for her fear of confronting her discontent and taking charge of her life. On the flight Isadora meditates on her frustrations that married life, society's prescription that women should seek definition and fulfillment through a man, has left her sexually restless and, as "half of something else," incomplete. Isadora confesses, "My response to all this was not (not yet) to have an affair and not (not yet) to hit the open road, but to evolve my fantasy of the Zipless Fuck," a "platonic ideal" in which zippers fall away "like rose petals" and underwear blows off "like dandelion fluff." Isadora's fantasy of faceless, anonymous sexual encounters with strangers becomes a form of liberation—of desire free of guilt and remorse—to scratch the itch she feels for both sex and solitude:

> The zipless fuck is absolutely pure. It is free of ulterior motives. There is no power game. The man is not "taking" and the woman is not "giving." No one is attempting to cuckhold a husband or humiliate a wife. No one is trying to prove anything or get anything out of anyone. The zipless fuck is the purest thing there is. And it is rarer than the unicorn. And I have never had one. Whenever it seemed I was close, I discovered a horse with a papier-mâché horn, or two clowns in a unicorn suit.

Fear of Flying begins by reversing expected gender roles. While women have long been objectified by men, Isadora fantasizes about becoming the sexual aggressor with men now the objects of desire. Violating the traditional goal of female fulfillment in marriage, Isadora begins to wonder whether her itch might be satisfied by sex without responsibilities or consequences. Isadora's fantasized alternative comes in the form of British Laingian analyst Adrian Goodlove, who seems to answer Isadora's dream of liberating and uncomplicated gratification. Adrian, a self-proclaimed free spirit, urges Isadora to cast off her marital ties and live under the sway of immediate sensation, as outlined by his self-directed existential philosophy. He appears to be Isadora's unicorn, and her struggle between faithfulness to Bennett and her urge to fly with Adrian is finally resolved in his favor when Isadora agrees to accompany Adrian on a hedonistic romp through Europe. What Isadora discovers, however, is not liberation but a different kind of confinement. She has simply exchanged one defining man, her husband, for another, her lover, and her odyssey turns into "desperation and depression masquerading as freedom." Adrian, the priapic principle, is all attitude without substance and is frequently impotent. His no-rules philosophy that calls for casting off all ties and responsibilities turns out to be a fraud as he abandons Isadora in Paris, after two weeks, to meet his wife and children for a prearranged vacation in Brittany.

Having cast off her husband and in turn been cast off by her lover, Isadora is forced into a reassessment of motive and identity:

> I said my own name to try to remember who I was: "Isadora, Isadora, Isadora, Isadora . . . Isadora White Stollerman Wing . . . Isadora Zelda White Stollerman Wing . . . B.A., M.A., Phi Beta Kappa. Isadora Wing, promising younger poet, Isadora Wing, promising younger sufferer. Isadora Wing, feminist and would-be liberated woman. Isadora Wing, clown, crybaby, fool. Isadora, wit, scholar, ex-wife of Jesus Christ. Isadora Wing, with her fear of flying. Isadora Wing, slightly overweight sexpot, with a bad case of astigmatism of the mind's eye. . . . Isadora Wing whose mother wanted her to fly. Isadora Wing whose mother grounded her. Isadora Wing, professional patient, seeker of saviors, sensuality, certainty. Isadora Wing, fighter of windmills, professional mourner, failed adventuress. . . .

Isadora's litany of identity contradictions eventually helps lead her to a truth: "I was trapped by my own fears. Motivating everything was the terror of being alone." Underlying her relationship with husbands and lovers was a fear of facing herself, unsupported or unvalidated by a mate: "I wanted to lose myself in a man . . . to be transported to heaven on borrowed wings." Accepting this truth about herself, Isadora takes her first steps toward real flight and freedom as her own person, resolved to put an end to "this nonsense of running from one man to the next." Accompanying this realization is the actualization of her fantasy of the zipless fuck with a stranger on a train that is far closer to rape than a platonic ideal of uncomplicated, mutually empowering sex. Isadora thereby realizes that liberation is not a simple matter of exchanging the prescribed female role for that of the male aggressor. Although the novel's sexual candor got all the headlines, the thematic trajectory of *Fear of Flying* has less to do with zippers than with identity, the way gender assumptions constrain and limit. Jong has declared that *Fear of Flying* is "not an endorsement of promiscuity at all." It is instead "about a young woman growing up and finding her own independence and finding the right to think her own thoughts, to fantasize."

As the novel closes, Isadora, soaking in the bathtub of Bennett's London hotel room while awaiting his return and the uncertain resolution of their marital status, manages to lose her fear of being herself. Cleansed of guilt and remorse about her past and present, Isadora is reborn on her own terms—flaws, fantasies, and all. Jong would later write of the ending of *Fear of Flying*:

> In the days when *Fear of Flying* was written it was still a novelty for a heroine to reach out for independence and not die as a result of her hubris. In the great novels about women of the nineteenth century, *Anna Karenina* and *Madame Bovary*, death was the inevitable result of a woman's quest for life beyond the bourgeois sphere (which invariably took the form of a love affair—the only stab at independence available to most women). I felt considerable pressure to kill off Isadora at the end of *Fear of Flying*. I contemplated the heroine's suicide a la *Madame Bovary* or *Anna Karenina;* I also contempated capitulation to bourgeois marriage, an out-of-wedlock pregnancy, and a then-fashionable trek into the wilderness to join a (female) commune. Thank the Goddess, I opted for none of these. My deepest hunch as a novelist was to stick with what the character of Isadora would *really* do under the circumstances. She would go home—chastened, changed, empowered, and redeemed by her adventure—and life would go on.

For all its bluster and the shock value of a fully fleshed heroine with graphic appetites and psychosexual hangups, *Fear of Flying* makes its strongest claim by dramatizing a character's hard-fought struggle toward female independence and autonomy. Isadora Wing would become the prototype for a new kind of literary heroine—no-nonsense, self-possessed, and self-determining—whose conflicts and triumphs, her fears and her flights, continue to resonate more than thirty years later.

AGAINST OUR WILL

by Susan Brownmiller

Until the 1970s, rape victims who brought charges against their attackers were at the mercy of antiquated, insensitive legal statutes that made convictions difficult and of male judges and juries who tended to blame the victim for inciting the act or failing to prevent it. In 1906, for example, a Wisconsin court of appeals acquitted an accused rapist, despite evidence that the sixteen-year-old victim had screamed, tried to get away from her attacker, and was nearly strangled. The court ruled that because she did not testify that she had used her hands, feet, or pelvic muscles to demonstrate her lack of consent and because she was not bruised and had no torn clothing, any claim that she offered "utmost resistance" was "well nigh incredible." Forty-three years later little had changed as a Texas court acquitted an accused rapist, ruling that the victim's "feigned and passive resistance" did not constitute sufficient grounds for a case of rape.

More than any other writer, Susan Brownmiller helped to change our understanding of and response to rape in her groundbreaking book, *Against Our Will: Men, Women and Rape* (1975), which grew out of the first public rape victims' speak-out, held in 1971, at St. Clement's Episcopal Church, in New York City, which Brownmiller helped to organize. Reviewer Mary Ellen Gale called Brownmiller's long overdue history of rape and its cultural significance a work that "deserves a place on the shelf next to those rare books about social problems which force us to make connections we have long evaded, and change the way we feel about what know." A year following the book's publication, the first rape crisis center opened in Berkeley, California. Other centers followed in Michigan, Los Angeles, and Washington, D.C, and by 1980, there were over four hundred rape crisis centers nationwide. In 1975, the Michigan state legislature enacted the first comprehensive rape law reforms, specifically eliminating the physical resistance requirement and limiting the circumstances and extent to which a victim's sexual history could be introduced. In the years following, Michigan's rape laws would serve as models for other states. The transformation of our understanding of what rape is and how its victims should be treated can be traced directly to *Against Our Will*.

Born in 1935, in Brooklyn, New York, Brownmiller, after graduating from Cornell University, worked as an actress before beginning her career as a journalist, in 1959, as assistant to the managing editor of *Coronet*. During the 1960s, she worked as a national affairs researcher for *Newsweek*, a staff writer for the *Village Voice*, a reporter for NBC and ABC, and a freelance journalist writing increasingly on feminist topics. One of the first politically active feminists in New York City, Brownmiller helped found the New York Radical Feminists, in 1968, and as a member of that group took part in a number of public demonstrations, including a sit-in at the offices of the *Ladies' Home Journal*, in opposition to the magazine's demeaning treatment of women. A magazine article on Shirley Chisholm, the first black United States congresswoman, led to her first book, a biography of Chisholm for young readers, published in 1970.

Brownmiller calls her exploration of rape "a once-in-a-lifetime subject that had somehow crossed my path," and explains the genesis of *Against Our Will* in a personal statement that prefaces the book. In 1968, writing a magazine article on an interracial rape case, Brownmiller approached her subject "from the perspective of a woman who viewed a rape case with suspicion. . . . Although I conducted scores of interviews for that article, I did not seek out nor did I attempt to speak with the victim. I felt no kinship with her, nor did I admit, publicly or privately, that what had happened to her could on *any* level happen to me." In discussion with her feminist friends on the topic of rape, Brownmiller recalls denying that rape was a feminist issue at all: "Rape was a sex crime, a product of a diseased, deranged mind. . . . The women's movement had nothing in common with rape victims. Victims of rape were . . . well, what were they? *Who* were they?" Answers to these questions emerged gradually from listening to other women "who understood their victimization whereas I understood only that it had not happened to me—and resisted the idea that it could. I learned that in ways I preferred to deny the threat of rape had profoundly affected my life." The crystalization of this awareness came at the "Speak-Out on Rape" that Brownmiller helped to organize in 1971. While listening to rape victims tell their stories, Brownmiller had a significant "moment of revelation." "There, in a high school auditorium," she recalls, "I finally confronted my own fears, my own past, my own intellectual defenses. Something important and frightening to contemplate had been left out of my education—a way of looking at male-female relations, at sex, at strength, and at power." Brownmiller's view of both what rape is and its cultural significance had undergone a radical reassessment, and she concludes her personal statement by confessing that "I wrote this book because I am a woman who changed her mind about rape."

The result of four years of research and writing, *Against Our Will* provides the first comprehensive study of rape that traces its prevalence and significance in war from biblical times through the world wars to Vietnam. Brownmiller considers the origin and nature of American rape laws, the persistence of interracial rape in America from slavery onwards, and the prevailing psychological, legal, and cultural understandings of rape. "From prehistoric times to the present," Brownmiller asserts, "I believe, rape has played a critical function. It is nothing more or less than a conscious process of intimidation by which *all* men keep *all* women in a state of fear." For Brownmiller, rape becomes an instrument of patriarchal rule and a deadly and demeaning metaphor for male-female relationships. Central to her thesis is a paradigm-shifting redefinition of rape, in which Brownmiller argues that it is not a sexual act but an assertion of power based on an "anatomical fiat," the result of early man's realization that women could be subjected to "a thoroughly detestable physical conquest from which there could be no retaliation in kind." As Brownmiller asserts, "For if the first rape was an unexpected battle founded on the first woman's refusal, the second rape was indubitably planned. Indeed, one of the earliest forms of male bonding must have been the gang rape of one woman by a band of marauding men. This accomplished, rape became not only a male prerogative, but man's basic weapon of force against woman, the principal agent of his will and her fear. His forcible entry into her body, despite her physical protestations and struggle, became the vehicle of his victorious conquest over her being, the ultimate test of his superior strength, the triumph of his manhood."

Having speculated on rape's origin and gender implications, Brownmiller documents the persistence of rape as an instrument of power and control over women, which is shown as an ever-present aspect of warfare, uprisings, riots, and revolutions throughout human history. Brownmiller records rape atrocities from Troy to Vietnam and in Bangladesh, where a quarter of a million women, ravaged by their enemies, were cast out by their husbands as unclean. She treats rapes by whites and Indians throughout the settling of America, as well as by white slaveholders on their human property, and speculates on the connection among rape, marriage, and family life. "Female fear of an open season of rape," Brownmiller asserts, "and not a natural inclination toward monogamy, motherhood or love, was probably the single causative factor in the original subjugation of woman by man. . . . The most important key to her historic dependence, her domestication by protective mating." The price of such protection, Brownmiller argues was legal subordination: "Man's historic desire to maintain sole, total, and complete access to woman's vagina, as codified by his earliest laws of marriage, sprang from his need to be the sole physical instrument governing impregnation, progeny, and inheritance right." Rape was conceived as theft, a violation of property laws in which the male protector, not the woman victim, was traditionally compensated. At the time *Against Our Will* appeared, rape statutes still exempted a woman's spouse from the prohibition of forcible sexual intercourse. The legal protection of a husband's right of unconditional access to his wife's body "gives the lie to any concept of equality and human dignity. . . . A sexual assault is an invasion of bodily integrity and a violation of freedom and self-determination wherever it happens to take place, in or out of the marriage bed." Far from being psychopaths acting out aberrant urges, Brownmiller suggests that "men who commit rape have served in effect as frontline masculine shock troops, terrorist guerrillas, in the longest sustained battle the world has ever known." Rape must be understood, Brownmiller declares, as a persistent factor of our social order, a fundamental aspect of male-female relations, supported by a culture and a legal system that blames the victim and exonerates (and even glamorizes) the perpetrator. "As man conquers the world," Brownmiller states, "so too he conquers the female. Down through the ages, imperial conquest, exploits of valor and expressions of love have gone hand in hand with violence to women in thought and deed."

Against Our Will concludes by suggesting some means to break what poet Adrienne Rich would call a "rape culture," including ending the protection of husbands who force their wives to have sex, overturning employed standards of resistance and consent in dealing with rape, and striving for gender equality among law enforcement to encourage women to come forward to make sexual assault complaints that will be believed and taken seriously. "Once we accept as basic truth that rape is not a crime of irrational, impulsive, uncontrollable lust, but is a deliberate, hostile, violent act of degradation to intimidate and inspire fear, we must look toward those elements in our culture that promote and propagandize these attitudes. . . ." These include prostitution and pornography, which, Brownmiller asserts, contribute to "the false perception of sexual access as an adjunct of male power and privilege" and dehumanize women. The ultimate protection, she argues, for women against rape is self-defense and fighting back. "That is the activity we must engage in, together, if we—women—are to redress the imbalance and rid ourselves and men of the ideology of rape." Brownmiller ends *Against Our Will* with a challenge: "My purpose in this book has been to give rape its history. Now we must deny it a future."

LOOKING FOR MR. GOODBAR

by Judith Rossner

Judith Rossner's chilling and complex exploration of the descent of her central character, Theresa Dunn, into a sexual hell that ends with her murder at the hands of one of her bedmates is very much a novel of its time. *Looking For Mr. Goodbar* is primarily set in the Manhattan of the 1960s, the decade in which the sexual revolution and singles bars coexisted with the beginnings of the women's movement. It was published in 1975, at the height of what had come to be widely known as "women's lib," when drugs, rock 'n' roll, self-help, and a distaste for permanent commitment together with a fear of intimacy had been firmly ensconced in American culture, and the overheated "disco" era of Studio 54 and sex clubs like Plato's Retreat—all of which would help to define the 1970s as the "Me Decade"—was about to begin. *Looking For Mr. Goodbar* is one of the most important women's novels to come out of the 1970s, not only because it is an illuminating and cautionary tale of its time, but also because of Rossner's ability to make the reader feel the intensity of Theresa's thoughts, feelings, and experiences as she copes with her lack of self-esteem and a painful loneliness dating from childhood by rejecting love and

218   A BOOKSHELF OF OUR OWN

companionship in favor of the promiscuous sexuality that will eventually cause her death.

Looking For Mr. Goodbar was Rossner's fourth novel. A native New Yorker, Judith Perelman Rossner (born in 1935) was early encouraged to become a writer by her mother, who was a teacher. At nineteen she dropped out of City College to marry Robert Rossner, a teacher and writer; the couple would have two children and later divorce. She worked in the advertising department of *Scientific American*, work she enjoyed but which she felt distracted her from the novel she was writing. She later opted for a less demanding job in real estate and finished her manuscript, which she did not publish. In 1966, she produced her first published novel, *To the Precipice*, the account of a Jewish woman raised in a New York tenement, who marries a wealthy gentile rather than commit herself to a self-made lawyer she has known from childhood and with whom she feels a more passionate attachment. The theme of separation and the conflict between selfishness and altruism is explored in *To the Precipice* and in Rossner's next two novels: *Nine Months in the Life of an Old Maid* (1969), the story of a self-absorbed insane woman who lives in isolation with her sister, and in *Any Minute Now I Can Split* (1972), a darkly comic tale of commune life. It is also seen in *Looking For Mr. Goodbar*. The genesis of Rossner's fourth novel was a piece she was asked to write for a women's issue of *Esquire* magazine on Roseann Quinn, a twenty-seven-year-old teacher who had recently been murdered by a man she had taken home with her from a singles bar. After *Esquire*'s lawyers decided not to let the story run, Rossner decided to write it as a novel.

Looking For Mr. Goodbar begins with the background of Gary Cooper White, the young drifter who has fled to New York to avoid arrest in Florida for armed robbery, and who has killed Rossner's protagonist after meeting her in a singles bar called Mr. Goodbar and taking her back to her apartment for sex. Rossner gives us White's taped confession while he is in police custody, then relates the story of the victim, Theresa Dunn, from her lower-middle-class Irish-American childhood in the Bronx to her murder on New Year's Day, 1970. Theresa, a first-grade teacher, has grown up with a sense of being damaged, both physically and emotionally. At four she contracted a mild case of polio, which was followed by scoliosis and surgery that resulted in a year spent in the hospital; this has left her overly sensitive about the wormlike scar on her back, her slight limp, and her weight. She has grown up with the belief that her parents do not love her, and she is emotionally detached from them, as well as from her outgoing, tomboyish younger sister, Brigid, who is happily married and has produced several offspring.

Theresa's closest family ties have been to her older siblings, Thomas and Katherine. She was especially fond of Thomas, who was eleven years older than her and her mother's favorite. It was Thomas who visited her in the hospital and read to her throughout her illness; his death in a training-camp gun accident at eighteen devastated the family. Theresa's relationship with Katherine, while close, is strained: she resents Katherine's beauty, the ease with which she obtains what she wants, and what Theresa feels is her status as their father's favorite. Theresa's family and the other characters in the novel are stereotypes that help to reveal the author's themes through her central character. Katherine, for example, typifies a certain kind of sixties woman: self-confident and sophisticated, she has aggressively taken part in whatever has been on offer in the New York bohemian world of the early-to-mid years of the decade and the hippie culture of the late sixties. Experimental, yet careful to make appropriate choices, Katherine has a gift for surviving and thriving that is lacking in her sister.

Theresa's first sexual experience is with her cynical City College English professor, Martin Engle, who takes an interest in her writing and hires her, ostensibly as a secretary, but in reality to seduce her. When she tells him, "I love you so much, Martin," he replies with his customary irony, "Ah, yes. . . . Love." Before she sleeps with Martin, Theresa envisions a romantic scenario concerning him that also contains a hint of her sexual predilection: "In her fantasies his wife had just died in an automobile accident and he had sent for her. He made love to her passionately after explaining that all love had gone from his marriage for years. Sometimes they played a game called Threshold of Pain, in which he and many assistants tested her to see where pleasure ended and pain began. . . ." During their affair, Martin fulfills a requirement that is important to Theresa in her romantic relationships: he talks to her. She values this quality in James Morrisey, her would-be fiancé and the only person to whom she can confess her love of teaching (she has difficulty sharing her feelings with her few women friends and avoids joining a women's "consciousness-raising" group).

When her affair with Martin Engle predictably ends, Theresa, disillusioned by love and fearful of rejection, turns to what becomes her drug of choice: sex. Finding bed partners in bars is all too easy, and she embarks on a series of casual one-night encounters with a variety of men, most of them nameless. The men we meet include Eli, a former Hassidic Jew who has changed his named to Ali, rejected his community, and lives in an untidy loft; and Victor, who is in New York on business, and with whom she shares a weekend of sex at his hotel. Theresa feels both comforted and constricted by her secret sexual roundelay and almost incredulous concerning the duality of her life:

> Actually, when she thought about it at all, she didn't really feel that she *had* a life, one life, that is, belonging to a person, Theresa Dunn. There was a Miss Dunn who taught a bunch of children who adored her ("Oh, that's Miss Dunn," she'd heard one of her children say once to a parent. "She's one of the kids. A big one.") and there was someone named Terry who whored around in bars when she couldn't sleep at night. But the only thing those two people had in common was the body they inhabited. If one died, the other would never miss her—although she herself, Theresa, the person who thought and felt but had no life, would miss either one.

Theresa's longest lasting and most sexually satisfying relationship is with Tony, an Italian-American garage attendant who makes love to her to the blare of rock 'n' roll. The couple never talks and never goes out, preferring instead to stay in bed. The one time Theresa ventures out with him as his girlfriend, it is to the Bronx for his mother's birthday. There, Tony physically attacks his mother's boyfriend and hits Theresa, thus essentially ending their relationship. With Tony gone, Theresa becomes closer to the patient, forbearing James, who loves her but who does not give her the sexual pleasure she craves. She cannot commit to him because she feels he does not see her realistically; that is, as the damaged person she truly is. When James gives her a ring at Christmas, Theresa has a panic attack, and he takes her home, where she voices her resentment of the ring as an emblem of ownership and control. However, after he leaves, she becomes distraught at the thought that she has lost him and admits to herself that "if James disappeared from her life he would leave an enormous gap that couldn't easily be filled."

All alone at New Year's, Theresa feels a sense of panic: "She felt as though she were walking a tightrope and certain moves would send her plunging, but she had no way of knowing exactly what they were." She resolves to begin a diary and starts to write, but her thoughts roll back to Martin Engle and she cannot get beyond the date: "How could you begin a diary not long before your twenty-seventh birthday without ever saying anything about what happened before? And what could she say about what had happened before? What was there to say about her life?" Overwhelmed by loneliness and feeling in desperate need of sex, Theresa visits Mr. Goodbar, where she picks up the man who will shortly murder her. Her last thoughts are calls for help from James and from Mommy and Daddy, who cannot save her now.

Looking For Mr. Goodbar was a best-seller praised by reviewers for its great sensitivity and skill. *The New York Times* book reviewer observed, "It is a measure to 'Mr. Goodbar's' richness and complexity that it can be viewed on many levels. Catholics might view it as a passion play: feminists might consider Theresa a political victim of rape." In truth, Theresa *is* a victim—of her childhood, her religion, and the culture of sexual freedom. Judith Rossner has masterfully evoked a culture that glorified sensation without understanding in a novel that calls into question the true meaning of "women's liberation."

THE WOMAN WARRIOR

by Maxine Hong Kingston

Maxine Hong Kingston's *The Woman Warrior* (1976) is one of the singular achievements of modern American literature. The first work by an Asian-American writer to gain widespread popularity and critical acclaim, it revolutionized accepted literary forms, creating a new genre that has been called "the creative memoir," and spawning an ongoing and important exploration of the American experience from personal, ethnic, cultural, and gender perspectives. Subtitled "Memoirs of a Girlhood Among Ghosts," *The Woman Warrior* presents the coming-of-age and coming-to-terms saga of an Asian-American woman's attempt to achieve an authentic identity and liberation against the cultural and gender restrictions imposed by the intimidating and threatening specters of both Caucasian-American life and her often mystifying and stultifying Chinese heritage. The work has been described as the first postmodern autobiography in which chronological, objective narrative is abandoned in favor of fragmented, subjective moments of illumination, mixing fact and fiction that blurs the distinction between biography and legend, reality and fantasy, truth and myth. A work of remarkable originality and popular appeal, *The Woman Warrior* has become one of the most assigned texts on contemporary college campuses, appearing on syllabi in course offerings in English, ethnic studies, women's studies, American studies, Asian studies, Asian-American studies, anthropology, sociology, history, and psychology. Clearly, the relevance and resonance of *The Woman Warrior* has exceeded the reach of the standard memoir of growth and development from a particular ethnic, cultural, historical, or regional perspective. As scholar Sau-Ling Wong has observed, "It is safe to say that many readers who otherwise do not concern themselves with Asian American literature have read [*The Woman Warrior*]." Through the remarkable poetic and vibrant quality of her prose, her daring, experimental mixture of fictional and nonfictional elements, and her balancing of rival cultural imperatives in pursuit of synthesis, Kingston has moved in *The Woman Warrior* from the particular to the universal, chronicling an Asian-American woman's personal and family story that is also a profound exploration of gender, cultural, and human identity.

Born Maxine Ting Ting Hong in Stockton, California, in 1940, the writer was the first of six American-born children of Chinese immigrants Chew Ling Yan and Tom Hong. Her father was trained in China as a scholar and teacher, and immigrated to the United States in 1925. Working as a laborer, he was eventually able to save enough to invest in a laundry in New York's Chinatown. Maxine's mother (Brave Orchid in *The Woman Warrior*) remained in China and was separated from her husband for fifteen years. During the interim, she trained in medicine and midwifery, and worked as a physician, a remarkable accomplishment for a Chinese woman of the time. She joined her husband in the United States in 1939 in Stockton, California, where Tom Hong had become the manager of an illegal gambling house owned by a wealthy Chinese immigrant. Maxine was named for an often lucky blond gambler. During World War II, the Hongs started a laundry in Stockton, where Kingston and her siblings were put to work as soon as they were old enough to help. The laundry became an informal Chinese community center where Kingston heard the "talk-stories" she would later draw on in her writing and characterized as "a tradition that goes back to prewriting time in China, where people verbally pass on history and mythology and genealogy and how-to stories and bedtime stories and legends. . . . [At the laundry] I would hear talk-story from everyone who came in. So I inherited this amazing amount of information, culture, history, mythology, and poetry." Speaking only Chinese until she

started school, Maxine failed kindergarten in part because she refused to speak. Gaining fluency and an increased mastery of expression in English, Kingston eventually excelled as a student,
publishing her first essay, "I Am an American" in *American Girl*,
in 1955, when she was still in high school. She attended the
University of California at Berkeley on a scholarship, graduating
in 1962 with a degree in English. The same year she married Earll
Kingston, an actor and fellow Berkeley graduate. Earning a
teaching certificate, Kingston taught English and mathematics in
a California high school for five years. Disillu-sioned with the
1960s drug culture and the ineffectiveness of the protest movement against the Vietnam War, the couple, with their young son,
left California, in 1967, en route to Japan. Stopping off in Hawaii,
they would remain there for the next seventeen years. Kingston
taught English, language arts, and English as a second language
at several high schools and business and technical colleges, and
for two and a half years she worked on the manuscript that would
become *The Woman Warrior*.

Kingston originally intended the work to be combined with the
stories that eventually made up *China Men* (1980) as "one big
book," exploring identity formation and cultural conflict faced by
Chinese Americans, based on her own experiences and her relationship with her mother and father and her relatives. Avoiding
the restrictions of "standard autobiography," which she identified
as dealing with "exterior things" or "big historical events that you
publicly participate in," Kingston concentrated instead on what
she called "real stories," narratives mixing facts and the imagination, dramatizing "the rich, personal inner life." Her publisher
insisted that the project be divided into two volumes and catego-
rized as nonfiction. *The Woman Warrior* was published in 1976, to
universal acclaim, winning the National Book Critics Circle
Award and establishing Kingston as a major writing talent. The
book was described by reviewer William McPherson as "a strange,
sometimes savagely terrifying and, in a literal sense, wonderful
story of growing up caught between two highly sophisticated and
utterly alien cultures, both vivid, often menacing and equally
mysterious." *The Woman Warrior* explores the forces of heritage,
family, and personal experience that impact the lives of women
and must be confronted before any genuine autonomy and liberation can be achieved. "Chinese-Americans," Kingston writes,
"when you try to understand what things in you are Chinese, how

do you separate what is peculiar to childhood, to poverty, insanities, one family, your mother who marked your growing with stories, from what is Chinese? What is Chinese tradition and what is the movies?" *The Woman Warrior* attempts to answer these questions, dealing in imaginative terms with the status of Asian women in America and the various burdens and responsibilities faced by all women.

Divided into five sections, each centered on a talk-story, *The Woman Warrior* provocatively begins with a family secret and a warning:

> "You must not tell anyone," my mother said, "what I am about to tell you. In China your father had a sister who killed herself. She jumped into the family well. We say that your father has all brothers because it is as if she had never been born."

Told to the narrator by her mother, Brave Orchid, as a "story to grow up on," the fate of "No Name Woman," who bears a child two years after her husband's departure for America, is intended as a sobering lesson to a maturing daughter of the dangers of unsanctioned sexuality and the consequences of a Chinese woman's transgressing the traditional gender rules—subservience to male authority and repression of personal desires—she is expected to obey. For her sexual indiscretion, the narrator's aunt provokes the community's wrath, and the villagers kill the family's livestock and destroy their possessions. A pariah who has caused her family shame and misery, No Name Woman gives birth unattended in a pigsty, kills herself and her newborn, and is sentenced by her own family to the anonymity of a nonperson; even her name is obliterated. This striking story establishes the costs and consequences of challenging the established, patriachal values of Chinese tradition, while the narrator's breaking the taboo of silence and imaginatively restoring aspects of her aunt's history and identity establish central themes of *The Woman Warrior*, including the repression faced by Chinese women and the harsh retribution suffered by transgressors, as well as the redemptive power of the imagination to restore the life of the voiceless and forgotten.

The second section, "White Tigers," recasts the legendary story of Fa Mu Lan—a woman warrior who takes her father's place in battle and avenges her family's wrongs that are carved onto her back—as an alternative Chinese myth in contrast to the submissive, subservient female myth revealed by the fate of No Name Woman. For the narrator, the thrilling adventures of a fantasized woman warrior invites a sustaining identification. Refusing to be the passive victim of racist and sexist acts, the narrator, like Fa Mu Lan, sees her writing as a different kind of fighting, declaring:

> The swordswoman and I are not so dissimilar. May my people understand the resemblance soon so I can return to them. What we have in common are the words at our backs. The idiom for *revenge* are "report a crime" and "report to five families." The reporting is the vengeance—not the beheading, not the gutting, but the words. And I have so many words—"chink" words and "gook" words too—that they do not fit on my skin.

The middle chapter, "Shaman," presents a biographical sketch of the narrator's mother, Brave Orchid, as the story of a modern woman warrior. Like Fa Mu Lan, who went "away ordinary and came back miraculous, like the ancient magicians who came down from the mountains," Brave Orchid earns a medical degree, bravely exorcises the malevolent "Sitting Ghost" that threatens her school, and establishes a respectable career as a physician in China before joining her husband in America. In contrast, "At the Western Palace" presents the fate of Brave Orchid's sister, Moon Orchid, a victim of sexual manipulation and submissiveness that leads to madness. Moon Orchid has been left in Hong Kong by her husband, who has come to America and bigamously married a young assimilated Chinese-American woman. Brought to America by her sister to reclaim her rights as her husband's first wife, Moon Orchid's passivity, timidity, and subservience to established Chinese values prohibits her reaching a positive settlement with her husband, and the radically different values she finds in America lead to her gradual loss of sanity and self-identity, and eventual confinement to a mental asylum.

The silence and madness of No Name Woman and Moon Orchid, therefore, stand in sharp contrast for the narrator to the liberating possibilities of Fa Mu Lan and Brave Orchid; and the conflict among competing gender and cultural assumptions are applied in the book's concluding section, "A Song for a Barbarian Reed Pipe," to the narrator's development through several events in her childhood and adolescence. Silence and its cost is the dominating theme of this portion of *The Woman Warrior* as the narrator recalls "the worst thing [she] had yet done to another person," cruelly trying to force a silent classmate to speak, a metaphor for the narrator's own inner trauma of inarticulateness, being suspended between the opposing ghosts in her life—her Chinese heritage and American life. "Once upon a time," the narrator recalls, "the world was so thick with ghosts, I could hardly breathe; I could hardly walk, limping my way around the White Ghosts and their cars." The narrator's haunting is a result both of her parents' refusal to acknowledge the reality of their American life and their imposition of the shadowy world of their Chinese past and childhood on their offspring. Regarded by the older generation of Chinese immigrants as not completely Chinese, at school the narrator finds herself insufficiently American; she is therefore alienated both from her ancestral past and her Amerian present. She is also female, judged inferior and a burden by Chinese standards, and an outsider by the dominating American patriarchy. The disjunction makes the narrator a double victim of the sexual stereotypes and racist stigmatism that threatens to destroy one's identity if one is unable to resolve these contradictions. As the narrator achieves the power to confront her mother for imposing silence on her, and is able to speak out against the various gender and racial forces that threaten her, she finds a new model, in the second-century Chinese woman poet Ts'ai Yen, to displace the swordswoman Fa Mu Lan. A prisoner of the barbarians for twelve years, Ts'ai Yen is able to recover her voice as she listens to the music of barbarian flutes and is inspired to write poetry that distills her experiences into an enduring voice that challenges her repression and achieves valuable communication:

> Ts'ai Yen sang about China and her family there. Her words seemed to be Chinese, but the barbarians understood their sadness and anger. Sometimes they thought they could catch barbarian phrases about forever wandering. Her children did not laugh, but eventually sang along when she left her tent to sit by the winter campfires, ringed by barbarians.

Ts'ai Yen is the final version of the woman warrior who, like the narrator, lives among people of a different race and offers the narrator, as a word warrior, a model for using self-expression as a means of reclaiming identity, liberation, and autonomy. By setting

Ts'ai Yen's story—along with those of No Name Woman, Fa Mu Lan, Brave Orchid, and Moon Orchid—in the context of her own experiences, the narrator ultimately achieves the means to exorcise her own ghosts, to find her own voice, and to achieve self-definition out of the various forces of gender and culture that silence, repress, and destroy. *The Woman Warrior* functions, therefore, both as a crucial record of Chinese-American experience and a dramatization of the process by which a woman, of whatever ethnicity, is forced to fashion an identity out of gender and cultural imperatives.

OF WOMAN BORN

by Adrienne Rich

Adrienne Rich, one of the most acclaimed contemporary American poets, is also an important prose writer, whose essays are collected in *On Lies, Secrets and Silence* (1979) and *Blood, Bread and Poetry* (1986), and whose most significant contribution to the debate over women's identity and empowerment is *Of Woman Born: Motherhood as Experience and Institution* (1976), one of the groundbreaking works in feminist theory. In it, Rich sets out to "examine motherhood—my own included—in a social context, as embedded in a political institution: in feminist terms." The result is one of the first attempts to understand motherhood as a cultural rather than a biological phenomenon, drawing an important distinction between "two meanings of motherhood, one superimposed on the other: the *potential relationship* of any woman to her powers of reproduction and to children; and the *institution*, which aims at ensuring that that potential—and all women—shall remain under male control." Rich calls institutionalized motherhood "a keystone of the most diverse social and political systems," which "has withheld over one-half the human species from the decisions affecting their lives; it exonerates men from fatherhood in any authentic sense; it creates the dangerous schism between 'private' and 'public' life; it calcifies human choices and potentialities. . . . It has alienated women from our bodies by incarcerating us in them." *Of Woman Born* traces the implications of this assertion and examines the role that motherhood has played in history and culture to shape the destinies of women.

Because *Of Woman Born* intentionally mixes personal testimony with research and theory, the biographical details of Rich's life and development are central to an understanding of the work. Born in Baltimore, Maryland, in 1929, Rich was the eldest of two daughters. Her father was a pathologist working as a professor and researcher at Johns Hopkins Medical School. Educated at home until the fourth grade and encouraged in her writing, her first book, *Ariadne,* was a three-act play and poems, privately printed when she was only ten. Rich would graduate with honors from Radcliffe College, in 1951, the same year that her first collection of poetry, *A Change of World,* was published in the prestigious Yale Series of Younger Poets. W.H. Auden, who selected Rich's collection for the series, declared that her poems "speak quietly but do not mumble, respect their elders but are not cowed by them, and do not tell fibs." In 1953, Rich married Alfred Conrad, an economics professor at Harvard University, and had three sons between 1955 and 1959. Preoccupied with her responsibilities as a wife and mother, Rich saw her writing languish; she broke her silence, in 1963, with the important collection, *Snapshots of a Daughter-in-Law.* "In the late fifties I was able to write," Rich recalls, "for the first time, directly about experiencing myself as a woman." The long title sequence was "jotted in fragments during children's naps, brief hours in a library, or at 3:00 A.M. after rising with a wakeful child" and explores for one of the first times in poetry the limitations faced by women in their restrictive domestic roles and in identities defined by masculine expectations. Rich's experience of motherhood would, as she declares in *Of Woman Born,* radicalize her and provide her with a central preoccupation in her poetry and prose.

When Rich's husband began teaching at New York's City College, the family relocated there, and Rich formed important relationships with fellow poets Audre Lorde and June Jordan. Rich also began her own teaching career, with stints at Swarthmore College, Columbia, Brandeis, and City College. In 1970, Rich's husband committed suicide, and, in 1976, Rich came out as a lesbian, beginning a long-term relationship with writer Michelle

Cliffe. During this period, Rich published some of her most important works, including *Leaflets* (1971), the National Book Award–winning *Diving into the Wreck* (1973), and *The Dream of a Common Language* (1977). Throughout, Rich captures in intense and striking images the challenges women face under a repressive social system that denies their human potential, while expressing the urgency to achieve a liberating and autonomous self-identity.

Many of the themes of Rich's poetry recur in *Of Woman Born*, which considers motherhood as the "experience by which women are expected to define themselves . . . and as an institution by which a male-dominated society controls and diminishes them." Calling motherhood "the great mesh in which all human relationships are entangled, in which lurk our most elemental assumptions about love and power," Rich surveys her subject from personal, anthropological, historical, and political perspectives, beginning with her own experiences as a mother of three boys. Relying on journal entries from the period, Rich, in powerful and candid language, records her ambivalence during her pregnancies and as the prime caregiver to her sons, in which she is "caught up in waves of love and hate, jealousy even of the child's childhood; hope and fear for its maturity; longing to be free of responsibility, tied by every fibre of one's being." Rich relates her guilt and anxiety over feeling inadequate as a homemaker and mother, and resentful that so much of her intellectual and artistic life was sacrificed to mind-numbing domestic chores. That she did not live up to the standard of the self-fulfilled, completed mother figure of myth led Rich to a realization: "I was effectively alienated from my real body and my real spirit by the institution—not the fact—of motherhood. This institution—the foundation of human society as we know it—allowed me only certain views, certain expectations, whether embodied in the booklet in my obstetrician's waiting room, the novels I had read, my mother-in-law's approval, my memories of my own mother, the Sistine Madonna or she of the Michelangelo *Pietà*, the floating notion that a woman pregnant is a woman calm in her fulfillment or, simply, a woman waiting. Women have always been seen as waiting: waiting to be asked, waiting for our menses, in fear lest they do or do not come, waiting for men to come home from wars, or from work, waiting for children to grow up, or for the birth of a new child, or for menopause." This insight leads Rich to consider how "the experience of maternity and the experience of sexuality have both been channeled to serve male interests." Patriarchy, she declares, "would seem to require, not only that women shall assume the major burden of pain and self-denial for the furtherance of the species, but that a majority of that species—women—shall remain essentially unquestioning and unenlightened." Patriarchal society idealizes woman as childbearer and enforces motherhood on many women who should never have had children; and it never prepares women for the contradictory emotions of loneliness and depression that is a consequence of the dissolution of sustaining kinship groups and the restriction of women from productive work outside the home. Patriarchal society, Rich asserts, has forcibly defined her and all women exclusively in maternal terms, with resistance against that restriction making her feel that she is "Kali, Medea, the sow that devours her farrow, the unwomanly woman in flight from motherhood."

A solution to this dilemma is the acceptance of a wider conception of women's identity, one in which motherhood is only "one part of the female process . . . not an identity for all time," and that alternative conceptions of maternity are possible. *Of Woman Born* juxtaposes the institution of motherhood under a patriarchal system with matriarchal systems of woman-centered beliefs and woman-centered social organizations. "Throughout most the world," Rich asserts, "there is archeological evidence of a period when Woman was venerated in several aspects, the primal one being maternal; when Goddess-worship prevailed, and when myths depicted strong and revered female figures. In the earliest artifacts we know, we encounter the female as primal power." As matriarchal society gave way to the patriarchal, women's power was restricted to childbearing alone, with women and motherhood controlled and domesticated. Woman "becomes the property of the husband-father," and a woman's value is defined exclusively by her ability to reproduce, particularly the sons who will inherit the patrimony. "Patriarchal man created—out of a mixture of sexual and affective frustration, blind need, physical force, ignorance, and intelligence split from its emotional grounding, a system which turned against woman her own organic nature, the source of her awe and her original powers."

In a review of obstetrics, Rich documents a demeaning process of control that dehumanizes women, in which childbirth is transformed from a natural process to a medical condition and the mother-to-be into a passive recipient of technology: "The loneliness, the sense of abandonment, of being imprisoned, powerless, and depersonized is the chief collective memory of women who have given birth in American hospitals." The institution of patriarchal motherhood both defines women exclusively as childbearers and limits their powers under a male-dominated birthing system. Rich similarly finds evidence of the patriarchy at work in the assumptions of child rearing in which women are expected to prepare their offspring to accept their appointed roles—males as active and aggressive; females as passive and subordinate.

Of Woman Born catalogs a number of suggested alternatives to the patriarchal institution of motherhood, "for the taking over by women of genetic technology; for the insistence on childcare as a political commitment by all members of a community," by the "return to a 'village' concept of community in which children could be integrated into the adult life of work; the rearing of children in feminist enclaves to grow up free of gender-imprinting," and a redefinition of fatherhood, "which would require a more active, continuous presence with the child." Many of these solutions, Rich writes, may be naïve and simplistic. Instead, she urges a fundamental "repossession by women of our bodies," which she states "will bring far more essential change to human society than the seizing of the means of production by workers." As Rich concludes:

> We need to imagine a world in which every woman is the presiding genius of her own body. In such a world women will truly create new life, bringing forth not only children (if and as we choose) but the visions, and the thinking, necessary to sustain, console, and alter human existence—a new relationship to the universe. Sexuality, politics, intelligence, power, motherhood, work, community, intimacy will develop new meanings; thinking itself will be transformed.
> This is where we have to begin.

THE WOMEN'S ROOM

by Marilyn French

One of the most influential novels of the modern feminist movement, Marilyn French's *The Women's Room* (1977) is a blistering indictment of gender conflict in America from the 1940s through the 1970s. The fictional counterpart to Betty Friedan's *The Feminine Mystique, The Women's Room* supplies a collective biography of a generation of American women, described by novelist Anne Tyler as "expectant in the 40's, submissive in the 50's, enraged in the 60's" who "have arrived in the 70's independent but somehow unstrung, not yet fully composed after all they've been through." Anchored by the self-realization process of Mira—a woman whose traditional upbringing leads to a conventional marriage that ends suddenly in divorce, forcing a painful reassessment of the gender assumptions that have dictated her and her peers' fates as women, wives, and mothers—*The Women's Room* documents and dramatizes ordinary women's daily lives; this subject, rare in novels, presents the challenges and risks of women's liberation. A controversial best-seller, *The Women's Room* was both praised for its uncanny, unvarnished recognition of the actuality of contemporary women's lives and decried as a polemical work of idealized female victims and male villains, described by critic Libby Purves as "a prolonged—largely autobiographical—yell of fury at the perversity of the male sex," in which "the men in the novel are drawn as malevolent stick figures, at best appallingly dull and at worst monsters." Observing in her own defense, French has stated, "That infuriates me. Every time I see that I see orange. The men are there as the women see them and feel them—impediments in women's lives. That's the focus of the book. Aristotle managed to build a whole society without mentioning women once. Did anyone ever say: 'Are there women in [Joseph Conrad's] *Nigger of the Narcissus?*' " The often vitriolic defensiveness that characterizes much of the critical response to *The Women's Room* reflects the novel's still-threatening power to challenge preconceived assumptions. As reviewer Christopher Lehmann-Haupt observed, the novel "seized me by my preconceptions and I kept struggling and arguing with its premises. Men can't be that bad, I kept wanting to shout at the narrator. There must be room for accommodation between the sexes that you've somehow overlooked." Lehmann-Haupt is finally persuaded that "the damnable thing is, she's right." Reviewer Brigitte Weeks has praised the novel for forcing "confrontations on the reader mercilessly" and as a "wonderful novel, full of life and passions that ring true as crystal. Its fierceness, its relentless refusal to compromise are as stirring as a marching song."

Placing *The Women's Room* in the cultural context of its time, Susan Faludi has argued that it was strikingly different from the other "women's novels" of the 1960s and 1970s that attempted to present feminist themes. Portraying "a weepy, wispy lady flailing ineffectually at fate, breaking a few kitchen appliances perhaps, but never straying far beyond the picket gate (or the gate of the mental hospital)," conventional women's novels depicted women's restricted roles and their psychological cost though a protagonist who "analyzed her life, but she didn't act on her analysis in any politically meaningful way—and she didn't inspire you to act either." In Faludi's view, French's novel manages to do both:

The Women's Room played out its most important and formative role as an agent for social and political action. It helped inspire sisterhood, by bringing women from the suburbs together by disclosing their commonly held grievances. It offered a political framework, by uncovering the gears and pulleys, the subtle social engineering of the fifties, that tried to reduce women and men to two-dimensional roles. And it gave women that ingredient essential to all social revolutions, large and small—a feeling of hope. By showing women that the "problem" wasn't all in their heads, *The Women's Room* opened the minds of women to the possibility that their lives were subject to change.

An assault on conventional ideals and a call to action and revolutionary gender change, *The Women's Room* was designed to incite and motivate. "My goal in life," French has argued, "is to change the entire social and economic structure of western civilization, to make it a feminist world." In her extensive survey of patriarchy, *Beyond Power: On Women, Men, and Morals* (1985), French has defined feminism as "the only serious, coherent, and universal philosophy that offers an alternative to patriarchal thinking and structures." Feminists, she asserts, "believe that women are human beings, that the two sexes are (at least) equal in all significant ways, and that this equality must be publicly recognized. They believe that qualities traditionally associated with women— the feminine principle—are (at least) equal in value to those traditionally associated with men—the masculine principle—and that this equality must be publicly recognized. . . . Finally, feminists believe the personal is the political—that is, that the value structure of a culture is identical in both public and private areas, that what happens in the bedroom has everything to do with what happens in the board room, and vice versa, and that, mythology notwithstanding, at present the same sex is in control in both places."

Dramatizing what feminists believe and why, *The Women's Room* derives its considerable power from its reflections of French's own experiences, and the developmental process that took her from stay-at-home spouse during the 1950s to divorced, single mother and Harvard graduate student in the radical 1960s. Born in 1929, in Brooklyn, French earned a bachelor's degree from Hofstra College (now University), in 1951. She gave up a plan to pursue a graduate degree, however, to marry Robert M. French, Jr., with whom she had two children. Living in a suburban Long Island town and feeling entrapped as a housewife, French would later point to reading, in 1956, Simone de Beauvoir's *The Second Sex*, with its indictment of women's sacrifice of their potential, choosing to live vicariously through men as a determining force in the resumption of her academic career. French returned to Hofstra to earn her master's degree in 1964, and, in 1967, she divorced her husband and enrolled in the English graduate program at Harvard, where she received her Ph.D., in 1972. Teaching English at the College of the Holy Cross in Worcester, Massachusetts, from 1972 to 1976, French converted her doctoral thesis into her first book, *The Book As World: James Joyce's Ulysses*, in 1976, and a year later she brought out *The Women's Room*. The book's phenomenal commercial success allowed French to pursue writing full-time, and her subsequent works include the novels *The Bleeding Heart* (1980), *Her Mother's Daughter* (1987), *Our Father* (1994), and *My Summer with George* (1996), as well as the volumes of nonfiction, essays, and criticism *Shakespeare's Division of Experience* (1981), *Beyond Power* (1985), *The War against Women* (1992), and *From Eve to Dawn: A History of Women* (2002–2003), and the memoir *A Season in Hell* (1998).

All of French's works attempt to break conventions, to show the reality of women's lives through history, culture, and her own life. French explained in an interview that her intention in *The Women's Room* was to "tell the story of what it is like to be a woman in our country in the middle of the twentieth century." Using her own experiences in realizing and resisting the patriarchal values that restricted possibilities for women, *The Women's Room* attempts to document the workings of this male-dominated system as it affects ordinary women's lives. "I sometimes think I've swallowed every woman I ever knew," French has observed. "My head is full of voices . . . clamoring to be let out." Central to her purpose was the desire "to break the mold of conventional women's novel," which she has described as books that "deal with young unmarried women. The action is her choosing a husband, the only choice she has the power to make and the final choice of her life—thus they always end with her marriage." *The Women's Room* set out to continue women's stories beyond the altar into the sobering reality of their domestic lives. "Books, movies, TV teach us false images of ourselves," French has written. "We learn to expect fairy-tale lives. Ordinary women's daily lives—unlike men's—have not been the stuff of literature. I wanted to legitimize it and I purposely chose the most ordinary lives—not the worst cases." French focuses on the growth of her protagonist, Mira, from her upbringing and childhood, through her college experience, marriage, suburban lifestyle, and eventual radical reorientation of her life and values following her divorce. Mira's experiences are presented as representative of an entire generation of women coming to terms with the gender assumptions that have damaged them, and the novel equally treats the complementary stories of Mira's friends and peers, who respond in different ways to their circumstances as wives, mothers, and workers, to produce a panoramic group portrait. As one reviewer notes, "It is as if French had been taking notes for twenty years. Her dialogue, her characterizations, her knowledge of the changing relationships, sexual and otherwise, between men and women in a complex world of shifting values are all extraordinary." The novel's popularity and persistence are based, in the words of another, on the author's "genuine sympathy for other women caught in life situations, trivial or deadly serious, for which they were never prepared."

Submissive and repressed, Mira subordinates her intellectual potential and ambition to work menial jobs to support her stolid husband, Norm, through medical school. With the arrival of babies, Mira's world shrinks even further to her housekeeping and nurturing chores. With Norm's success comes the ideal house in the suburbs. French presents the details of suburban life, described by Anne Tyler as "balky ice-cube trays and Cub Scout meetings" that "interlace with adulteries, attempted suicides and enforced stays in mental institutions." Mira encounters Natalie, who copes with her homebound frustrations by continually redecorating; Martha, who fights her boredom with housework by going back to school and falling in love with one of her professors; and Lily, whose honest assessment of suburban women's maddening restrictions leads to her own confinement in an asylum. Norm eventually is unfaithful, and Mira breaks free from the suburbs to experience the turbulent sixties and seventies as an English graduate student at Harvard. There she encounters gender bias in academia as well as among the radicals who supposedly advocate enlightened liberation. Both take their toll on several more of Mira's peers, such as Val, Kyla, Grete, Ava, Clarissa, and Iso, who to a greater or a lesser degree are destroyed and damaged by a male-dominated/female-subordinated system. Mira eventually achieves her doctorate and winds up teaching at a coastal Maine community college where "she walks the beach every day, and drinks brandy every night, and wonders if she's going mad." The ultimate literary convention of the happy ending is avoided. As French has stated, "No one at all, lives happily ever after. A woman may endure, but suffering never ends."

Reflecting on her accomplishment in portraying the reality of women's lives during the period that created the modern women's movement, Marilyn French ably summarizes: "*The Women's Room* shows women's work for the tedious, draining, menial, and occasionally brilliant and creative thing it is; it insists on the centrality of women's work to the world at large and to women themselves. It shows the actual importance of men to a variety of women. It offers no finality, no promised Eden, but only endurance, survival." *The Women's Room* stands as one of the great breakthrough works in which centuries of conventions that have ruled the way women are portrayed are overturned for a sobering reality upon which self-realization and true liberation can be more securely based.

SILENCES

by Tillie Olsen

Silences, Tillie Olsen's 1978 collection of essays, talks, notes, and excerpts from the diaries, journals, and letters of a wide range of writers, past and present, has been called by Alix Kates Shulman a "classic of feminist literature." Described by its author as a work "concerned with the relationship of circumstances—including class, color, sex; the times, climate into which one is born—to the creation of literature," *Silences* describes the "thwarting of what struggles to come into being, but cannot" that has prevented writers, particularly women, from being heard. Although the author of only a single volume of acclaimed short stories, *Tell Me a Riddle* (1961), and an unfinished novel, *Yonnondio: From the Thirties* (1974), Tillie Olsen is greatly admired both for the artistry of her works and the obstacles she has had to overcome to produce them. Margaret Atwood has asserted that "few writers have gained such wide respect on such a small body of published work." Among her peers, Atwood declares, the word "respect" is simply inadequate to describe the feelings Olsen evokes: " 'Reverence' is more like it. This is presumably because women writers, even more than their male counterparts, recognize what a heroic feat it is to have held down a job, raised four children and still somehow managed to become and to remain a writer." A groundbreaking and foundation document of the modern women's movement, *Silences* deals with the ramifications and consequences of Olsen's determination to define herself as a "worker-mother-writer," and, as Atwood summarizes, "The exaction of this multiple identity cost Tillie Olsen 20 years of her writing life. The applause that greets her is not only for the quality of her artistic performance but, as at a grueling obstacle race, for the near miracle of her survival."

Olsen was born Tillie Lerner, in 1913, to Russian-Jewish immigrant parents in Nebraska. Both her parents had been involved in the 1905 Russian Revolution against the czar and had fled to America when the uprising failed. To support his family, Olsen's father worked as a farm worker, painter, paperhanger, candy maker, and packinghouse worker while maintaining his political commitment by serving as state secretary of the Nebraska Socialist Party. Educated through the eleventh grade in public schools in Omaha, Olsen read Rebecca Harding Davis's *Life in the Iron Mills* (1861) (*see* Honorable Mentions) as a teenager and was so impressed by its depiction of working-class life that Olsen vowed, as a youthful protagonist in an unpublished story proclaimed, "I shall write stories when I grow up, and not work in a factory." However, to supplement her family's income, Olsen left school early for work in a variety of menial jobs while becoming active in socialist politics. She was arrested, in 1931, for encouraging Kansas City packinghouse workers to unionize. By 1934, Olsen had moved to San Francisco and again was jailed for participating in the infamous Bloody Thursday Longshoreman's Strike of that year. In 1943, she married printer and union organizer Jack Olsen and raised their four daughters in a working-class section of San Francisco, supporting the family by taking jobs as a waitress, secretary, and laundress.

Having abandoned a novel about the Great Depression, *Yonnondio*, in 1937, Olsen did not take up writing again until the 1950s, when she enrolled in a writing class at San Francisco State University and won a Stanford University creative writing fellowship. She published the acclaimed short story, "I Stand Here Ironing," in 1956, followed by "Hey Sailor, What Ship?" in 1957. Both were collected with the title work to form the universally praised *Tell Me a Riddle*, in 1961, which established Olsen's reputation as one of the contemporary masters of short fiction.

Olsen's stories, expressed in a dialect-rich verisimilitude, focus on the perspectives of working-class characters, particularly women, whose stamina and endurance are tested under the constricting conditions of their unglamorous lives. As a mother of four children, forced for many years to work at low-paying jobs in addition to her ceaseless labor as a wife and mother, Olsen draws on her own experiences in her fiction to give voice to those whose lives and experiences have gone largely unrecorded. It is both the fate of her characters to be silenced by their circumstances and the near-fate of Olsen herself that she explores in *Silences*.

A miscellany of talks, essays, and excerpts, "garnered over fifty years, near a lifetime" in which the thought "came slow, hard-won," *Silences* opens with the title essay and its eloquent opening line: "Literary history and the present are dark with silences." Unlike natural silences—"that necessary time for renewal, lying fallow, gestation, in the natural cycle of creation"—the unnatural silences Olsen speaks of are the conditions that thwart literary creation, such as the economic conditions that silenced Herman Melville or the "censorship silences" that caused Thomas Hardy to abandon novel writing. The most tragic of these unnatural silences are all the "mute inglorious Miltons," individuals who may have had the genius but not the conditions necessary to enable them to produce literature. Members of the working class, condemned to the drudgery of subsistence, have been unable to express their lives creatively due to the conditions of their lives. "Substantial creative work demands time," Olsen asserts, "and with rare exceptions only full-time workers have achieved it. Where the claims of creation cannot be primary, the results are atrophy; unfinished work; minor effort and accomplishment; silences." Women face the additional burdens of motherhood and household responsibilities that restrict the time and autonomy necessary for creativity. To prove her point, Olsen notes that important nineteenth-century women writers—Jane Austen, Emily Brontë, Christina Rosetti, Emily Dickinson, or Louisa May Alcott— never married or had children. In the twentieth century, Olsen argues, most of the significant women writers still have not married or have remained childless. Almost no mothers have created enduring literature because, in Olsen's view, "More than in any other human relationship, overwhelmingly more, motherhood means being constantly interruptible, responsive, responsible," qualities antithetical to writing that requires "constant toil" rather than constant interruption. By class and gender restrictions, therefore, the working classes and women have been silenced.

Olsen next treats her own life and writing career to illustrate her point. "In the twenty years I bore and reared my children," she points out, "I usually had to work on a paid job as well, the simplest circumstances for creation did not exist." After her youngest entered school, Olsen squeezed time for her writing on the bus to her job, at night, during and after housework, trying to balance the impossible combination of "worker-mother-writer." "In such snatches of time I wrote what I did in those years, but there came a time when this triple life was no longer possible. The fifteen hours of daily realities became too much distraction for the writing. I lost craziness of endurance. . . . My work died. What demanded to be written, did not." Finally rescued by a grant to resume her work uninterrupted, Olsen writes, "This most harmful of all my silences has ended." As a survivor, Olsen closes with a warning that "we are in a time of more and more hidden and foreground silences, women *and* men."

The next essay in *Silences,* "One Out of Twelve: Writers Who Are Women in Our Century," considers why, even after considerable gains for women in the twentieth century, including "access to areas of work and of life previously denied; higher education; longer, stronger lives," women writers are accorded so little recognition and why there is only "one woman writer of achievement for every twelve men writers so ranked." The answer rests in a persistent gender bias in which women have been "excluded, excluded, excluded from council, ritual, activity, learning, language, when there was neither biological nor economic reason to be excluded." Olsen argues that all writers must be convinced of the importance of their ideas, and self-confidence, difficult for the working classes and for men not born into privilege, is "almost impossible for a girl, a woman." Women, moreover, are faced with the "sexist notion that the act of creation is not as inherently natural to a woman as to a man," and in the past have been forced to choose between artistic achievement and fulfillment as women. "More and more women writers in our century," Olsen observes, "primarily in the last two decades, are assuming as their right fullness of work *and* family life." Of this change she states, "I hope and fear for what will result. I hope (and believe) that complex new richness will come into literature; I fear because almost certainly their work will be impeded, lessened, partial. For the fundamental situation remains unchanged. Unlike men writers who marry, most will not have the societal equivalent of a wife—nor (in a society hostile to growing life) anyone but themselves to mother their children." Added to this central challenge faced by women writers is the persistent devaluation of women's achievement by a male-dominated critical establishment. Olsen argues that the solution to the imbalance between male and female writers of significance is to "read, listen to, living women writers; our new as well as our established, often neglected ones. . . . Read the compass of women writers in our infinite variety. . . . Teach women's lives through the lives of the women who wrote the books. . . . Be critical. Women have the right to say: this is surface, this falsifies reality, this degrades. . . . Help create writers, perhaps among them yourselves."

If the first essay of *Silences* deals with the factors that silence working class and women writers, and the second examines the ways to increase women's voices, the third essay, Olsen's afterword to Rebecca Harding Davis's *Life in the Iron Mills,* pays tribute to the life and achievement of a talented, influential, but neglected American woman writer who deserves to be heard. By treating Davis's career Olsen embodies and dramatizes her previous points about the circumstances that constrain women writers and the importance of Davis's perspective on aspects of women's lives that have often been overlooked. *Silences* concludes with quotations "selectively chosen for maximum significance" to illustrate her previously discussed themes. Dealing with the various forms of unnatural silences that have afflicted writers, both male and female, the section provides a valuable collection of commentary on the nature, pressures, and possibilities of breaking through the silences that have thwarted creative expression.

The impact of *Silences* has been significant. Written in the early days of the women's movement of the 1960s and 1970s, the book offered a new perspective on gender and creativity, and an empowerment of neglected perspectives. Not since Virginia Woolf's *A Room of One's Own* had a woman writer offered such a radical gender and class-based conceptualization of literary history and literary possibilities. Olsen's admonition to "teach books by women" has been answered by the increasing number of books by women now found in print and taught in college courses. New and neglected women writers, such as Rebecca Harding Davis, are silent no longer. *Silences* came at a decisive moment, articulating both the challenges and potential of the second wave of the women's movement. "Probably she is not the first," critic Annie Gottlieb has argued, "but to me Tillie Olsen *feels* like the first, both to extend 'universal' human experience to females and to dignify uniquely female experience as a source of human knowledge."

WOMEN, RACE & CLASS

by Angela Davis

An activist, scholar, educator, and one-time fugitive on the FBI's "Ten Most Wanted List," Angela Davis has lived a life in opposition, challenging the forces of social injustice wherever she has found them. Perhaps best remembered as a radical lightning rod of the 1960s and 1970s, the subject of "Free Angela" rallies around the world, Davis is also an important, influential social theoretician who has framed the debate over women's rights in daringly original and expansive contexts. One of the foundation texts of black feminist theory, Davis's *Women, Race & Class* (1981) explores the origins of the women's movement in America from the campaign to abolish slavery, and draws connections between sexism, racism, and classism in the subsequent battles over suffrage, equal rights, civil rights, and such contemporary issues as sexual assault and reproductive rights. As one critic has observed, the work "helped to establish the guidelines for critical analysis in current American feminist scholarship through its insistence on the investigation of the historically specific ways in which the inequalities of race, gender and class interact." It is a work that challenges preconceptions, overturns conventional understandings, and clears the ground for a new paradigm for un-

derstanding the complex, interconnected forces that must be opposed in any serious effort to redress inequities and foment radical change in women's lives.

Davis's experiences as a black woman and a radical during one
of the most turbulent periods in American history has clearly
shaped her works; a knowledge of these experiences provides the
understanding essential for appreciating her perspective and
achievement in *Women, Race & Class*. Born in 1944, in Birmingham,
Alabama, Davis grew up in the segregated Jim Crow south. Her
mother was an elementary schoolteacher, and her father owned a
service station. When she was four years old, her family moved
into a formerly all-white neighborhood that became known as
"Dynamite Hill," after white supremacists bombed so many of
the houses of newly arrived black families. Participating with her
mother at civil rights demonstrations in Birmingham, Davis spent
summers in New York City, where her mother studied to earn her
master's degree. Davis gained scholarships to attend a private
school in Greenwich Village and Brandeis University, where she
majored in French literature. While studying abroad in Paris,
Davis met students from Algeria and other African nations who
had grown up under colonial rule; she began an intellectual
search for a conceptual means to correlate her experiences with
the burgeoning civil rights movement in the United States during
the period and wider international historical and cultural developments. The key was provided by Brandeis's Marxist philosopher Herbert Marcuse, who became Davis's mentor. "*The
Communist Manifesto* hit me like a bolt of lightning," Davis remembered in her autobiography. "I read it avidly, finding in it answers to many of the seemingly unanswerable dilemmas which
had plagued me. . . . I began to see the problems of Black people
within the context of a large working-class movement. . . . What
struck me so emphatically was the idea that once the emancipation of the proletariat became a reality, the foundation was laid
for the emancipation of all oppressed groups in society."

After graduating from Brandeis, in 1965, Davis did graduate
work in philosophy at the University of Frankfurt and finished
her master's degree in philosophy under Marcuse at the
University of California, San Diego, in 1968. Around the same
time, Davis joined the Communist Party, the Student Nonviolent
Coordinating Committee (SNCC), and the Black Panthers. Even
among these radical groups, publicly committed to overthrowing

traditional power hierarchies, Davis experienced sexism from the predominately male leadership: "I was criticized very heavily, especially by male members . . . for doing a 'man's job,' " she recalled. "Women should not play leadership roles, they insisted." Hired as an assistant professor of philosophy at UCLA, in 1969, Davis was fired by California Governor Ronald Reagan and the Board of Regents after word leaked out that she was a communist. Faculty members and the university president overwhelmingly condemned the dismissal, and Davis was reinstated by court order. However, when her contract expired the following year she was dismissed again. As she was fighting to regain her job, Davis organized a nationwide effort to free three prison inmates, known as the Soledad Brothers, who had been falsely accused of killing a Soledad Prison guard. In August 1970, a brother of one of the Soledad Brothers, using firearms Davis had purchased to protect herself from death threats, mounted a rescue and hostage taking at the Marin County Courthouse. The attempt was foiled in a firefight that claimed four lives, including that of a county judge. A federal warrant was issued for Davis's arrest, and she went into hiding. After a two-month search, during which Davis was placed on the FBI's "Ten Most Wanted List, " she was apprehended in New York and extradited to California, where she was imprisoned for sixteen months. Prosecutors accused Davis of masterminding the attack. Davis insisted on her innocence, claiming that she was a retaliatory target as a result of her political activism. Demonstrations of support took place around the world, and "Free Angela" buttons, bumper stickers, and billboards established a slogan that came to represent the plight of political prisoners worldwide. In 1972, after deliberating for thirteen hours, a jury of eleven whites and one Mexican American acquitted Davis on the three charges of murder, kidnapping, and conspiracy. Davis responded with a national lecture tour and her *Autobiography*, which appeared in 1974. Looking back on her time in jail and her trial, Davis has remarked, "That period was pivotal for me in many respects. I came to understand much more concretely many of the realities of the Black struggle of that period." Davis would embody her realizations into the call for a total reassessment of attitudes on race, class, and gender that she synthesized in *Women, Race & Class*.

Organized in a series of thirteen chapters that survey American history from slavery through modern times, *Women, Race & Class* offers an alternative and iconoclastic view of the intersection of race, class, and gender, which challenges standard versions and forces a reassessment of racism, classism, and sexism in America. Davis begins with a powerful account of slavery that contradicts the stereotype of most black women slaves as domestic servants. Davis shows instead that virtually all black women under slavery were field hands who worked side by side with men. Their experiences, in Davis's view, create a new paradigm for working women in America in which African-American women slaves "passed on to their nominally free female descendants a legacy of hard work, perseverance and self-reliance, a legacy of tenacity, resistance and insistence on sexual equality. . . ." She also skillfully draws the connection between the abolitionist movement and the burgeoning women's movement. The fight against slavery proved to be the training ground for the leaders of the women's rights movement such as Lucretia Mott, Elizabeth Cady Stanton, Susan B. Anthony, and others. However, Davis asserts that the solidarity and common cause between black liberation and women's liberation was short lived, undermined by racism and classism. Davis faults the framers of the landmark Declaration of Principles at the first Women's Rights Convention in Seneca Falls, in 1848, for ignoring "the circumstances of women outside the social class of the document's framers." Working women were not mentioned in the called-for reform in marriage, property law, and education, and black women were not in attendance at the convention.

Following the Civil War, the constitutional struggle to enfranchise black males widened the rift between race and gender among reformers, exposing the underlying racism of many women's rights leaders. Susan B. Anthony, for example, Davis points out, readily sought the support of southern white supremacists on behalf of the woman suffrage cause. While Elizabeth Cady Stanton, feeling resentful and betrayed by the enfranchising of black males over white women, is quoted declaring, "The representative women of the nation have done their uttermost for the last thirty years to secure freedom for the negro; . . . but now, as the celestial gate to civil rights is slowly moving on its hinges, it becomes a serious question whether we had better stand aside and see 'Sambo' walk into the kitchen first. . . . Are we so sure that he, once entrenched in all his inalienable rights, may not be an added power to hold us at bay?" Davis documents from many additional historical sources other instances of the racism that divided the movement for equal rights and the class bias that caused the early women's movement to ignore the plight of working women. Black women, in particular, she asserts, were left to struggle on their own, triply oppressed by their class, race, and gender.

For many in the women's movement of the nineteenth and early twentieth centuries, suffrage was the ultimate goal upon which women's liberation depended. Davis, however, makes clear that the vote was insufficient to resolve the oppression of workers, blacks, or women in America, and the nexus among race, gender, and class continues to qualify and complicate contemporary social justice issues. After a chapter on "Communist Women," which Davis devotes to profiles of neglected and forgotten women socialist reformers, *Woman, Race & Class* sets in perspective some contemporary social issues: rape, reproductive rights, and "women's work." In Davis's view, consideration of rape continues to rely on the myth of the black rapist; she argues that "the notion is accepted that Black men harbor irresistible and animal-like sexual urges, the entire race is invested with bestiality." In documenting the pervasiveness of this notion and its use to justify racial injustice, Davis asserts, "Racism has always served as a provocation to rape, and white women in the United States have necessarily suffered the ricochet fire of these attacks. This is one of the many ways in which racism nourishes sexism, causing white women to be indirectly victimized by the special oppression aimed at their sisters of color." Davis points out that the passage of the 1977 Hyde Amendment, mandating the withdrawal of federal funding for abortions, restricted reproductive rights on the basis of class privilege. "Black, Puerto Rican, Chicana and Native American Indian women, together with their impoverished white sisters, were thus effectively divested of their right to legal abortions." With class and race complicating the issue of reproductive rights, Davis suggests, "The abortion rights activists of the early 1970s should have examined the history of their movement. Had they done so, they might have understood why so many of their Black sisters adopted a posture of suspicion toward their cause. They might have understood how important it was to undo the racist deeds of their predecessors, who had advocated birth control as well as compulsory sterilization as a means of eliminating the 'unfit' sectors of the population." Davis concludes with a consideration of housework, childcare, and the economic and social factors that have continued to assign woman the role of "man's eternal servant," women being the "guardians of a devalued domestic life." Davis urges that housework should be "industrialized" and shifted from the private to the public sector. "For Black women today and for all their working-class sisters," she asserts, "the notion that the burden of housework and child care can be shifted from their shoulders to the society contains one of the radical secrets of women's liberation. Child care should be socialized, meal preparation should be socialized, housework should be industrialized—and all these services should be readily accessible to working-class people."

Although Davis can be charged with an overreliance on now-devalued communist theory to frame many of her arguments and solutions, *Woman, Race & Class* retains its importance and relevance in its repeated calls for inclusiveness in addressing issues of social justice, for a truly united black and women's liberation, and for a widened understanding of the complex interactions of race, class, and gender.

THE HOUSE OF THE SPIRITS

byIsabel Allende

It can be argued that the most distinctive, enduring methods and achievements of the novel in the second half of the twentieth century have been made by Latin American writers, beginning with Gabriel García Márquez's groundbreaking novel *One Hundred Years of Solitude*, published in 1967. It caused, in the words of fellow novelist Mario Vargas Llosa, "a literary earthquake in Latin America," the reverberations of which stunned the world. As critics in Europe and North America were lamenting the death of the novel in the face of the declining energy of literary modernism, García Márquez offered an invigorating renewal, synthesizing elements from Kafka, Joyce, Hemingway, Faulkner, and others from Hispanic oral and literary traditions with the novel's most basic resource—captivating storytelling. García Márquez fashioned an absorbing narrative that was simultaneously a family saga, historical chronicle, and universal symbolic myth. In combining everyday events with supernatural occurrences, he also pioneered the subsequently often imitated fictional technique of "magic realism." Among the writers who followed García Márquez's artistic lead, Isabel Allende became the first significant woman contributor to the so-called Boom of Latin American literature. Her remarkable first novel, *La casa de los espíritus* (1982), translated as *The House of the Spirits* (1985), established her distinctive voice and the reputation that would make her the best-known Latin American woman novelist, and perhaps the most widely read contemporary Latina writer in the world.

The House of the Spirits is an ambitious debut, weaving together family and national history derived from Allende's ancestors, background, and experiences. Allende was born in 1942, in Lima, Peru, where her father, a first cousin of the future socialist president of Chile Salvador Allende, was a Chilean diplomatic attaché. After her parents divorced when Isabel was two years old, she and her mother returned to Santiago and moved in with her maternal grandparents. They would serve as the models for the characters Esteban and Clara Trueba, and their home the central locale in *The House of the Spirits*. After her mother remarried, again to a diplomat, Allende accompanied her family on his assignments to Bolivia, Europe, and the Middle East. Returning to Chile when she was fifteen, Allende subsequently worked as a journalist, on television programs, and appeared in newsreels. She wrote a satirical column, "Los Impertinentes" (The Impertinents), for the radical women's magazine *Paula*, hosted a weekly television program, produced plays, and wrote short stories for children.

On September 13, 1973, Allende's life abruptly changed when her uncle and godfather, President Salvador Allende, was assassinated in a military coup, led by General Augusto Pinochet Ugarte, that toppled the elected socialist government and ushered in a period of brutal military repression. "I think I have divided my life [into] before that day and after that day," Allende would later recall. "In that moment, I realized that everything was possible—that violence was a dimension that was always around you." For the next fifteen months, at the risk of her own life, Allende assisted the victims of the Pinochet regime in escaping persecution, witnessing many of the events that she would later incorporate into her first novel. "Because of my work as a journalist," Allende wrote in an essay, in 1984, "I knew exactly what was happening in my country, I lived through it, and the dead, the tortured, the widows and orphans, left an unforgettable impression on my memory. The last chapters of *The House of the Spirits* narrate those events. They are based on what I saw and on the direct testimonies of those who lived through the brutal experience of the repression." In 1975, fearful that her life and family were in jeopardy, Allende left Chile for Caracas, Venezuela, with her husband and teenage children. Unable to resume her creative writing, she worked as a teacher and administrator before she was able to begin work as a reporter on one of Venezuela's leading newspapers.

The genesis for *The House of the Spirits* came in the form of a letter written to her nearly one-hundred-year-old dying grandfather, who had remained in Chile. "My grandfather thought people died only when you forget them," Allende observed. "I wanted to prove to him that I had forgotten nothing, that his spirit was going to live with us forever." Although the letter was never sent to her grandfather, who soon died, Allende's reclaiming her memories of her family and her country formed the core of her first novel. "When you lose everything, everything that is dear to you," she has written, "memory becomes more important." With *The House of the Spirits* Allende achieved "the recovery of those memories that were being blown by the wind, by the wind of exile."

Like García Márquez's *One Hundred Years of Solitude, The House of the Spirits* is a family saga with recognizable historical circumstances in an unnamed Latin American country. References to well-known incidents, however, such as the disastrous earthquake of 1933, the agrarian reforms of the 1960s, the election of Salvador Allende, and the death of poet Pablo Neruda, clearly locate the action of the novel in Chile. Both novels present a synthesis of realism and the uncanny, depicting characters caught between fact and fantasy, a world in which dreams, ghosts, and the irrational are grafted onto a panoramic documentation of modern Latin American history. However, Allende provides more than a worthy imitation of García Márquez's subject and technique. As reviewer Antony Beevor has perceptively observed, Allende has taken up García Márquez's genre "to flip it over." "The metaphorical house," Beevor argues, "the themes of time and power, the *machista* violence and the unstoppable merry-go-round of history: all of these are reworked and then examined from the other side—from a woman's perspective." Allende counters the male-dominated perspective of her fellow Latin American writers with, in the words of critic Bruce Allen, "an original feminist argument that suggests women's monopoly on powers that oppose the violent 'paternalism' from which countries like Chile continue to suffer." If historical fiction traditionally focuses on male protagonists and major events, *The House of the Spirits* redirects attention to the story of women's seemingly mundane lives and their transformative, heroic capacities. *The House of the Spirits* thereby deconstructs the traditionally dominating patriarchy of Latin American culture and substitutes a powerful, alternative female ethos in which recent Latin American history can be reimagined from a new visionary perspective.

Dedicated to her mother, grandmother, and "all the other extraordinary women of this story," *The House of the Spirits* reflects Chilean history during the first three-quarters of the twentieth century from the vantage point of four generations of women in the del Valle/Trueba family. Beginning with feminist matriarch Nívea del Valle, the novel concentrates on her descendents, Clara, Blanca, and Alba Trueba, the wife, daughter, and granddaughter of the domineering family patriarch Esteban Trueba. He is a self-made man who ruthlessly acquires land, wealth, and political power and combines both the character strengths and weaknesses that Allende shows as characterizing Latin American patriarchal society. Each of the extraordinary del Valle/Trueba women counterpoint and challenge his values, while his brutal, violent behavior, fear of change, and hypocritical double standard indirectly leads to his downfall.

Following the poisoning death of Nívea del Valle's beautiful daughter Rosa, Esteban, her fiancé, dedicates himself to restoring his family's estate, Tres Mariás, while Rosa's clairvoyant and telekinetic sister Clara begins a nine-year-long silence, which is broken only when she announces that she will marry Esteban. Clara's uncanny sensitivity and empathy helps to humanize the driven Esteban, who has become the archetypal *patrón*, a feudal lord who determines his peasants' lives and rapes and impregnates the young women on his estate. After Esteban and Clara's daughter Blanca falls in love with Pedro Tercero García, the son of the estate's foreman, and Esteban learns of the affair, he strikes Clara, who has pleaded on behalf of the young couples' love. Clara responds to his action by leaving Tres Mariás for her parents' home, vowing never to speak to her husband again. As Esteban successfully pursues a political career as a conservative senator, Blanca gives birth to Pedro Tercero's child, Alba. After

Clara dies, when her granddaughter is seven, Esteban concentrates on his beloved granddaughter's upbringing amid the growing political turmoil that challenges his reactionary views. Blanca resumes her relationship with Pedro Tercero, who has become a socialist revolutionary and political singer, while Alba becomes involved in student demonstrations on behalf of the insurgent populist movement that wins the national election despite the opposition of Esteban's conservative coalition of business interests, the military, the church, and CIA backing. Esteban supports the military coup that assassinates the new president and topples the elected government. He then is horrified by the political repression of the new regime and decides to help Blanca and Pedro Tercero leave the country. Alba is arrested and tortured by her grandfather's bastard son, Esteban Garciá, who has come to power under the coup. She is sustained by Clara's spirit, who urges her to counter her pain with the stories of her family and those of her ancestors. Released, a pregnant Alba forsakes vengeance and recrimination in the del Valle home of Nívea, Clara, and Blanca. Inspired by her grandmother's and mother's writings and her own memories, she reveals herself as the chronicler of her family's story, which becomes *The House of the Spirits*. Esteban dies in Alba's arms, invoking Clara's name and her spirit that has recalled him to his humanity:

> At first she was just a mysterious glow, but as my grandfather slowly lost the rage that had tormented him throughout his life, she appeared as she had been at her best, laughing with all her teeth and stirring up the other spirits as she sailed through the house. She also helped us write, and thanks to her presence Esteban Trueba was able to die happy, murmuring her name: Clara, clearest, clairvoyant.

Over the course of multiple life stories, *The House of the Spirits* has refracted Chilean history through the alternative perspective of the del Valle and Trueba women whose affirmation of love, spirit, and the future ultimately triumphs over the life-denying and destructive patriarchy typified by Latin American history and Esteban Trueba. The novel presents a series of strong women who oppose their male-dominated society with a visionary willfulness. Nívea del Valle fights for women's suffrage; Clara opposes her husband's dominance with a mystical sense of life's harmonies;

both Blanca and Alba break from the narrow and self-serving assumptions of their class and gender to embrace the greater good and liberating possibilities. *The House of the Spirits* supplies a moving and compelling treatment of female empowerment that opposes a cycle of violence and repression with cathartic and healing transcendence.

BELOVED

by Toni Morrison

One of the most emotionally compelling and intellectually complex treatments of the legacy of slavery ever explored in fiction, *Beloved* (1987) is thus far Toni Morrison's most ambitious and most fully realized novel, a masterpiece of almost unbearable power and seemingly inexhaustible cultural and psychological relevance. In this remarkable attempt to come to terms with the enormity of slavery and the American past, racial, personal, and national history comes together in an essential myth that probes a collective scar and suggests how healing can begin.

Beloved is Toni Morrison's fifth novel. She had published her first novel, *The Bluest Eye*, in 1970, when she was thirty-nine and had been working as a senior book editor at Random House since 1967. She had previously taught English courses at Texas Southern University and Howard University, where she had received her undergraduate degree in 1953; after graduation, she went on to obtain a master's degree from Cornell University. *The Bluest Eye*, a lyrical exploration of racial and gender identity, was followed by *Sula* (1974). Both novels were critically praised for their poetic prose, emotional intensity, and unique interpretation of African-American experience from the largely neglected woman's perspective. Neither book was a popular success and both novels were out of print when Morrison published *Song of Solomon* (1977), the breakthrough novel that established her reputation as a dominant voice in contemporary fiction worldwide. With *Song of Solomon*, Morrison extended her range, employing a male protagonist for the first time, Milkman Dead, whom critic Margaret Wade-Lewis has called "undoubtedly one of the most effective renderings of a male character by a woman writer in American literature." His quest to find a family legacy and to decipher his racial identity is a complex and resonant interweaving of myth and history that draws on black folklore, oral tradition, and classical archetypes. This expansiveness is continued in her next novel, *Tar Baby* (1981), in which Morrison continues an imaginative search for identity in the confrontation between blacks and whites, along with her characteristic fusion of realism with fantasy derived from the black American folktale, both of which are placed in a global setting that encompasses the entire African diaspora.

Tar Baby was a best-seller and prompted *Newsweek* to do a cover story on the writer. Ironically, Morrison felt at the time that her writing days were over. "I would not write another novel to either make a living or because I was able to," she later recalled. "If it was not an overwhelming compulsion or I didn't feel absolutely driven by the ideas I wanted to explore, I wouldn't do it. And I was content not to ever be driven that way again." The compulsion came reluctantly as Morrison began to confront the legacy of slavery, a subject obscured, in Morrison's words, by a "national amnesia." *Beloved* would become the deliberate act of reconstructing what has been forgotten, which the author defined as "a journey to a site to see what remains have been left behind and to reconstruct the world that these remains imply." In an act of bearing witness, of giving voice to the unspeakable, Morrison set out "to fill in the blanks that the slave narrative left," to "part the veil that was frequently drawn," in which the full ramifications of the slave experience could be probed, and its costs embodied in psychological, emotional, social, and cultural terms.

The inspiration for her story came from Morrison's editorial work on Middleton Harris's documentary collection of black life in America, *The Black Book*. Morrison became fascinated by a historical incident from a newspaper clipping contained in Harris's collection entitled "A Visit to the Slave Mother Who Killed Her Child." It concerns a journalist's report on a runaway slave from Kentucky, Margaret Garner, who, in 1855, tried to kill her children rather than allow them to be returned to slavery. Successful in killing one, Margaret Garner would provide the historical access point for Beloved, allowing Morrison to explore in fiction the conditions that could have led to such a horrific act and its consequences to the survivors.

Narrated in a series of flashbacks, assembled gradually from the limited perspective of its characters, *Beloved* opens in 1873, eighteen years after the defining trauma in the life of Sethe—a former slave on a Kentucky farm called Sweet Home. Sethe lives in an isolated house outside Cincinnati with her eighteen-year-old daughter, Denver, and the ghost of Sethe's dead baby girl, named by the inscription on her tombstone, "Beloved." The novel's present during the Reconstruction period is symbolically appropriate for a novel that will concern the search for wholeness, the effort to rebuild an identity, a family, and a community from one that has been shattered by the enormous human wastage and dehumanization of slavery. A clear chronology of events in Sethe's life emerges only eventually as numerous characters—Sethe's mother-in-law, Baby Suggs, the black river man Stamp Paid, and Sethe's fellow slave, Paul D., the last of the Sweet Home Men, and others—allow their experiences to be revealed, painfully, through the curtain of protective repression.

In 1848, the teenage Sethe is sold to Mr. Garner at Sweet Home as the replacement for Baby Suggs, whose freedom has been purchased by her son Halle, whom Sethe marries. When Mr. Garner dies, in 1853, the farm is placed in the hands of an overseer called "Schoolteacher," who transforms Mr. Garner's more benign regime with a brutal and calculated indifference to the humanity of the Sweet Home slaves. When one is sold, the rest plot their escape. On the eve of departure, the pregnant Sethe is attacked by Schoolteacher's two nephews. As one holds her down, the other submits her to "mammary rape," sucking the milk from her breasts. Unknown to Sethe, this violation is witnessed by Halle, who is incapable of assisting his wife. The event leads to his derangement and disappearance. Sethe sends her three children to join the emancipated Baby Suggs in Ohio and eventually reaches freedom there herself after giving birth to her daughter, Denver. The four other Sweet Home men are either brutally killed or imprisoned. Sethe enjoys only twenty-eight days of freedom before Schoolteacher arrives to take her back. Rather than allowing her children to be returned to slavery, Sethe tries to kill them. Three children are saved from death, but Sethe cuts Beloved's throat. Arrested and sentenced to hang, Sethe is pardoned due to the intervention of abolitionists and allowed to return to Baby Suggs's home at 124 Bluestone Road in Cincinnati, where she is shunned by the black community. The vengeful spirit of her murdered child also takes up residence, drives away Sethe's two sons, contributes to Baby Suggs's death after she despairingly retreats to her bed, and holds Sethe and Denver in her spell until the arrival, in 1873, of Paul D.

Paul D is able to expel the ghost, temporarily breaking the hold of debilitating grief and despair that has condemned Sethe and Denver to seclusion. Paul D offers the possibility of family and future, but neither he nor Sethe is truly ready to put the past behind them. As if to insist that both must confront that past, the ghost returns in bodily form as a young woman the age Beloved would have been had she survived, and she claims sanctuary. A sinister presence, Beloved's voracious obsession with food and Sethe's love splits the developing family apart. The revelation that Sethe has killed her daughter shocks Paul D and drives him away, leaving Beloved to claim complete dominance over Sethe as the physical embodiment of her uneasy conscience. Increasingly obsessed with righting the wrong to Beloved that cannot be corrected, Sethe loses her job as a cook and drops all contact with the outside world. Neglected and starving, Denver is forced to reach out to the larger community for assistance, an act that finally will break the hold Beloved has over Sethe. As the black women of the community who had previously ostracized Sethe for her murder now come to her assistance, a version of Schoolteacher's arrival at the house at 124 Bluestone is reenacted: the elderly Mr. Bodwin, who had gained Sethe's pardon in 1855, is mistaken by the deranged Sethe as a slave catcher. She is prevented from stabbing him with an ice pick, but her climactic gesture of striking out, not at the victims of slavery in her earlier assault on her children but at its presumed agent, does cause Beloved to vanish; it prepares the way for the novel's concluding reconciliation and affirmation. Sethe at first despairs at losing her child yet again, but her complete breakdown and retreat from life, following the previous example of Baby Suggs, is halted by the return of Paul D, whose acceptance of Sethe and the past asserts Sethe's ability to face the future. Contrary to Sethe's belief that her children were her "best things," that her all-encompassing love was the essential justification for her to kill them rather than allow them to be returned to slavery, Paul D insists, "You your best thing, Sethe. You are." The revelation he offers Sethe suggests that the past need not tyrannize but must be fully confronted, with wholeness being the result of self-respect *and* selflessness, of individual autonomy and participation in a sustaining wider human community.

Morrison was awarded the Pulitzer Prize for *Beloved*, 1988, and it is considered her masterpiece. In the novel Morrison buried a repressed, traumatizing past and then allowed it only gradually to emerge in disjointed, lethal images. In a present haunted by the past, a spirit from the host of the anonymous dead magically appears and compels an exorcism. Morrison's protagonists are left to celebrate their resilience and survival, yet what remains unresolved are the effects of the systematic cruelty and devastation of slavery upon the black community. In a work of shattering emotional intensity and historical synthesis Morrison has crafted one of the essential novels of the second half of the twentieth century.

THE SHAWL

by Cynthia Ozick

Dealing almost exclusively with the challenges faced by Jews in the modern world, Cynthia Ozick has turned her subject into a profound and universal exploration of the struggle for spiritual survival and affirmation in the face of seemingly insurmountable obstacles. Critic Diane Cole has asserted, "Few contemporary authors have demonstrated her range, knowledge, or passion," while Elaine M. Kauvar has described Ozick as a "master of the meticulous sentence and champion of the moral sense of art." The author of four novels—*Trust* (1966), *The Cannibal Galaxy* (1983), *The Messiah of Stockholm* (1987), and *The Puttermesser Papers* (1997)—Ozick has gained perhaps her most acclaim for her short fiction, collected in such volumes as *The Pagan Rabbi* (1971), *Bloodshed and Three Novellas* (1976), and *Levitation: Five Fictions* (1982). As critic Carol Horn has observed, "Her stories are elusive, mysterious, and disturbing. They shimmer with intelligence, they glory in language, and they puzzle." Two of her greatest achievements are the harrowing "The Shawl" and its sequel, the novella, *Rosa*, collected in the volume *The Shawl*, published in 1989. There are few better imaginings of the impact of the Holocaust or more striking introductions to this important writer's work.

Ozick was born in New York City, in 1928. Her parents, Russian-Jewish immigrants, were the owners of the Park View Pharmacy in the Pelham Bay section of the Bronx, where Ozick helped out by delivering prescriptions. At age five, Ozick was taken to Hebrew school by her grandmother, who was told by the rabbi not to bring her back because "a girl doesn't have to study." Ozick later traced the origins of her feminism to this experience and has expressed gratitude to her grandmother who rejected the rabbi's order and insisted that her granddaughter be allowed to stay in his class. Ozick would subsequently impress the rabbi with her "golden head," which quickly mastered her lessons. Attending public school in the Bronx, Ozick found it "brutally difficult to be a Jew" there; she remembers having stones thrown at her, being called a Christ-killer, and being publicly humiliated for refusing to sing Christmas carols. She excelled academically, however, at the all-girl Hunter College High School in Manhattan, where she mastered Latin poetry. She graduated from New York University, in 1949, and received a master's degree from Ohio State University, in 1950, writing a thesis entitled "Parable in the Later Novels of Henry James." Although Ozick has stated that her decision to become a writer dates "from the first moment of sentience," it was with her discovery of Henry James at the age of seventeen that she received the calling "to serve as a priest at the altar of literature."

In 1952, she married Bernard Hallote, an attorney. After a year in Boston, where Ozick worked as a department store copywriter, the couple moved into her parents' home in the Bronx. Ozick, using her childhood bedroom as a study, worked for a number of years on an ambitious philosophical novel called *Mercy, Pity, Peace, and Love,* which echoed James's *The Ambassadors.* She finally abandoned it and devoted seven years, from 1957 to 1963, to what would be her first published novel, *Trust*—a nuanced exploration of identity and self-discovery through the search for a biological father; in it Ozick's own unique voice and subjects began to emerge from the influences of James, E.M. Forster, and F. Scott Fitzgerald. "In writing *Trust*," Ozick has stated, "I began as an American novelist and ended as a Jewish novelist. I Judaized myself as I wrote it." She would evolve through her first novel the repeated theme that would dominate her subsequent work: the opposing claims of two dominating impulses, the pagan and the holy. As writer Eve Ottenberg has observed, Ozick's "characters struggle, suffer, perform bizarre feats, even go mad as a result of remaining or finding out what it means to remain—culturally, and above all, religiously—Jewish. . . . Her characters are often tempted into worshiping something other than God—namely, idols. And this struggle marks her characters with a singular aloneness—the aloneness of people who are thinking a great deal about who they are, and for whom thinking, not doing, is the most emotional and engaging aspect of their lives."

Ottenberg's characterization of the moral dynamic of Ozick's fictional universe is helpful for an understanding of *The Shawl*, which crystallizes many of Ozick's themes of Jewish identity, idolatry, isolation and community, and the crippling impact of the past. Both the story and the novella in it center on Rosa Lublin, a Polish Holocaust survivor who, in "The Shawl," witnesses the death of her baby daughter, Magda, in a Nazi concentration camp. Rosa's story is resumed thirty-five years later in *Rosa*. Now living in Miami, still unable to face the fact of her daughter's brutal murder, Rosa struggles to come to grips with her past and her present, providing the reader with an intimate and illuminating exploration of a psyche still haunted by a horrific experience, as she fights to cope with the costs and consequences of her memories.

Only eight pages long, "The Shawl" is one of the most powerful attempts to depict the horrors of the Holocaust in literature. On the march to a concentration camp, Rosa, accompanied by her teenage niece Stella, attempts to protect her infant daughter Magda by hiding her in her shawl. The shawl serves both as a protection for Magda, concealing her from the view of the Nazis, and as a pacifier, which the baby sucks after Rosa's milk dries up, silencing the cries that might give her away. After arriving in the camp, Rosa hears Magda's cry as she crawls, shawless, on the ground outside. Rosa runs back into the barracks to retrieve the comforting shawl to stifle Magda's cries and discovers that Stella has taken the baby's shawl to keep from freezing. Rosa seizes the shawl, hurries back to Magda, but it is too late. A German officer has picked up the baby and is headed to the electrified fence. Rosa's maternal instinct to save her child battles with her instinct for self-preservation, aware that she will be shot if she screams. As Magda is flung against the electrified fence to her death, Rosa stifles her cries by stuffing the shawl into her mouth:

All at once Magda was swimming through the air. The whole of
Magda traveled through loftiness. She looked like a butterfly
touching a silver vine. And the moment Magda's feathered round
head and her pencil legs and balloonish belly and zigzag arms
splashed against the fence, the steel voices went mad in their
growling, urging Rosa to run and run to the spot where Magda
had fallen from her flight against the electrified fence; but of
course Rosa did not obey them. She only stood, because if she ran
they would shoot, and if she tried to pick up the sticks of Magda's
body they would shoot, and if she let the wolf's screech ascending
now through the ladder of her skeleton break out, they would
shoot; so she took Magda's shawl and filled her own mouth with it,
stuffed it in and stuffed it in, until she was swallowing up the wolf's
screech and tasting the cinnamon and almond depth of Magda's
saliva, and Rosa drank Magda's shawl until it dried.

In language that is as precise as it is poetic, Ozick captures the
unimaginable horror of the Holocaust with a focus on the crippling paralysis and contradictions of the survivors.

To penetrate what Elie Wiesel has called "Rosa's dark and devastated soul," Ozick revisits her protagonist in *Rosa* some thirty-
five years later. Rosa and Stella have survived the camps and
made it to America, where Rosa operates an antique shop in New
York. Refusing to accept her daughter's death, Rosa creates a
bright future for Magda in her mind while turning the shawl that
protected her into a kind of holy relic, a means to evade the awful
truth of her experience. Infuriated when her customers show no
interest in the story of Jewish suffering she feels compelled to re-
count to them, unable and unwilling to adapt to life after her
traumatic experience, Rosa smashes up her store. Stella arranges
for her aunt's relocation to Miami Beach, where she lives in a
rundown retirement hotel. Resembling a "madwoman and a
scavenger," Rosa is disengaged from the life around her, rarely
venturing outside her tiny room, spending her time writing long
letters to her niece and to Magda, whom she imagines enjoying a
happy, productive life. She has requested that Stella send her the
shawl, and her niece responds: "Your idol is on its way. . . . Go on
your knees to it if you want. . . . You'll open the box and take it
out and cry, you'll kiss it like a crazy person. Make holes in it with
kisses. You're like those people in the Middle Ages who worshipped a piece of the True Cross, a splinter from some old out-
house. . . ." Like so many of Ozick's characters, Rosa copes with

reality as an idol worshiper, substituting a more pleasing or necessary myth for the truth.

On the day that *Rosa* begins, her routine and her increasing retreat into isolated fantasy is halted when she meets at the laundromat an old man with false teeth, a red wig, and a Polish accent. He introduces himself as Simon Persky, "a third cousin to Shimon Peres, the Israeli politician." Unlike Rosa's indifferent customers in New York, Persky is fascinated by Rosa's story and sympathetically claims kinship with her. Like her, Persky is a native of Warsaw, and he exposes the prejudices Rosa has long had about her Jewish identity. Rosa had been raised by assimilated Polish Jews, and everything about Persky—from the Yiddish paper he read, to his heavy accent, to what she imagines is the stink of the Warsaw ghetto that he must have inhabited—are objectionable characteristics she has rejected. However, in a series of ironically achieved insights, Rosa begins to see herself more clearly in Persky's reflection, including her own inadequate English, unkempt appearance, and old woman's odors. It is a shock of self-recognition that helps to break the spell of the past that has robbed Rosa of a present and future. When Magda's shawl arrives from Stella, its power as a relic that has imprisoned Rosa is broken. It is finally seen for what it is, a "colorless cloth" with "a faint saliva smell." As Rosa admits Persky to her room, and presumably to her reengaged life, the story concludes with an acknowledgement that the child who has haunted Rosa has finally been put to rest: "Magda was not there. Shy, she ran from Persky. Magda was away."

Rosa's recovery of herself in Ozick's view begins with facing the truth and accepting it in all its contradictions and ambiguities. Looking deeply beneath the exterior of a "madwoman and a scavenger," Ozick has uncovered an extraordinary character trying to cope with the unspeakable, unrelenting realities of modern existence. Ozick's remarkable volume justifies Elie Wiesel's description of *The Shawl* as "dazzling and staggering pages filled with sadness and truth."

BACKLASH

by Susan Faludi

Susan Faludi's *Backlash: The Undeclared War Against American Women* (1991) sets out to expose a troubling anomaly: why is it that, in the 1980s, after American women's apparent victories in the fight for equality, "another message flashes. You may be free and equal now, it says to women, but you have never been more miserable." Faludi identifies a persistent, media-driven "counterassault on women's rights, a backlash, an attempt to retract the handful of small and hard-won victories that the feminist movement did manage to achieve for women. This counterassault is largely insidious: in a kind of pop-culture version of the Big Lie, it stands the truth boldly on its head and proclaims that the very steps that have elevated women's position have actually led to their downfall." A controversial bestseller, *Backlash* has evoked comparisons with Simone de Beauvoir's *The Second Sex* and Betty Friedan's *The Feminine Mystique* as "feminism's new manifesto" in which, in the words of reviewer Laura Shapiro of *Newsweek*, "Once you've read this hair-raising but meticulously documented analysis, you may never read a magazine or see a movie or walk through a department store the same way again." The book made Faludi a sought-after guest on talk shows and a feminist spokesperson, though she rejected her elevation "as a sort of seer," preferring her role as a reporter and emphasizing the importance of her book as investigative journalism that corrects damaging falsifications. "To the extent that *Backlash* arms women with information and a good dose of cynicism," Faludi has asserted, "I think it will have served its purpose." She adds a secondary use for *Backlash*: "It's also very large, so it can be thrown at misogynists."

Susan Faludi was born in 1959, in New York City, the daughter of photographer Steven Faludi and Marilyn Faludi, a dynamic and outspoken woman who gave up her career ambitions to become a traditional housewife until she divorced her husband, in 1976. Faludi, who dedicated *Backlash* to her mother, has credited her mother's frustrations with her husband's "old-world belief that women should stay home, be decorative, make elaborate meals, and do all the traditional duties of wifedom," with teaching her about the circumscribed lives of women. "My mother has been cheated," she has said, "and the world's been cheated of her talents." Faludi's interest in journalism and her willingness to court controversy began in high school, when she surveyed her classmates on such hot-button topics as the Vietnam War, abortion, and the Equal Rights Amendment; for this she was accused of having "incited communism." As managing editor of the *Harvard Crimson*, Faludi reported on sexual harassment on campus, implicating a Harvard professor. Despite pressure from the professor and the administration to abandon the story, Faludi refused to back down, and the professor was eventually forced to take a leave of absence.

Faludi's first job after college was as a copy clerk for *The New York Times*, where her efforts to rise up in the ranks were rebuffed by a male reporter who told her that, because women were able to carry a baby for nine months, they were "biologically more patient," and she should defer to the more urgent need of male ambition. Faludi left *The Times*, in 1982, for a job with *The Miami Herald* and then a general reporting position at *The Atlanta Journal-Constitution*. After moving to the California, in 1985, Faludi worked for *West*, the Sunday magazine of the *San Jose Mercury News*, and, in 1990, became a staff writer for the San Francisco bureau of *The Wall Street Journal*. She wrote on how President Ronald Reagan's budget cuts impacted poor children and how companies in California's Silicon Valley were replacing older employees with younger, more cost-effective workers. In 1991, she won the Pulitzer Prize for her investigative reporting on the human cost of the $5.65 billion leveraged buyout of the Safeway Stores.

The genesis of *Backlash* began with Faludi's reaction to a 1986 study, featured as a cover story in *Newsweek,* that had been conducted by a research team from Harvard and Yale; it claimed that college-educated women at age thirty had only a twenty percent chance of getting married; by age thirty-five, the study found, their chances dropped to only five percent, and by age forty, the study asserted, a woman was "more likely to be killed by a terrorist" than find a husband. This so-called "marriage crunch" among women who had put off marriage for careers was widely reported, and its conclusion accepted that women would be wise to set aside their careers in favor of a quest for marriage. "What was remarkable to me," Faludi recalled, "was that there was so little interest in finding out whether the study was true or false. The story simply fit the notion of where women were at that point in history." Faludi investigated and discovered that the methodology used to generate the marriage study was flawed, and the study's unrepresentative sampling suggested that the report's conclusions were suspect. Despite contrary evidence, the myth of the marriage crunch and the warning to career women had taken hold. *Backlash* was written during an eighteen-month leave from Faludi's reporting assignments. During her leave she investigated the accuracy of other widely reported trend stories about women's status in the 1980s, including accounts of professional women leaving the workforce in large numbers to care for their homes and children, and increasing instances of single career women suffering from depression, nervous breakdown, and burnout. Faludi concluded that these were misrepresentations and misinterpretations, instances of a larger trend to discredit the women's movement. Faludi called these anti-liberation myths about single and working women are "the chisels of a society-wide backlash. They are part of a relentless whittling-down process—much of it amounting to outright propaganda—that has served to stir women's private anxieties and break their political wills." Describing her book's title, Faludi explains that

> *Backlash* happens to be a title of a 1947 Hollywood movie in which a man frames his wife for a murder he's committed. The backlash

against women's rights works in much the same way: its rhetoric charges feminists with all the crimes it perpetrates. The backlash line blames the women's movement for the "feminization of poverty"—while the backlash's own instigators in Washington pushed through the budget cuts that helped impoverish millions of women, fought pay equity proposals, and undermined equal opportunity laws. The backlash line claims the women's movement cares nothing for children's rights—while its own representatives in the capital and state legislatures have blocked one bill after another to improve child care, slashed bullions of dollars in federal aid for children, and relaxed state licensing standards for day care centers. The backlash line accuses the women's movement of creating a generation of unhappy single and childless women—but its purveyors in the media are the ones guilty of making single and childless women feel like circus freaks.

Backlash supplies a compendium of examples of the ways in which an attack on the women's movement and its achievements has been perpetuated in print, on television, in the movies, by the fashion and cosmetic industries, and in national politics. Faludi shows how the media and politicians present women's liberation as the source of women's problems, by distorting the facts and perpetrating myths that undermine equality and autonomy for women. "The backlash is at once sophisticated and banal," Faludi concludes, "deceptively 'progressive' and proudly backward. It deploys both the 'new' findings of 'scientific research' and the dime-store moralism of yesteryear; it turns into media sound bites both the glib pronouncements of pop-psych trend-watchers and the frenzied rhetoric of New Right preachers. The backlash has succeeded in framing virtually the whole issue of women's rights in its own language. Just as Reaganism shifted political discourse far to the right and demonized liberals, so the backlash convinced the public that women's 'liberation' was the true contemporary American scourge—the source of an endless laundry list of personal, social, and economic problems."

Backlash is particularly insightful (and entertaining) on how the depiction of women in the media helps to undermine gains made by the women's movement—by reporting dubious trends like the flight of women from the workforce to a more fulfilling life as homemaker or the mythical 1980s "baby boom" spawned by a "terror" of infertility and anxiety over the ticking biological clock. As Faludi concludes, the press was "not only dictating to women how they should feel, but persuading them that the voice barking orders was only their uterus talking." The demonizing of the single career woman, and the apotheosis of the post-liberation housewife, are ably demonstrated by Faludi on television and the movies. Faludi insightfully details how one of the most popular films of the 1980s, *Fatal Attraction,* was transformed from a story of how a married man must take responsibility for destroying the life of a single woman with whom he has an affair to the pathology of a single woman who must be killed to save a traditional household. "In the end," Faludi observes, "the attraction is fatal only for the single woman."

Backlash also features profiles of a number of antifeminists, including George Gilder, author of *Wealth and Power* and a former speechwriter for President Reagan, Allen Bloom, the author of *The Closing of the American Mind,* a book that decries feminism's supposedly pernicious influence in higher education, Robert Bly, author of *Iron John* and a founder of the men's movement in the United States, Sylvia Ann Hewlett, author of *A Lesser Life: The Myth of Women's Liberation in America,* and Michael Levin, author of *Feminism and Freedom,* a work that denounces feminism as an "antidemocratic, if not totalitarian, ideology." As Gayle Greene observed in her review of *Backlash,* "Faludi must be a crackerjack interviewer, letting subjects babble on until they blurt out marvelously self-incriminating revelations, offering up the real reasons they hate and fear feminists—motives that are self-serving, silly, often sinister—which Faludi simply, deadpan, recounts."

Backlash counters the myths by showing how contemporary women's anxieties and frustrations stem not from too much freedom and equality but from too little. Contrary to the backlash myths, Faludi demonstrates that women must still struggle for equality in politics, the workplace, at school, and at home, the real cause for women's discontent. The average women college graduate, Faludi demonstrates, still earns less than the average man with a high school diploma, and American women "face the worst gender-based pay gap in the developed world." This is exacerbated by insufficient childcare and family-leave policies. Women, Faludi shows, "still shoulder 70 percent of the household duties. . . . Furthermore, in thirty states, it is still generally legal for husbands to rape their wives; and only ten states have laws mandating arrest for domestic violence—even though battering was the leading cause of injury of women in the late '80s." While some of the statistics have changed in the years since *Backlash* was published, the need for countering misleading myths with truth remains fundamental. Women still are bombarded by contrary messages about marriage, motherhood, and careers, as well as new obstacles to achieving social justice and equality. *Backlash* helps its reader understand the ways in which popular culture and politics work out agendas that must be understood and confronted.

THE BEAUTY MYTH

by Naomi Wolf

Named by *The New York Times* as one of the seventy most influential books of the twentieth century, and hailed as "a provocative new feminist tract which should take its place alongside such polemics as Betty Friedan's *The Feminist Mystique*," Naomi Wolf's *The Beauty Myth: How Images of Beauty Are Used Against Women* (1991) suggests that the feminine mystique, which defined women by their domestic role, has been succeeded by a beauty mystique that dictates that women must be slim, young, conventionally good-looking, and subservient to men. As Wolf argues, "We are in the midst of a violent backlash against feminism that uses images of female beauty as a political weapon against women's advancement." The beauty myth, which promulgates an unrealistic (and unhealthy) ideal of female beauty, is "undermining—slowly, imperceptibly, without our being aware of the real forces of erosion—the ground women have gained through the long, hard, honorable struggle," according to Wolf. She asserts that the beauty myth has been one of the fundamental means of social control for men to secure patriarchal dominance. "I contend that this obsession with beauty in the Western world . . . is, in fact, the last way men can defend themselves against women claiming power." She suggests that the beauty myth is destroying women physically and psychologically. It is responsible for the rise of eating disorders, an increase in unneeded and dangerous cosmetic surgery, a general decline in women's self-esteem, with envy and competition growing among women, as well as a morbid fear of aging, and the addition of a "third shift"—after career and domestic chores—to overwhelm women with pursuing beautification at the expense of gaining real social power and achieving gender equality. As a result of the beauty myth, "in terms of how we feel about ourselves physically," Wolf concludes, "we may actually be worse off than our unliberated grandmothers."

The Beauty Myth offers a powerful and challenging way to view the cultural coding of beauty and its impact on women, raising awareness and provoking positive social change. "What I've tried to do," Wolf explained in an interview, "is make an argument so powerful that by the end the reader either has to find a situation we take for granted intolerable and take steps to change it—or kill the messenger."

The messenger was born in 1962, the daughter of academic parents in San Francisco, who grew up, in her words, "as a baby of the counterculture." The Wolf family lived in the Haight-Ashbury neighborhood, the epicenter of the free-love and "flower power" upheavals of the 1960s. As Wolf recalled in her book *Promiscuities: The Secret Struggle for Womanhood* (1997), "The city made us feel that we were not alive if we were not being sexual." During her teens, Wolf became obsessed with her body image and developed anorexia. "Adolescent starvation," Wolf writes in *The Beauty Myth,* "was for me a prolonged reluctance to be born into woman if that meant assuming a station of beauty." Despite serious health problems, Wolf excelled academically and graduated from Yale University in 1984. She became a Rhodes scholar, studying English at Oxford University and working on a doctoral thesis that focused on male and female writers of the nineteenth and twentieth centuries and how they "used beauty differently." In it, she demonstrated that "male writers often used beauty not to illuminate, but to silence women characters." Wolf's literary research became personal when she overheard a colleague say that she had won her Rhodes scholarship because of her looks. "I had an image of the documents I had presented to the committee— my essay, book of poems I had written, letters of recommendation—and the whole of it being swept away by that one sentence," she recalled in a 1991 interview. Although she never completed her Oxford degree, Wolf extended her research into the culturally inscribed standards of female beauty and their consequences, turning her thesis into *The Beauty Myth,* which created a sensation when it was first published in England in 1990, and in the United States in 1991.

Widely reviewed and discussed, *The Beauty Myth* was praised for raising important points and offering a new perspective on the obstacles faced by women in achieving good self-esteem and empowerment. As Caryn James observed in a *New York Times* review, "No other work has so forcefully confronted the anti-feminism that emerged during the conservative, yuppified 1980's, or so honestly depicted the confusion of accomplished women who feel emotionally and physically tortured by the need to look like movie stars." The book was also attacked for making sweeping generalizations at the expense of more objective, careful documentation. Some critics complained that Wolf's conception of the beauty myth confused a symptom with a cause. Betty Friedan criticized Wolf for dealing with the superficial rather than coming to grips with the modern-day political and social challenges that confront women; while Diane Johnson commented that Wolf "ultimately attributes all social evils . . . to the frenzied thrashings of threatened manhood, and here it is possible that she has not cast her net wide enough." Ironically, confirming Wolf's thesis that beauty is often used to silence women, the author's own good looks were held against her by several of the book's critics. As writer Lynn Darling observed, "The book that Wolf saw as 'a tribute to women's beauty and power' became, in flip media shorthand, a beautiful woman's condemnation of other women's attempt to be beautiful." Wolf remained undaunted by the controversy *The Beauty Myth* generated, confidently insisting to an interviewer, "I'm trying to seize this culture by its collar and say 'Stop! Look what you're doing!' To the extent that people get angry, I know I've done a good job."

The Beauty Myth mounts its case by identifying the pressures women face to look beautiful, in which an impossible ideal of eternal, youthful beauty has replaced the prefeminist goal of perfect domestic bliss. Women have left the home for careers, but little has changed to replace physical perfection as women's true source of fulfillment and constant anxiety. "The closer women come to power," Wolf asserts, "the more physical self-consciousness and sacrifice are asked of them." She summarizes the persistence of the beauty myth to undermine female empowerment: "During the past decade, women breached the power structure; meanwhile, eating disorders rose exponentially and cosmetic surgery became the fastest-growing medical specialty. During the past five years, consumer spending doubled, pornography became the main media category . . . and thirty-three thousand American women told researchers that they would rather lose ten to fifteen pounds than achieve any other goal." The beauty myth originates, according to Wolf, from men whose power is threatened by feminist gains, and it is internalized by women because the myth "exploits female guilt and apprehension about our own liberation." As Wolf explains, "The beauty myth of the present is more insidious than any mystique of femininity yet: A century ago, Nora slammed the door of the doll's house; a generation ago, women turned their backs on the consumer heaven of the isolated multi-applianced home; but where women are trapped today, there is no door to slam. The contemporary ravages of the beauty backlash are destroying women physically and depleting us psychologically. If we are to free ourselves from the dead weight that has once again been made out of femaleness, it is not ballots or lobbyists or placards that women will need first; it is a new way to see."

Wolf proceeds to show how the beauty myth operates in the workforce and the marketplace, draining time, attention, and money from women to satisfy what Wolf labels a Professional Beauty Qualification (PBQ) that has been added to their career aspirations. "For every feminist action," Wolf observes, "there is an equal and opposite beauty myth reaction. In the 1980s it was evident that as women became more important, beauty too became more important. The closer women come to power, the more physical self-consciousness and sacrifice are asked of them. 'Beauty' becomes the condition for a woman to take the next step. You are now too rich. Therefore, you cannot be too thin." The beauty myth is enforced by cultural ideals that profit a $20 billion-a-year cosmetics industry, a $33 billion diet industry, and a $300 million cosmetic-surgery industry (75 percent of whose patients are women), and a $7 billion pornography industry. Wolf draws a connection between women's subjugation to the beauty myth and a cult psychology that gives over personal power in order to achieve an illusive promise of thinness, youth, and an approved standard of beauty. Women, in Wolf's view, are complicit in their own objectification to male dictates. "Placing female pleasure, sex or food or self-esteem into the hands of a personal judge turns the man into a legislator of the woman's pleasure, rather than her companion in it," Wolf contends. " 'Beauty' today is what the female orgasm used to be; something given to women by men, if they submitted to their feminine role and were lucky." Wolf measures the cost to women of subscribing to the beauty myth in the rise of eating disorders, in the growing popularity of expensive and often dangerous cosmetic surgery, and in the unreasonable percentage of women's earnings spent on dubious cosmetics, dieting products, and impractical clothing. All contribute not only to a physical but a psychological torment of women, who find themselves chasing an unrealistic and unrealizable phantom of perpetual, perfect beauty.

Wolf concludes *The Beauty Myth* with an alternative set of choices proceeding from the rejection of the beauty myth and the release of a "feminist third wave." We must, Wolf concludes, "dismantle the PBQ; support the unionization of women's jobs; make 'beauty' harassment, age discrimination, unsafe working conditions such as enforced surgery, and the double standard of appearance, issues for labor negotiation; women in television and other heavily discriminatory professions must organize for wave after wave of lawsuits; we must insist on equal enforcement of dress codes, take a deep breath, and tell our stories." Seeing the beauty myth for what it is, Wolf insists, will break its power and allow for a reinterpretation of beauty that is "noncompetitive, nonhierarchical, and nonviolent." To achieve this goal, Wolf urges women to "be shameless. Be greedy. Pursue pleasure. Avoid pain. Wear and touch and eat and drink what we feel like. Tolerate other women's choices. Seek out the sex we want and fight fiercely against the sex we do not want. Choose our own causes. And once we break through and change the rules so our senses of our own beauty cannot be shaken, sing that beauty and dress it up and flaunt it and revel in it: In a sensual politics, female is beautiful."

BRIDGET JONES'S DIARY

by Helen Fielding

Bridget Jones's Diary by Helen Fielding records the romantic, professional, and personal trials and tribulations of a bright, klutzy, often neurotic, thirty-something single woman. Sound familiar? From *Friends,* to *Ally McBeal,* to *Sex in the City* the single woman in the postfeminist world seems ubiquitous, dominating the new genres of "chick lit" and "chick flicks." *Bridget Jones's Diary* (published in England in 1996 and the United States in 1998), though not the first novel to tackle the subject of the "singleton," defined and set the standard for the form. One of the most popular novels of the 1990s, *Bridget Jones's Diary* became a cultural phenomenon, with its heroine proclaimed an iconic, hapless but endearing everywoman, and her creator praised for seizing the comic zeitgeist of postmodern courtship, lifestyles, and the self-actualizing rituals of the urban hip. *Bridget Jones's Diary* is a witty, hilarious survey of contemporary mores and mantras that allows its readers vicariously to court social and relationship disasters with Bridget while seeing themselves reflected in the exaggerated lens of her manias and obsessions. Bridget's missteps and consumer- and media-driven angst certainly make us laugh and, although it is always dangerous to dissect a joke or to belabor the search for meaning in a work that its creator has insisted was motivated strictly by a spirit of fun, can still claim intriguing cultural significance. As Elizabeth Glieck observed in *The New York Times*, "People will be passing around copies of *Bridget Jones's Diary* for a reason: It captures neatly the way modern women teeter between 'I am woman' independence and a pathetic girlie desire to be all things to all men." The novel takes as its subject the peculiarly modern phenomenon of the nontraditional single household and post–women's liberation gender identity, and finds its humor in the disjunction between the female ideal and lifestyle rewards Bridget strives for and actuality, between the conception of the modern superwoman—self-possessed, empowered, fulfilled in the bedroom, nursery, and boardroom—and the reality that turns seekers of feminine perfection like Bridget into train wrecks of needy, self-absorbed inadequacy. "Women today are bombarded with so many messages," Fielding has observed, "like we should have Naomi Campbell's body and Madeline Albright's career. Here's someone saying, 'I can't be all these things!' but trying anyway." Therein lies both the fun of *Bridget Jones's Diary* and its extraordinary resonance among readers. "Bridget is groping through the complexities of dealing with relationships in a morass of shifting roles," Fielding has observed, "and a bombardment of idealised images of modern womanhood. It seems she's not the only one who's confused."

Fielding has deflected the suggestion that her protagonist is based on herself by calling Bridget "an imaginary amalgam of insecurities," contrasting herself with the Chardonnay-drinking, nicotine-addled, relationship-deprived Bridget by stating, "I don't drink, I don't smoke and am a virgin . . . yeah, right!" There are in fact sufficient correspondences between creator and creation to see Bridget at least as an alter ego. Born in 1959, in Yorkshire, Fielding is the daughter of a mill manager and a homemaker. After graduating from Oxford University, in 1979, she worked for a decade as a producer for the BBC before becoming a freelance writer. Her first novel, *Cause Celeb* (1994), is based on her experiences producing the Comic Relief charity telethon on behalf of African famine relief for the BBC. In 1995, an editor for London's *Independent* newspaper, where she was working as a feature writer, approached her to provide a weekly column based on her life as a single professional woman. She instead opted for the anonymity of a fictional persona. "You can be so much more honest if it's not supposed to be your own life," Fielding has explained. "You can shamelessly detail exactly what goes on in the three hours between waking up and leaving for work late." *Bridget Jones's Diary* debuted on February 28, 1995. After the first few columns, she thought, "This is self-conscious, stupid, who wants to read this? Then people started to say they liked it, and, being, as my agent says, as shallow as a puddle, I immediately admitted it was me since it was praise." Fielding drew on her own experiences and those of her single and married friends, for material to capture the 1990s London lifestyle. She also consulted some of her old diaries and duplicated her tendency to record caloric, alcohol, and nicotine intake that she uses to preface each diary entry as a gauge to Bridget's emotional states. A typical entry begins: "129 lbs. (excellent progress)—2 lbs. of fat spontaneously combusted through joy and sexual promise), alcohol units 6 (v.g. for party), cigarettes 12 (continuing good work), calories 1258 (love has eradicated need to pig out)."

To produce her novel, Fielding reformulated material from her columns into a year in the life of Bridget Jones with a romantic narrative structure echoing Jane Austen's *Pride and Prejudice*. Austen's sparkling courtship drama in which the sharp-tongued, quick-witted Elizabeth Bennet resists and later falls in love with the presumed arrogant Mr. Darcy is one of the most beloved romantic novels of all time, a realistic fairy tale in which a disadvantaged heroine manages to claim the hand of a gentleman of means and stature after the lovers readjust their distorted views of the other and of themselves. As a story that submits romance to the conditioning influences of family, class, economics, and identity, *Pride and Prejudice* is the perfect model for Fielding's purposes in which satire, love, and self-obsession are so inextricably mixed. Commenting on *Pride and Prejudice* and her borrowing from it, Fielding has observed, "I thought that it had been very well market-researched over a number of centuries." Bridget becomes a modern self-improvement-obsessed version of Elizabeth Bennet, starting the new year resolved to lose weight, stop smoking, get a grip on her drinking, learn to program her VCR, and develop "inner poise and authority and sense of self as a woman of substance, complete *without* boyfriend, as best way to obtain boyfriend." Despite her best intentions, she will through the course of the year consume 5,277 cigarettes, 3836 "alcohol units," gain seventy-four pounds while losing seventy-two, secure a boyfriend (the roguish Daniel Cleaver), lose him through his fecklessness, and finally gain another, Mark Darcy. She spends much of the year annoyed with Mark and humiliated in his presence.

Bridget begins her year in torment over her independent status as a single professional woman with a deep-seated need for fulfillment in a relationship, hoping to relieve the singleton's greatest fear of perishing "all alone, half-eaten by an Alsatian." Beset by the "Smug Marrieds" and family and friends who delight in making ticking biological clock sounds and impertinent inquiries about her love life ("We wouldn't rush up to *them* and roar, 'How's your marriage going? Still having sex?' "), the newly resolved Bridget first must endure a New Year's Day Turkey Curry Buffet at Geoffrey and Una Alconbury's suburban home, the first in a series of public disgraces that will test Bridget's "inner poise." There she encounters her intended setup, distinguished human rights lawyer Mark Darcy. The irony is not missed by Bridget: "It struck me as pretty ridiculous to be called Mr. Darcy and to stand on your own looking snooty at a party. It's like being called Heathcliff and insisting on spending the entire evening in the garden, shouting 'Cathy' and banging your head against a tree." Needless to say, the two do not hit it off. ("It's not that I wanted him to take my phone number or anything, but I didn't want him to make it perfectly obvious to everyone that he didn't want to.") Back at work as a publicist at a London publishing firm, Bridget conducts a protracted flirtation with her bad-boy boss, Daniel Cleaver, which features suggestive e-mails, a short skirt, and eventual sex but with insufficient follow-up phone calls.

By spring, however, Daniel assumes full boyfriend status. Instead of a summer of love, Bridget gets to watch cricket with Daniel in a baking apartment with curtains drawn. Even the promise of a romantic mini-break provides little fulfillment, other than watching Match of the Day inside their quaint room at an inn. Meanwhile, Bridget's ditzy mother, Pam, has rebelled against her suburban life as a homemaker, managed to wrangle a better job than Bridget's as a television presenter, and begun an affair with a shady operator named Julio. Humiliations continue when Bridget arrives at a Tarts and Vicars fancy-dress lawn party at the Alconburys in black lace stockings, suspenders, and a cotton rabbit's tail, having missed the message that the dress up has been canceled. Again Mark Darcy is in attendance, and they quarrel over his animosity toward Daniel. Returning from the party unannounced to Daniel's apartment, Bridget discovers his American lover. Inner poise gives way to disintegration: "I'm falling apart. My boyfriend is sleeping with a bronzed giantess. My mother is sleeping with a Portuguese. . . . Prince Charles is sleeping with Camilla Parker-Bowles. Do not know what to believe in or hold on to anymore."

Bridget breaks with Daniel and lands a new job on the current affairs television program *Good Afternoon!* where bad timing causes a live on-air spot of her sliding down a fireman's pole to show her trying to climb back up. Inexplicably, an invitation arrives for Bridget to attend the celebration of Mark Darcy's parents' ruby anniversary, where Bridget spends much of her time embarrassed by her family. Despite learning that Mark was not responsible for the invitation, Bridget does receive a date request from him and a major concession: " 'Bridget,' " Darcy declares, " 'all the other girls I know are so lacquered over. I don't know anyone else who would fasten a bunny tail to their pants . . .' " Mark sounds the novel's moral point that the imperfect Bridget is preferable to the lifeless paragons she aspires to become. This is a lesson that Bridget still must learn while reassessing her previous assumptions about Mark. To win him, Bridget tries to prove herself a stylish hostess only to endure the humiliation of a dinner party in which the soup turns blue, the tuna steaks mysteriously disappear, and the confit of oranges turns into marmalade. Her burgeoning relationship with Mark is further tested when Bridget's mother gets involved with Julio's phony time-share scheme, which bilks the savings of the Joneses and their friends, including Mark's parents. Mark's efforts to save Mrs. Jones make clear the points of both his worthiness and his willingness to accept Bridget as is—flaws, family, and all. Bridget, a Cinderella-also-ran, wins a Prince Charming after all, despite impossible obstacles, and in defiance of all her resolutions and self-help advice.

It is unclear as the novel concludes what, if anything, Bridget Jones has learned over the course of her year. Unlike Elizabeth Bennet, who realizes that she has been "blind, partial, prejudiced, and absurd" while recognizing the superiority of Darcy's judgment and experience and the expanded possibilities that his prospects offer, Bridget is, though rewarded in love, still far from stability and self-possession. The perfect harmony and blending of spirit and sense that delight the reader of *Pride and Prejudice* are

beyond the reach of Bridget, and the reader suspects her battle
with calories, cigarettes, alcohol units, and neuroses will delight-
fully continue (as indeed they do in Fielding's 2000 sequel, *Bridget
Jones: The Edge of Reason*). As Bridget admits, "I am a child of
Cosmopolitan culture, have been traumatized by supermodels and
too many quizzes and know that neither my personality nor my
body is up to it if left to its own devices. I can't take the pressure."
It is Bridget's battles that endure and endear, not her victories.

Despite praise for the novel's spot-on accuracy in depicting
how contemporary single women in their thirties actually think
and feel, many have resisted Bridget as everywoman as cartoonish
and a feminist betrayal. Alex Kuczynski has called Bridget "a
sorry spectacle, wallowing in her man-crazed helplessness," who
has been constructed "out of every myth that has ever sprung
from the ground of *Cosmopolitan* and television sitcoms. To wit,
that men are, in the words of one character, 'stupid, smug, arrogant, manipulative and self-indulgent'; that women are obsessed
with boyfriends, diets and body hair, and that every emotional reversal is cause for a chocolate binge." In defense, it can be argued
that Bridget is hardly presented as a role model but as a comic
striver beset by the contemporary contradictions of gender in
which female independence and autonomy battle with the need
to be rescued and validated by a male. Imelda Whelehan, in considering the "chick lit" phenomenon of the 1990s, has observed
that "its writers are a generation of women too young to be in the
vanguard of the 1970s, and yet aware enough to have absorbed
the cultural impact of *The Female Eunuch* and *Fear of Flying. . . .*
These women are a part of a generation who felt that feminism
did not speak to their needs and hadn't kept apace with its own
victories. They perhaps even bought into the idea that it was feminism that had oppressed women by making them lose contact
with the pleasures derived from celebrating femininity—dressing
up, wearing makeup, and feeling glamorous. There was a significant feeling from the late 1980s onwards that feminism might be
restricting women's choices, because it was mistakenly regarded
as anti-sex and anti-glamour." Bridget may be a sorry excuse as a
feminist, but her perspective on the gender battleground of the
postfeminist world is as unavoidable as it is illuminating.

THE BITCH IN THE HOUSE

Compiled and edited by Cathi Hanauer

From 1854 to 1862, English poet Coventry Patmore (1823–1896) published *The Angel in the House*, a long and much-admired poetic sequence celebrating wedded love and the ideal of woman as domestic deity that dominated the nineteenth-century cultural imagination. Patmore's conception of the saintly female paragon, worshipped on her home-bound pedestal, would be later attacked by Virginia Woolf in a 1931 essay in which she states, "You who come of a younger and happier generation may not have heard of her. You may not know what I mean by 'the angel in the house.' She was intensely sympathetic. She was immensely charming. She was utterly unselfish. She excelled in the difficult arts of family life. She sacrificed herself daily. If there was chicken, she took the leg. If there was a draft, she sat in it. In short, she was so constituted that she never had a mind or a wish of her own, but preferred to sympathize always with the minds and wishes of others." In Woolf's view, for a woman to reach her potential, the myth of the all-sacrificing, subordinate woman—the angel in the house—must be killed. In the essay collection, *The Bitch in the House: 26 Women Tell the Truth About Sex, Solitude, Work, Motherhood, and Marriage* (2002), the angel is dead, re-

285

placed by her enraged alter ego, telling tales and naming names in the postfeminist gender wars.

The Bitch in the House was conceived and edited by Cathi Hanauer, a novelist (*My Sister's Bones*) and magazine writer who has been the book columnist for *Glamour* and *Mademoiselle,* and was the relationship advice columnist for *Seventeen.* "This book was born out of anger—specifically, my own domestic anger," she states in the introduction, "which stemmed from a combination of guilt, resentment, exhaustion, naiveté, and the chaos of life at the time." Hanauer, in her mid-thirties, moved with husband and two children, from their cramped New York apartment to their dream house in Northampton, Massachusetts, to enjoy the fruits of a less-stressed, egalitarian marriage and coparenting idyll. Hanauer had ostensibly achieved the mythical goal of "having it all." As she recalled, I "had everything I'd ever worked hard to have and everything I'd ever wanted—the husband, the kids, the job—and I found myself, rather than appreciating and being able to enjoy my life, sort of overwhelmed by the juggling act that my life had become. I was stressed out and tired, and I was basically a bitch in the house. And the more I talked to other women, the more I realized how many of us were feeling this way." As a means of understanding her frustrations in dealing with the gap between the contemporary woman's ideal of career-fulfillment, marriage, and motherhood and the often maddening reality, Hanauer solicited reflections on the current temperature of women from "mostly novelists and professional writers, but also a handful of other smart, thinking women who I knew had a story to tell. I requested of these potential contributors that they explore a choice they'd made, or their life situation—or their anger, if they felt it— in an essay; that they offer an interesting glimpse into their private lives, as if they were talking to a friend at a café." Contributors to *The Bitch in the House,* ranging in age from twenty-four to sixty-five, single, married, divorced, with children and without, candidly discuss the challenges they have faced and the revelations they have gained. The book's emphasis is less on self-help advice than on an at times brutally honest assessment of the expectations and disappointments that define a new, virulent strain of "domestic anger." Writers include Pulitzer Prize–winner Natalie Angier, poet Jill Bialosky, essayist Hope Edelman, fiction writers Ellen Gilchrist, Daphne Merkin, Elissa Schappell, and Helen Schulman, and memoirists Veronica Chambers and Vivian Gornick.

The result is a witty, intriguing, and often illuminating look at the lives and values of postfeminist lovers, wives, mothers, and independent women struggling to come to terms with gender expectations, both new and old, and the realities of women's lot in the post-liberation age.

This confessional exercise can be dismissed easily as the self-indulgent whines and gripes of those who seem to have it all and want even more. Such is the reaction of reviewer Joan Smith, who boils down the essence of *The Bitch in the House* to the generic, greedy refrain: "Why can't I have a gorgeous husband, fantastic sex, a fulfilling job, several adorable children, be a full-time mother and a have a few moments left over to write a bestselling novel?" However, *The Bitch in the House* manages to claim both relevance and importance by framing some of the possible terms of the next phase of feminism. As Maria Russo and Alexandra Wolfe write in their review of the collection, "The plight of the unhappy professional woman with children in her late 30's and early 40's has profound dimensions: Pulled between her biological and intellectual destinies, she essentially shortchanges her future if she doesn't pursue either one. But there are only so many hours in the day, so much emotional energy to go around, and part of her knows all too well that she's stuck in a zero-sum game. What sounds like a mere complaint about too many worldly burdens—by someone who's ridiculously privileged, as the human lot goes—is also an expression of a kind of post-feminist social and emotional reckoning." *The Bitch in the House* serves as *The Feminine Mystique* revisited forty years later. Betty Friedan similarly found herself discontented and frustrated conforming to the prescribed gender roles for women of her era as glamorized full-time housewives and mothers. She also surveyed other women to diagnose a common complaint, the "problem with no name" that Friedan labeled the feminine mystique, the myth of femininity—the pleasing of and subordination to men—as the ultimate goal of a woman's life. Nearly a half century later, from the chorus of voices Hanauer has collected in *The Bitch in the House*, it is apparent that the myth still lives and, in the words of writer Sandra Shea, "It's just been super-sized, to include children, a sensitive husband to co-parent them, and a fulfilling career. And women trying to reach these ideals are mad as hell at what they're finding instead." Hanauer's fellow "bitches" express their anger that the women's movement that Friedan and others touched off has done little to alter essential expectations that women can only be fulfilled with a mate, marriage, and motherhood, while adding to their burden new expectations for careers and the self-actualization that feminism has helped to foster. As Friedan herself pointed out in her book *The Second Stage* (1981), the feminine mystique has been succeeded by a "feminist mystique" of the superwoman who is expected to cope effortlessly with her relationships, career, and family. When women fail, guilt, resentment, and anger result, and the bitch in the house is unleashed.

Offering revealing examples of what happens when the post-feminist myth collides with reality, the collection is divided into four sections, treating relationships, marriage, motherhood, and general enlightenment. In the first, "Me, Myself, and I," writers take on the subject of women on their own, in and out of relationships. Mating remains the illusive goal for many of these women, despite the disillusionment several experience when lovers become roommates and solitude gives way to partnership. Daphne Merkin, whose "Memoirs of an Ex-Bride" compares her life before, during, and after marriage, captures the common feeling of the unattached woman from whose perspective "everyone else suddenly seems to be married—safely tucked in for the night in their tidy Noah's Ark of coupledom—while you're out in the lonely forest scavenging for a warm body to huddle up against." If single women seem ready to trade in their independence for coupledom, many of the married writers in the second section, "For Better and Worse," would gladly exchange their lives with them, resenting the compromises and sacrifices of married life and its costs in autonomy and passion. As several of the essayists make clear, domestic life remains, with all the consciousness-raising and gender enlightenment, grindingly routine, with a disproportionate burden still falling on the woman of the house. Add to the mix dual careers and kids, and things quickly turn toxic. Kristin van Ogtrop in "Attila the Honey I'm Home" identifies among married couples a "mobius strip of guilt and resentment, and more guilt because of the resentment" developing around the central dilemma of "who is doing more." Others, such as Hope Edelman and Laurie Abraham, explore the myth of coparenting; while Elissa Schappell in "Crossing the Line in the Sand: How Mad Can Mother Get?" confesses that "some days . . . all I do is yell at my kids, then apologize for yelling at them, then feel guilty for being such a lousy mother, then start to feel resentful about being made to feel like a bad mother." Susan Squire in "Maternal Bitch" is even more blunt: "If you avoid motherhood, you avoid activating the Bitch."

Three-quarters of the way through *The Bitch in the House* the venting about the flash points of being single, married, and with children gives way to perspectives gained and conclusions reached in the final section, "Look at Me Now." If the curse of many of the writers' lives is discovered to be unrealistic expectations about women's roles and responsibilities promulgated by both the feminine and feminist mystique, the concluding essays begin with an earned sense of compromises and self-acceptance needed to defuse the rage that results in the illusory pursuit of perfection as lover, wife, and mother. Nancy Wartik in "Married at 46" helps to clarify why one should marry and why one should not, particularly from the perspective of someone who has resisted coupledom to her mid-forties. Ellen Gilchrist's "Middle Way" offers a Zenlike armistice in the war between family and work. Advocating joy and patience with less rather than striving to have it all, Gilchrist provides the commonsensical observation that "I think I'm happy because I have quit trying to find happiness through other people. . . . Happiness is self-derived and self-created." Vivian Gornick's "What Independence Has Come to Mean to Me" assesses a lifetime alone that is sustained by a process of self-knowledge, and Pam Houston's "The Perfect Equality of Our Separate Chosen Paths" suggests that contentment rests not in fantasies subscribed to, such as a culturally shared timetable and proscription for women's happiness and fulfillment, but in the acceptance of limits and the small enjoyments—friends, family, health, and even pets—that sustain and redeem a life.

The Bitch in the House offers the reader an excellent opportunity to eavesdrop on the intimate revelations of contemporary women. If Woolf is right and the angel in the house must be conquered, it is no less true that the bitch in the house needs to be grappled with and her rage understood. Naming a problem is the first step in curing it, and *The Bitch in the House* helps to diagnose a "problem with no name" for the next wave of feminism to treat.

HONORABLE MENTIONS

Jane Addams, *Twenty Years at Hull House* (1910)
Dorothy E. Allison, *Bastard Out of Carolina* (1992)
Lisa Alther, *Kinflicks* (1976)
Julia Alvarez, *How the Garcia Girls Lost Their Accents* (1991)
Margaret Atwood, *The Handmaid's Tale* (1985)
Jane Austen, *Pride and Prejudice* (1813), *Persuasion* (1818)
Elizabeth Bowen, *The Death of the Heart* (1938)
Charlotte Brontë, *Villette* (1853)
Emily Brontë, *Wuthering Heights* (1847)
Rita Mae Brown, *Rubyfruit Jungle* (1973)
Pearl Buck, *Pavilion of Women* (1946)
Fanny Burney, *Evelina* (1778)
Anton Chekhov, *The Three Sisters* (1901)
Sandra Cisneros, *The House on Mango Street* (1991)
Laurie Colwin, *Happy All the Time* (1978)
Michael Cunningham, *The Hours* (1998)
Rebecca Harding Davis, *Life in the Iron Mills* (1861)
Daniel Defoe, *Moll Flanders* (1722)
Annie Dillard, *Pilgrim at Tinker Creek* (1974)
Daphne du Maurier, *Rebecca* (1938)
Charles Frazier, *Cold Mountain* (1997)
Betty Friedan, *The Second Stage* (1981), *The Fountain of Age* (1993)
Margaret Fuller, *Women in the Nineteenth Century* (1845)
Elizabeth Gaskell, *Wives and Daughters* (1866)
Carol Gilligan, *In a Different Voice: Psychological Theory and Women's Development* (1982)
Nadine Gordimer, *Burgher's Daughter* (1979)
Carolyn Heilbrun, *Writing a Woman's Life* (1988)
Lillian Hellman, *The Children's Hour* (1934)
Hayden Herrera, *Frida* (1983)
Henry James, *The Portrait of a Lady* (1881)

Jamaica Kincaid, *At the Bottom of the River* (1983)
Jhumpa Lahiri, *Interpreter of Maladies* (1999)
Clare Booth Luce, *The Women* (1937)
Mary McCarthy, *The Group* (1963)
Carson McCullers, *The Member of the Wedding* (1946)
Marsha Norman, *'Night Mother* (1982)
Joyce Carol Oates, *them* (1969)
Marjorie Rosen, *Popcorn Venus* (1973)
May Sarton, *The Magnificent Spinster* (1985)
Alix Kates Shulman, *Memoirs of an Ex-Prom Queen* (1972)
Jane Smiley, *A Thousand Acres* (1991)
Amy Tan, *The Joy Luck Club* (1989)
Anne Tyler, *Breathing Lessons* (1988)
Paula Vogel, *How I Learned to Drive* (1997)
Alice Walker, *The Color Purple* (1982)
Wendy Wasserstein, *The Heidi Chronicles* (1990)
Eudora Welty, *Delta Wedding* (1946)
Virginia Woolf, *Mrs. Dalloway* (1925)

SELECT BIBLIOGRAPHY

Aquiar, Sarah Appleton. *The Bitch Is Back: Wicked Women in Literature*. Carbondale: Southern Illinois University Press, 2001.

Arcana, Judith. *Grace Paley's Life Stories: A Literary Biography*. Urbana and Chicago: University of Illinois Press, 1993.

Auerbach, Nina. *Romantic Imprisonment: Women and Other Glorified Outcasts*. New York: Columbia University Press, 1985.

Bair, Deidre. *Simone de Beauvoir: A Biography*. New York: Summit Books, 1990.

Banner, Lois W. *American Beauty*. New York: Knopf, 1983.

Barlowe, Jamie. *The Scarlet Mob of Scribblers: Rereading Hester Prynne*. Carbondale: Southern Illinois University Press, 2000.

Beers, Patricia. *Reader, I Married Him*. New York: Barnes & Noble, 1974.

Bowlby, Rachel. *Virginia Woolf: Feminist Destinations*. New York: Blackwell, 1988.

Brabant, Margaret, ed. *Politics, Gender and Genre: The Political Thought of Christine de Pizan*. Boulder, Colorado: Westview Press, 1992.

Brownmiller, Susan. *In Our Time: Memoir of a Revolution*. New York: Dial Press, 1999.

Brumberg, Joan. *The Body Project: An Intimate History of American Girls*. New York: Random House, 1997.

Casagrande, Peter J. *"Tess of the d'Urbervilles": Unorthodox Beauty*. New York: Twayne, 1992.

Cohen, Marcia. *The Sisterhood*. New York: Simon & Schuster, 1988.

Danahy, Michael. *The Feminization of the Novel*. Gainesville: University of Florida Press, 1991.

Davis, Angela. *Angela Davis: An Autobiography*. New York: International Publishers, 1988.

Durbach, Errol. *"A Doll's House": Ibsen's Myth of Transformation.* Boston: Twayne, 1991.

Elbert, Sarah. *Hunger for Home: Louisa May Alcott's Place in American Culture.* Philadelphia: Temple University Press, 1984.

Erens, Patricia, ed. *Sexual Strategies: The World of Women in Film.* New York: Horizon, 1979.

Evans, Mary. *Reflecting on Anna Karenina.* New York: Routledge, 1989.

Evans, Sara M. *Born for Liberty: A History of Women in America.* New York: Free Press, 1989.

Fraiman, Susan. *Unbecoming Women: British Women Writers and the Novel of Development.* New York: Columbia University Press, 1993.

Freedman, Rita Jackaway. *Beauty Bound.* New York: Lexington Books, 1986.

Frye, Joanne S. *Living Stories, Telling Lives: Women and the Novel in Contemporary Experience.* Ann Arbors: University of Michigan Press, 1986.

Gilbert, Sandra M., and Susan Gubar. *The Madwoman in the Attic.* New Haven: Yale University Press, 1979.

——— *No Man's Land: The Place of the Woman Writer in the Twentieth Century.* New Haven: Yale University Press, 3 vols., 1988–1994.

Gordon, Lyndall. *Charlotte Brontë: A Passionate Life.* New York: Norton, 1995.

Gwin, Minrose. *The Woman in the Red Dress: Gender, Space, and Reading.* Urbana: University of Illinois Press, 2002.

Haight, Gordon S. *George Eliot: A Biography.* New York: Oxford University Press, 1968.

Hanson, Claire. *Hysterical Fictions: The 'Woman's Novel' in the Twentieth Century.* New York: St. Martin's Press, 2000.

Hanson, Elizabeth J. *Margaret Mitchell.* Boston: Twayne, 1990.

Heilmann, Ann. *New Woman Fiction: Women Writing First-Wave Feminism.* New York: St. Martin's Press, 2000.

Hemenway, Robert E. *Zora Neale Hurston.* Urbana: University of Illinois Press, 1977.

Horowitz, Daniel. *Betty Friedan and the Making of the Feminine Mystique.* Amherst: University of Massachusetts Press, 1998.

Isaacs, Neil David. *Grace Paley: A Study of the Short Fiction.* Boston: Twayne, 1990.

Jacobs, William Jay. *Women in American History.* Beverly Hills, California: Benziger Bruce & Glencoe, 1976.

Kaplan, Louise J. *Female Perversions: The Temptations of Madame Bovary.* New York: Doubleday, 1991.

Kaurar, Elaine. *Cynthia Ozick's Fiction: Tradition and Invention.* Bloomington: Indiana University Press, 1993.

Kawashima, Terry. *Writing Margins: The Textual Construction of Gender in Heian and Kamakura Japan.* Cambridge: Harvard University Press, 2001.

Kirkham, Margaret. *Jane Austen, Feminism and Fiction.* Atlantic Highlands, New Jersey: Athlone Press, 1997.

Larch, Jennifer. *Mary Wollstonecraft: The Making of a Radical Feminist.* London: Berg, 1990.

Lee, Hermione. *Willa Cather: A Life Saved Up.* London: Virago, 1989.

Levine, Linda Gould. *Isabel Allende.* New York: Twayne, 2002.

Macpherson, Pat. *Reflection on* The Bell Jar. New York: Routledge, 1991.

Maraini, Dacia. *Searching for Emma: Gustave Flaubert and Madame Bovary.* Chicago: University of Chicago Press, 1998.

Matteo, Sherri. *American Women in the Nineties: Today's Critical Issues.* Boston: Northeastern University Press, 1993.

Moglen, Helene. *The Trauma of Gender: A Feminist Theory of the English Novel.* Berkeley: University of California Press, 2001.

Morgan, Robin. *Going Too Far: The Personal Chronicle of a Feminist.* New York: Random House, 1977.

Nebeker, Helen. *Jean Rhys, Woman in Passage.* St. Albans, Vermont: Eden Press, 1981.

Orr, Elaine Neil. *Tillie Olsen and a Feminist Spiritual Vision.* Jackson: University Press of Mississippi, 1987.

Peters, Pearlie Mae Fisher. *The Assertive Woman in Zora Neal Hurston's Fiction, Folklore, and Drama.* New York: Garland, 1998.

Rosenman, Ellen Bayuk. *A Room of One's Own: Women Writers and the Politics of Creativity.* New York: Twayne, 1995.

Rothman, Sheila. *Woman's Proper Place: A History of Changing Ideals and Practices, 1870 to the Present.* New York: Basic Books, 1978.

Rupp, Leila J., and Vera Taylor. *Survival in the Doldrums: The American Women's Rights Movement, 1945 to the 1960s.* New York: Oxford University Press, 1987.

Sawaya, Francesca. *Modern Women, Modern Work.* Philadelphia: University of Pennsylvania Press, 2004.

Searles, Patricia, and Ronald J. Berger, eds. *Rape and Society.* Boulder, Colorado: Westview Press, 1995.

Shapiro, Anne R. *Unlikely Heroines: Nineteenth-Century American Women Writers and the Woman Question.* New York: Greenwood Press, 1987.

Showalter, Elaine. *A Literature of Their Own.* Princeton, New Jersey: Princeton University Press, 1977.

Smith, Sidonie. *A Poetics of Women's Autobiography.* Bloomington: Indiana University Press, 1987.

Spacks, Patricia Meyer. *The Female Imagination.* New York: Knopf, 1975.

Taylor, Barbara. *Mary Wollstonecraft and the Feminist Imagination.* New York: Cambridge University Press, 2003.

Templin, Charlotte. *Feminism and the Politics of Literary Reputation.* Lawrence: University of Kansas Press, 1995.

Thurman, Judith. *Secrets of the Flesh: A Life of Colette.* New York: Knopf, 1999.

Tidd, Ursula. *Simone de Beauvoir: Gender and Testimony.* New York: Cambridge University Press, 1999.

Tomalin, Claire. *The Life and Death of Mary Wollstonecraft.* New York: Harcourt, 1974.

Wallace, Christine. *Germaine Greer, Untamed Shrew.* Boston: Faber and Faber, 1998.

Ward Jouve, Nicole. *Female Genesis: Creativity, Self, and Gender.* New York: St. Martin's Press, 1998.

Willard, Charity Cannon. *Christine de Pisan: Her Life and Works.* New York: Persea Books, 1984.

Wilson, Anna. *Persuasive Fictions: Feminist Narrative and Critical Myth.* Lewisburg, Pennsylvania: Bucknell University Press, 2001.

Wolf, Cynthia Griffin. *A Feast of Words: The Triumph of Edith Wharton.* New York: Oxford University Press, 1977.